HOW TO SELF-PUBLISH YOUR OWN COMIC BOOK

HOW TO SELF-PUBLISH YOUR OWN COMIC BOOK

TONY C. CAPUTO

WATSON-GUPTILL PUBLICATIONS/NEW YORK

Page 2 (frontispiece): Inked art for *Vespers* #1. Penciled by Tony Caputo, inked by David Mowry.

Senior Editor: Candace Raney
Associate Editor: Alisa Palazzo
Designer: Jay Anning
Production Manager: Hector Campbell

First published in 1997 in the United States by Watson-Guptill Publications, a division of BPI Communications, Inc., 1515 Broadway, New York, N.Y. 10036.

Library of Congress Cataloging-in-Publication Data
Caputo, Tony.
    How to self-publish your own comic book / Tony Caputo.
        p.   cm.
    Includes bibliographical references and index.
    ISBN 0-8230-2455-5 (paperback)
    1. Comic books, strips, etc.—Marketing. 2. Comic books, strips, etc.—Publishing. 3. Self-publishing. I. Title.
    PN6714.C28 1996
    741.5'068—dc21   96-37271
                              CIP

Printed in the USA

First printing, 1997
1 2 3 4 5 6 7 8 /04 03 02 01 00 99 98 97

A WORD FROM THE AUTHOR

I was born in Chicago, the first of three sons of Italian immigrants. Because reading (at least in English) wasn't a very popular activity in my household, I didn't really discover the joys of reading until I was about 11 years old. It was a DC Comics special edition, which I begged my parents to buy for me, that first caught my eye as a young boy. It was full of color, creativity, fantasy, monsters, villains, and heroes—and, it was fun to read. That's what I learned from comic books—that it is truly enjoyable to just read. In my years of publishing comic books, if I've introduced that same joy to another person, then I feel I've done my job successfully.

Today, the comic book industry is an entertainment business not unlike Hollywood. Just as there are popular actors, there are also the star comic book creators, writer, and pencilers, who attract crowds of hundreds—sometimes thousands—of eager, autograph-seeking fans at every comic book convention they attend. And, Hollywood producers and other executives are now interested in developing comic book story lines into movies, making comic book publishing, potentially, a very profitable business endeavor. So, in this exciting industry it's not unlikely for a creator to come up with a story, publish it as a profitable comic book, and, a few years later, find it on the big screen as a major motion picture. And it's the unbridled creativity and minimal production expenses of the medium that can enable all this skill to end up in the hands of the right people at the right time. It's a tidal wave; you just have to ride it at the right speed with the right knowledge, product, business savvy, and resources, and eventually, you'll make it to the beach.

This book gives you all the tools you'll need to publish a successful comic book. It shows you how to avoid the mistakes and miscalculations that countless others have experienced and go on to become a successful publisher. The information provided here reflects over a decade of comic book publishing experience and history, including analyses of what makes a comic book successful, discussions of the numerous changes in industry trends, and an examination of market gluts. When I look back 10 years ago, I remember how I was forced to learn firsthand from my errors and oversights, as well as my successes, and I remember thinking, "I could really use a comic book publishing course or a how-to book, and there isn't one." But now, there is!

Tony Caputo

CONTENTS

GETTING STARTED

The single most important thing a new publisher must have to succeed is commitment to a project. It's nice to know all the finer points of art production, pre-press, distribution, and promotion, but without the constant drive and vision throughout, the dream will not become a reality.

—Marc Hansen, creator and publisher of
Weird Melvin and *Ralph Snart Adventures*

In any situation, if you're genuinely dedicated to your goals, you have a better chance at attaining them. When starting a business, it is also important to keep in mind that if you aren't adequately prepared for what lies ahead, you will be more likely to fail. In order to be successful in your business endeavor, you must research and analyze the market that you plan to enter. You must be committed to your dream and also committed to gathering as much useful information as you can. You should evaluate any growth opportunities and the products already out there, and then identify and examine the niche you hope to fill. This book will help you do this, as well as show you how to create and sell your unique product. It provides invaluable tips to help your comic book thrive in a marketplace filled with competition, and will enable you to understand every channel of distribution and every avenue of promotion and advertising, and how to exploit them for maximum sales. Armed both with knowledge and dedication, you will be prepared for success.

Researching current market conditions requires footwork and a keen sense of foresight. To learn everything you can about the comic book industry, read trade publications, and ask numerous comic book store managers about current sales as compared to a year, or even two years, ago. Ask them specifically what products are selling and at what quantities. Comic book conventions are also a gold mine for market analysis. (For a list of the nation's largest shows, see Appendix, page 169.) Dealers are never shy in exploiting the latest "hot" trend, and you can also discover the failures by scanning through any bargain boxes. If your concept is similar to a bargain-box title, consider it a hard-sell item—one that will be difficult, but not impossible, to sell. Quite a few of today's hits were yesterday's low-order titles. Don't immediately discount your own concept because similar ideas ended up in the bargain box; those titles may be missing that one tiny element of success that yours contains.

THE COMIC BOOK INDUSTRY

In any situation, information is a weapon, and so, as I said above, you should arm yourself with as much knowledge about the comic book market as you possibly can so that you have a better chance at success. This is an exciting industry, and in recent years comic book sales have exceeded $4 billion worldwide. Approximately $800 million of that was generated in North America. The huge Japanese comic book industry alone is estimated at about $3 billion, with the remaining world markets adding another $500 million dollars. The foreign comic book markets have, traditionally, been dominated by foreign publishers, with American publishers accounting for only a small portion of total worldwide sales.

In the United States in the past five years there has been a continual fluctuation in comic book sales and profits as the industry struggles to expand. These market changes can be viewed as growing pains, and as a result of these efforts, the country can now boast a serious business with "big-money" investors who demand returns on their investment interests. These investors see huge comic book hits that seem to pop up out of nowhere, and they want that kind of success, too.

In the past year the industry has received a dramatic face-lift, and the strong will continue to become even stronger while the weak will give up and wither away. Those who give up don't realize that this billion-dollar-a-year-worldwide industry was only generating a mere $160 million as recently as 1984, and that with this kind of growth there will also be growing pains. This book will give you hints on weathering any kind of storm, and change, in the market.

There are four main segments of the comic book industry: superhero comics, licensed-property comics, mature-reader comics, and children's comics. The largest and fastest-growing one is the *superhero* category, which accounts for an estimated 75 percent of the entire domestic market. Despite the occasional violence in some of these comic books, these are mostly basic "good-versus-evil" stories and usually are not considered objectionable by the general public. The market leaders in this group are Marvel Comics (a public company—one that trades stock shares on the New York Stock Exchange), which produces among others *X-Men* and *Spider-Man,* and DC Comics (a Time-Warner Entertainment company), which produces *Superman* and *Batman.* This segment attracts a large, affluent audience, mostly of males between the ages of seven and 40, and these buyers, particularly the teenagers and collectors, are among the most avid and loyal customers in the entire entertainment industry.

The second largest comic book category consists of titles based on *licensed-property* characters that usually originated in movies, television shows, or games (such as board games and video or computer games). Once you sell the rights to one of your characters to other companies to manufacture related merchandise and pay royalties for that privilege to the rights holder, your character becomes a licensed property. Through an exclusive licensing agreement with the rights holder of an established property (or character), a publisher, for example, can acquire the right to create and market products based on that property. The instant recognizability of these characters often guarantees the publisher immediate success with that comic book. This category accounts for approximately 12 percent of the total national comic market and includes such comic book titles as *The Terminator, The Real Ghostbusters, Speed Racer,* and *Aliens.*

The third largest grouping, *mature-reader* comics, is classified as such due either to excessive violence or gore, sexually suggestive material, or adult humor. This category makes up approximately 8 percent of the total domestic market, and because of ever-changing fads, the titles in this segment tend to be short-lived. The primary buyers here are young males, ages 13 to 40, and titles in this category include *Sin City, Vertigo, Ralph Snart Adventures,* and *SNARF.*

Finally, the fourth and smallest classification consists of *children's* comics. These are "G-rated" titles, which appeal mainly to elementary school children. Many titles in this group are licensed properties that are the latest "hot" (or popular) characters with children. For example, *Casper, Mickey Mouse, Archie,* and *Bugs Bunny* comics all fall in this category. This group accounts for only about 5 percent of the market but has been steadily growing for several years due to the introduction of more contemporary licensed properties into the comic book format.

Industry Outlook

Domestic comic book sales are expected to grow at an average rate of 15 percent over the next five years. This figure is based on the national market growth from 1989 through 1993, which averaged approximately 16 percent even after the Black-and-White Implosion of 1987 (when a glut of comic books flooded the market and supply outweighed demand). And the demographics continue to be excellent—the core group of buyers (males, ages 12 to 19) is projected to increase 17 percent by the year 2000.

Another reason for this 15-percent market growth projection is that the number of publishers who have acquired 70 percent of the market has tripled within the past five years, and the number of comic book stores is expected to continue to grow steadily, reaching 4,000 by the end of 1999. In the early eighties, Marvel Comics had over 70 percent of the entire comic book market, DC Comics had approximately 20 percent, with the remaining 10 percent divided up between Archie, Harvey, and Gladstone (Disney publishing). The introduction of new, independent publishers (such as Now Comics), expanded the industry beyond those traditional companies and characters, which were all over 25 years old. The fresh new businesses and characters took a bite out of the market pie, shrinking Marvel's share down to 30 to 40 percent. The new publishers, such as Dark Horse, Image, Mirage, Caliber, Now Comics, and First, all successfully contributed to the toppling of Goliath, making room for self-publishers with original ideas. And today, even with continuing market changes and gluts, it's apparent that owning and operating a comic book specialty store is attractive to the retail-minded entrepreneur.

The comic book's connection with movies, television, and related merchandising continues to endure, attracting interest from Hollywood. Crossover comic books include *Batman* (which was made into a television cartoon and several feature films), *X-Men* (which inspired a television cartoon), *The Crow* (now also a full-length feature film with a sequel), and *The Tick* (also a popular television cartoon). Currently, there are a few dozen movies, based on comic book characters, that are now in development or production in Hollywood.

The enormous public and private investments made in the comic book industry within the past several years indicate that market experts believe more long-term profitable growth is possible. In July of 1991, Marvel Comics went public at an initial offering price of $8.25 per share. Just a few months after going public in 1992, Harvey Comics, which had weak characters at the time (such as Casper and Ritchie Rich) and three years of heavy operating losses, was selling for about 25 percent above its initial public offering price of $7.50 per share. Why is this? Comic books are clearly much more than 32-page periodicals; they're also "intellectual properties," which become far more recognizable and valuable over time. For example, you might ask yourself, Who hasn't heard of *Casper the Friendly Ghost*? No one, and these recent company share prices reflect this popularity.

Lately, there has also been turmoil in the comic book industry due to the Internet and other new-media developments. The future of the industry continues to involve the direct (or retail) market's struggle with ordering hundreds of products on a non-returnable basis. The age-old consignment formula of the traditional "newsstand" market, on the other hand, puts all the risk on the publisher rather than on the retailer. And, the consistent untimely shipping of favorite titles has always had a devastating effect on the market. Still, although the comic book industry peaked at about one billion dollars in 1990 but then dropped to half that in 1994, the domestic annual revenue is still expected to grow back to about $1 billion by 1999. The aftermath of the aforementioned 1987 Black-and-White Implosion created similar uncertainties within the comic book industry. The largest direct market distributor even filed for bankruptcy, but just a few years later, the industry generated over a billion dollars in revenue, up from $140 million in 1985. So, the comic book market has been known to bounce back with a vengeance.

Also keep in mind that if there are cries of agony from the large publishers and distributors about the state of the industry, it's because the smaller independent or alternative comic book publishers (with less exorbitant operational costs than the big companies) have made their mark and won't go away. They have acquired a big enough chunk of the market share to alarm the big boys, who have been swimming in the lap of luxury with 70 percent of the market for decades.

Online Comic Books

The Internet is following in the footsteps of the traditional comic book industry explosions of the late '80s and early '90s, with one very important difference: The Internet is changing the way we communicate, acquire information, find entertainment, and the way we publish.

The most attractive feature about the Internet is that it provides direct access to the consumer, eliminating the need for the printer, shipper, distributor, and retailer. There is also the lack of problems created by exclusive international formats (for example, the various size differences and constraints between domestic and foreign comic books or the problems with PAL versus VHS systems in video formats), which is a plus since the Internet is global, with an estimated 200 million users worldwide. Online comic books will definitely bring back those millions of comic fans who have lost themselves in cyberspace.

YOUR BASE OF OPERATIONS

With any business, you need a base of operations. This is your new home away from home—the place where everything is at your fingertips. Whether you are self-publishing a single comic book or planning to introduce multiple titles, having a centralized location with all the necessary equipment and materials will enable you to operate in a more effective and timely manner, whether it be handling correspondences or making important creative or production decisions. Your main office can be a spare bedroom in your house, a corner in your basement, or an entire floor (that you rent) in an office building. Organize your business base and plan your office space as efficiently as possible within your budget. As your company grows, you'll appreciate having invested all this time organizing when, for example, you need to find documentation in your files from three months ago.

OFFICE FURNITURE AND EQUIPMENT

Once you determine where your office space will be, you'll need all the office essentials. If you don't already have them, you can purchase many of these items at local used office-furniture stores, garage sales, or going-out-of-business sales for a fraction of their retail prices. There is no need to spend too much money on these items. With some determination, you should be able to find all the furniture you need for a total of about $500. With expenses/expenditures for computer equipment, you should run no more that $5,000, or possibly only a fraction of that depending on what you already have. Check your local papers or yellow pages for used furniture stores, or even ask your Aunt Gertrude if she has any unwanted furniture sitting in her garage. The plan is to set up an efficient office space without going beyond your financial reach.

Whether you are simply self-publishing one monthly title or planning to produce an entire line of comic books, starting with humble office beginnings will leave your capital available for other, more valuable company investments. You can always upgrade your office after generating revenue, and keeping your overhead low prior to publication is a safety net for your (or your investors') investment. You should always inspect your sales forecasts and then measure them up to your actual sales before putting money into a $40,000 computer system, a $3,000 telephone system, or any other major purchase. There may be a few final hurdles that you need to clear, once you begin the monthly publication process, before your company runs like a well-oiled machine.

If you have the capital investment to start a multiple-title comic book company, and you're worried about creating an image of affluence in your office—don't. Nothing impresses distributors, retailers, and customers more than a high-quality, timely *product*. Focus on your comics and how to inform the market of their availability, and don't spend money you don't yet have on unnecessarily fancy office equipment.

Note that a telephone line is, obviously, a must, as is an answering machine. You must give people the opportunity to communicate with you directly at any time. Also worthwhile is the call-waiting feature, which you can add on to your phone for a nominal monthly charge. An answering machine or service will ensure that you never miss an important call when you're out of your office. The lists below include the basic equipment for either a one- or multiple-title publishing facility; the only difference would be the number of individual employee work stations that you need to furnish to fit your planned manpower and output. Again, it isn't necessary to purchase every item listed here in one huge weekend shopping spree. Accumulate items gradually, taking the time to find the right products at the right prices. If you have to include office rent and utilities in your budget, start small and grow as your company's profits grow.

Furniture

Desk

Comfortable desk chair

Bright desk lamp

Drawing table (also with chair and lamp)

Taboret or cabinet (for office materials such as brushes, paint, pencils, drawing pads, and the like)

Bookshelves (for reference books, samples, other materials)

Four-drawer file cabinet

Production table (for cutting boards, handling large drawings)

Equipment

Telephone

Answering machine or service

Computer

Laser printer

Fax machine

Photocopy machine

Calculator

Typewriter

Computers and Laser Printers

I would bet that computers will eventually become more important to society than automobiles, so if you don't know how to use them, you should definitely learn now. The computer is certainly the most valuable piece of office equipment to the entrepreneur. With a computer and laser printer you can produce reproduction-quality book pages, advertisements, and logos. (*Reproduction-quality* and also *camera-ready* are printing terms indicating that the materials and images have the sharpest, crispest, photographic quality and can be used to make the film from which the metal printing plates will be produced.) You can write, edit, and spell-check all correspondences more efficiently on a computer than you can with any typewriter. And, with the right hardware and software, you can even professionally letter and color your comic book, producing the highest-quality, camera-ready pages.

The type of computer you buy is based on your budget. One alternative to buying a computer is to go to your local photocopying/computer center (such as a Kinko's copy center) and use the computers there (or use the printers, if you only own a computer); note that this can cost about $9 an hour with laser prints at about $.50 each. To find copy centers in your area, look in your local yellow pages under "Photo Copying"; prices may vary so you should always check with the salespeople. I wouldn't really suggest doing this in lieu of buying a computer; it's not very practical or cost efficient, although it may be your only alternative if you can't yet afford a computer of your own.

An alternative to buying a new computer is to purchase a used one with a monochrome screen from your local computer outlet. This might cost as little as $200. In ads in your local paper you'll probably be able to find an IBM-compatible XT/AT or 286 or an Apple Macintosh, with a 30mg hard drive, for about $300 to $500. (Note that these prices are only estimates, so you should check your local newspapers.) Although these models might be considered slow and out-of-date, they still produce. Computer technology is ever changing, and chances are, if you do purchase a new model, that it will also be slow and out-of-date in a couple of years; computers are continually becoming smaller, more powerful, faster, and inexpensive. Decide what your budget is and shop around; check the *Trading Times* (a national, classifieds-only newspaper) and your local newspaper classifieds.

A new laser printer for a PC (personal computer) sells for about $600. Laser printers produce a page of camera-ready art for about a penny, whereas even the inexpensive typesetting service bureaus charge $10 per page to do this. A laser printer will pay for itself within a few months. Again, if you shop around, you may be able to find a used one for $200 to $400.

Leasing a computer is another alternative. You may be able to rent-to-own an entire state-of-the-art system (without a printer) for about $250 per month. Check your yellow pages under "Computers—Renting & Leasing." If the businesses listed there can't help you, ask them who can; they usually can refer you somewhere else.

Computer Software

Publishing computer software varies greatly, and what software you get depends on the size of your organization and your production output. If you have a PC, you can effectively produce all business correspondences, mailing lists, forms, and other word processing with WordPerfect or Microsoft Word. For your desktop publishing needs, you can use Pagemaker or Microsoft Word 6.0+ software. These are easy to use and can create outstanding reproduction-quality masthead and letters-to-the-editor pages, as well as advertisements and other promotional pieces.

If you are already computer proficient, you may also want to pick up a book-keeping software program, such as Excel or Lotus 1-2-3. I don't recommend doing a crash course in number crunching with these programs if you're not familiar with computers. Learning how to use a computer is in itself a very time-consuming process; tackling complicated or advanced software, in addition to your basic word-processing and desktop-publishing programs, may consume the remaining time and energy you intended to focus on your product (not to mention your family, if you have one). Bookkeeping duties involve keeping track of order-entry and billing, inventory control, a general ledger of accounts receivable (money coming in) and accounts payable (money going out), sales analysis and forecasts, royalties, and a shipping manifest. This is where the calculator steps into the picture. You can do all your self-publishing bookkeeping with a calculator, typewriter, ledger pad and pencil, so special bookkeeping software is not a requirement. (See chapter 9 for more information on bookkeeping.)

A computer database listing is a very valuable asset to your company. You can use it to develop mailing lists and to keep tract of your business contacts. Every person whose business card you acquire can become a potential collaborator, whether today or 10 years from now, and all these contacts should go into your database. Always handle your contacts with extreme care, and always update your database whenever possible with new addresses, phone and fax numbers, and e-mail addresses. If a contact changes companies or positions, keep in touch and congratulate them—you never know when one of your contacts (who still reads your comic book) will leave his or her present job to head a major motion picture company! I have used many of my contacts even a decade after we first met, so don't underestimate your business relationships—they may end up being very valuable in years to come. My absolute favorite database software is ACT! by Symatek. It's sold wherever high-quality software is sold and is worth every penny. It can create instant letters and memos and can even fax contacts directly from your computer to theirs, if they have compatible fax software.

One computer issue you may end up considering is whether to get an Apple Macintosh system or an IBM PC with Microsoft Windows. My feeling is that the Macintosh is a "smart" computer for "stupid" people—people who want a highly intelligent "appliance" that is very user-friendly. It is a machine geared for people who are a bit intimidated by computers. The IBM PC with MS-DOS, on the other hand, is a "stupid" computer for "smart" people—people who will use their computers for more than just balancing their checkbook or playing card games, understand computer technology and are not intimidated by it, and will make more of an effort to get the most of their computers. The IBM PC is, therefore, a little less user-friendly ("stupid," in that the interface is not as self-explanatory).

You may also be wondering why, despite the fact that the vast majority of creative offices use the Apple Macintosh rather than the IBM PC, the Macintosh makes up only 6 percent of the entire computer market. Obviously, the cloning of the IBM PC by various other companies created an inexpensive option for the consumer neophyte. Apple's biggest mistake, I think, was not to license its computers for cloning (which would have lowered their prices, making them more accessible to the average computer user). The PC clones were much more affordable and could do most of what the average consumer or office worker needed them to do; as a result, the PC acquired more of the market than the Macintosh. Use of the more expensive Apple Macintosh was limited mostly to the creative fields or company art departments.

Now, Bill Gates and his company, Microsoft, have created a software program that gave the PC owner Macintosh-like windows programs. This simple application not only made Bill Gates one of the richest men in the world, but made the PC more user-friendly. The computer is no longer just an intimidating fancy appliance that sits on your desk in the den, used only to balance the household budget; it is the newest, hottest entertainment and infotainment gadget today. And, with the latest Microsoft Windows 95 program (which in some aspects even surpasses the interface of the Macintosh), computers are becoming much more accessible to everyone.

I've used both the PC and the Macintosh. The Macintosh is, by far, a better piece of equipment for creative development and applications, but the vast majority of the corporate world does use the PC. However, Microsoft Windows '95 gives the PC user a wonderful user-friendly interface very similar to the Macintosh. For my money, nothing beats the Macintosh—except, of course, Bill Gates—but, the Mac's programs are lean and mean with no extra "fat" to cause problems; they were designed to handle extensive color graphics work. With the explosive advent of electronic communications and transfers of electronic data via e-mail and the Internet, a less-expensive PC would be the way to start. (See chapter 8 for more on computers and the World Wide Web.)

Fax Machines, Photocopiers, and Other Items

Along with your computer and phone, another essential piece of equipment for business communication is the fax machine. The luxury of having instant written documentation assists in timely correspondences, production, and troubleshooting. You can pick up a new fax machine on average for $500. Prices for used equipment range from $150 to $400, depending on model and age. You can also lease fax machines or rent them on a rent-to-own plan (renting with the option to buy), but I'd recommend buying one rather than renting, if you can afford it.

Having a photocopy machine is a complete luxury. Most likely, your local drug store has one and only charges $.10 per copy. If you'd like the convenience of having one at your fingertips, consider buying a used one. A small used copy machine can cost about $300. Be very prudent when shopping for a used copy machine; maintenance costs can be quite high. As with purchasing a used car, check how many copies the machine has run in the course of its life. It's similar to buying a used car, when you don't want anything with over 100,000 miles. The copier should be able to produce multiple clean and crisp copies of your original without creating faded or spotted images and without jamming. You can also lease a copier, and I suggest doing this, but this usually requires a spotless and extensive credit history.

Another office item is a print calculator (one that prints your calculations out on paper as you type them), which is a minimal expense at about $30. A basic typewriter costs about $70, although used ones often only run about $30 (and don't forget to check with Aunt Gertrude). These two items will be valuable for bookkeeping, so you should definitely have them. Other standard office supplies include a stapler and staples, a tape dispenser and tape, phone message pads or Post-Its, a Rolodex, envelopes, stationery, file folders, file storage boxes (for old files), paper clips, pens, pencils, markers, computer printer paper, computer disks, reference books (dictionary, thesaurus, etc.), labels, packing tape, scissors, and anything else you think you might need.

COMPANY STRUCTURE

There are four main types of companies: sole proprietorship, partnership, C corporation, and sub-chapter S corporation. You should investigate each possibility and then choose the one with the organizational structure that best suits your needs, capabilities, and objectives. The most important difference between all these options is how you pay your federal and state income taxes.

Sole Proprietorship

This is a simple and easy way to begin and run your own business. It is, primarily, going into business for yourself (by yourself) under a company name (such as Spotman Comics, for example). The official name that appears on bank records or income tax records would be "Jane Doe DBA Spotman Comics." The DBA stands for "doing business as." You will pay taxes as an individual (using your social security number), with *all* your company expenses being tax deductions. As a sole proprietorship, you are the company, its income, and its debts. To obtain more information on taxes and sole proprietorships, call the I.R.S. (Internal Revenue Service) Distribution Center in your area, and ask for free copies of Publications 334, 463, and 550, which will help you prepare your sole proprietorship.

In a sole proprietorship, there is no mandatory obligation for liability insurance, stocks, shareholders, separate business bank accounts, or paychecks (with your company's share of payroll taxes). This means that you're not required by law to have any of these things in your business. Unfortunately though, a sole proprietorship doesn't offer the perpetual existence of a corporation. In other words, a corporation is considered a legal entity in and of itself, separate and apart from its shareholders. Corporation stockholders are, therefore, protected from any lawsuits filed against the corporation. This is not the case with a sole proprietorship, in which you would be personally liable for business losses. You could insure yourself against equipment damage, but any debt the company incurs passes directly to you. Most entrepreneurial entities start as a sole proprietorship. It's far more cost effective than the other three choices and gives you a lot of flexibility. The key is to be sure you've handled all your income taxes perfectly, with multiple receipts (if possible) for all deductions.

DON'T MESS WITH THE I.R.S. ALWAYS TAKE LEGITIMATE TAX DEDUCTIONS. IF YOUR COMIC BOOKS ARE A HUGE SUCCESS, THE I.R.S. MAY AUDIT YOU TO DISCOVER HOW YOU MADE ALL THAT MONEY.

WATCH WHAT YOU SAY IN PRINT!

The content in your letters-to-the-editor and other editorial comments, or even your business correspondences, may be protected by the first amendment, but the legal fees you might have to expend to defend yourself in slander/libel suits can eat you alive, so always choose your words carefully. This means that you should also be careful what you let your comic book characters say in your stories, and you should always pay attention to anything that you're signing your name to.

In order to do business under a company name other than your own name, you must register with your county clerk's office. This requires filling out a "Doing Business Under an Assumed Name" application, which costs about $5, plus taking out a classified advertisement in three consecutive issues of your local city newspaper to finalize the documentation. These requirements may vary nationwide, so you should call your local county clerk's office for exact instructions. You'll also have to add your company name to your checking account, or open a separate, company bank account under your business name.

Partnership

This form of company structure consists of two or more individuals working under a company name. A partnership has no perpetual existence (as discussed above under Sole Proprietorships), although many have won lawsuits to the contrary. Individuals, or shareholders, are only liable for the amounts they contributed to the company as capital. "Silent" partners (individuals who invest capital with complete anonymity) are safe from any legal liabilities—until they're discovered, that is. All partners are legally liable for any debts and are affected by any legal action taken against the company. Each partner also shares in the net income, which can be in either a bonus or salary form.

Partnerships are rarely recommended because one partner usually ends up working more (or thinking he's working more) than the other, thus causing conflicts that can destroy the business. If your company has more than one initial creator and owner, I would suggest entering into a C corporation or subchapter S corporation, in which the distribution of shares immediately specifies the percentage of ownership and responsibilities. This separation of the business into its own entity can help in separating the business from your personal identity and self, and with everyone focused on this new corporation, everyone will be working toward a collective goal.

C Corporation

A corporation represents the greatest possible separation of business from personal identity, both legally and financially. The traditional C corporation is its own entity, pays its own taxes (based on profits), and also protects its shareholders from any legal liabilities. This is, by far, the safest format for any company, but it can be expensive to structure and maintain. It has its own Federal Employer Identification Number (FEIN), address, checking account, and board of directors, which must hold board meetings regularly and file minutes (written transcripts) of the meetings in a corporate minute book.

To become incorporated, you file a registration of incorporation with your state and then receive a FEIN for tax purposes. This is like a social security number for your corporation. Since a corporation is its own entity, don't commingle personal and business funds; pay yourself a paycheck, withhold taxes, and pay the percentage of payroll taxes and FICA (social security) on that amount, as with any other employee. Your salary can be anything you want as long as the shareholders agree to it and it's written in the corporate minutes. Note that casually putting money in and taking it out of a corporate account can be considered embezzling. For more information on incorporation, write your state department and ask for the articles of incorporation.

51/49

Fifty-one percent of the business shares is the minimum needed to maintain control of a company. So, the above split of 51/49 is an example of a percentage of shares two partners may own (of any partnership or corporation) for one party to maintain the controlling interest in that situation. The individual who holds the most shares of the company is the majority interest and the person in charge. Although the board of directors or the officers of the corporation may make most company decisions, the majority shareholder has the right to veto anything at anytime. If you begin as a sole proprietorship, keep this in mind; you'll want to remember it when the vultures start circling above you. Always try to keep control of your business when other people or companies want to buy a piece of it, because investors are only interested in seeing a strong return on their money as quickly as possible—not in building a dream. If you maintain control, you'll have a better chance of realizing *your* goals. (See chapter 10 for more information on investors and acquiring capital.)

Sub-Chapter S Corporation

A sub-chapter S corporation has all the characteristics of a regular corporation, including stocks, multiple shareholders, a board of directors, paychecks, payroll taxes, and legal registration with the state. The primary difference between a sub-chapter S corporation and the C corporation is that a sub-chapter S corporation and its shareholders pay taxes once (as one combined amount), whereas a traditional C corporation pays taxes as its own legal entity and its shareholders pay separate taxes as employees (hence the W-2 form).

The advantage to the sub-chapter S status is the capability to deduct the company's annual losses against the shareholders' federal and state taxes. Any capital gains or dividends can also be more easily absorbed by the shareholders. For more tax information on a sub-chapter S corporation, call the I.R.S. Distribution Center in your area and ask for Publications 550 and 589, which are free.

COMPANY IDENTITY

When conceptualizing a company name you should think mainstream. You're not going to get serious, worthwhile attention from Hollywood executives or the public with a company called, let's say, HellHole Comics. Important clients will sooner consider looking into a company called Chicago Publishing, Inc., or New York Media Company, Inc. Don't limit yourself. If your comic book is a horror title, HellHole Comics could be a good, dramatic business name, but it may be inappropriate a year later when you want to publish a licensed title from a wholesome Saturday morning children's cartoon. For example, imagine the following situation:

> **You:** Hello, I'm interested in purchasing the rights to produce a comic book based on the *Those Wonderful Bears* cartoon.
>
> **Licensor:** Oh, great. . . . What's your company name, again?
>
> **You:** HellHole Comics.
>
> **Licensor:** Come again?
>
> **You:** HellHole Comics.
>
> **Licensor:** (silence)
>
> **You:** Hello?
>
> **Licensor:** Oh, I'm sorry, but we've already sold those rights.

The licensor paused because he had to figure out how he was going to sell and explain the idea of having a company called HellHole Comics publish a comic book of Reverend Scott's *Those Wonderful Bears*. Without even looking at your other products, he may be envisioning a satanic, bastardized version of the show. While this may be an extreme example, you get the point. Of course you can be creative, but you should also consider the fact that your company will deal with other businesses, investors, and individuals. You are a professional company, whether you're publishing a single title from your basement or producing 10 monthly titles from a Main Street office, and you should project a professional, credible image. You also can't always foresee future business opportunities, but if you have a presentable, more versatile company name, you'll ensure that you are better prepared for whatever opportunities do arise.

Before getting too involved with a name (whether it be a company name or a comic book title), you should check it with a quick scan in *The Overstreet Comic Book Price Guide* (your library should have a copy of this) and also on the computer system at your local library, to make sure no one else is already using it. Many computer online services offer trademark searches; just go to your favorite search engine and type "trademark search." Using your own name for a corporation name and identity can initially be an appropriate and inspiring motivational tool, especially if you have the controlling interest in the company; but if the shareholder structure changes, so should the company name. You don't want to be the figurehead of a company in which decisions are being made by committee, because if there's a negative reaction from the public or the business community to a decision or product, it's you who'll be attacked (since your name's on the door).

As a comic book publisher, you are, or have a partner who is, the artist for your books. Brainstorm visually to come up with a company name and logo, as well as the comic book titles. A logo can be as important as the company name itself, so make sure that it's clear and legible. Note that any logo must be easily readable whether it's one or 12 inches wide.

PROTECT YOUR PRIVACY!

When you print a company mailing address in your publication for the general public to see, you open your doors to the world. Although you want to encourage reader correspondence and business opportunities, you don't want someone knocking on your front door at dinnertime. If you don't have the budget for separate office space, get a post office box and use this rather than your home address. A box at your local post office costs about $20 for anything from six months to a year. In this way, you have some anonymity and are still available to receive company mail. You should also make sure your home telephone number is unlisted; you don't want any eager (or, even worse, crazy) fans calling you collect from Alaska. Hey, it happens!

TRADEMARKS, COPYRIGHTS, AND LICENSES 2

TRADEMARKS AND COPYRIGHTS

Trademark and copyright laws were established to protect against any unauthorized use of intellectual property names, titles, logos, art, or stories and to solidify legal ownership of these things. A trademark will protect the concept, name, and logo, while a copyright will protect the story, script, and visual artistic representation. Note that you cannot copyright a name or title; these things can only be protected by a trademark. Also note that you cannot trademark a story in which the trademarked name or title appears; you can only copyright that story concept to protect it. For your overall protection, I suggest having a lawyer help you in accurately securing trademarks and copyrights.

You can either have a reputable law firm trademark and copyright your titles and concepts for you, or you can do it yourself for a fraction of the cost a law firm would charge for the service. To do it yourself, write for the appropriate forms from the addresses on page 169, and check your local library (or the Internet) for more information on trademark availability and how to trademark your own titles. The United States Patent and Trademark Office (also listed on page 169) will file a trademark for you; if it finds no active trademark already in use for the name you want, it will register that name, title, and/or logo to you, and you will be the legal rights holder. If there already is an active trademark in use for that name, your application will be null and void.

To avoid submitting a void application, you should do a trademark search to see if the name or logo you want to use is already trademarked. To have a complete trademark search done through a reputable law firm costs about $100. You can search for existing trademarks yourself, but your search will probably not be as thorough. It's worth the expense to have a law firm do it, because without an absolutely complete search to clear the use of the trademark, you may find yourself changing the title of your comic book after the first few issues when the real trademark owner surfaces.

Although a copyrighted story may protect an intellectual property from being used unlawfully, proof of legal copyright may have to be proven in a court of law. Upon legal notification of copyright violation, the offender might opt *not* to discontinue the illegal use of the property and to have a court decide who has the rights to the concept, name, or logo. In many recent court cases, a trademark rights holder has won the case over an existing user of the same name, title, or logo who didn't file and hold the legal trademark. If another company or individual decides to use and trademark your name, title, or logo— and you don't hold the trademark—they could (intentionally or unintentionally) legally steal it. This could also happen with copyrights, as well; someone could copyright your story, thereby stealing it from you, unless you have proof that you wrote it first and are willing to spend tens of thousands of dollars fighting legal battles. To avoid those enormous legal fees, and the possibility of losing the rights to your concept, you must follow the legal steps to solidify that protection. If you're investing time and money into the production of a concept, it's worthwhile to also invest in protection of the rights of ownership.

Traditionally, you have a window of two years after their release to trademark a concept, name, and logo, but until 1988, there was no adequate protection prior to release. At that time, the Trademark Law Revision Act of 1988 was developed, allowing organizations to register a trademark with the "intent to use." This completely new trademark law, which went into effect on November 16, 1989, enabled creators to trademark a name, title, or logo *before* ever producing a product.

This act helped me in the summer of 1989, when I was developing a comic book concept called *Supercops*. It involved a story of America's future law enforcement. My inspiration for the idea came from an article in *Newsweek* magazine about how the nation's police department was outgunned, outmanned, and out of control in the war on drugs. *Supercops* had all the elements for commercial success: a catchy name, interesting characters, weapons, and a violent betrayal of the war on drugs. I immediately contacted my trademark lawyer to process a search on the name to see if it was already trademarked. (Note: Any lawyer can do this, but it's usually better and cheaper to use a trademark specialist.) Even after doing my own research on this at the library and finding nothing, I wanted more assurance and information. It seemed unbelievable that such an outstanding title was free of any trademark protection. The lawyer's computer trademark search only cost $150 and cleared the name for production.

When the Trademark Law Revision Act went into effect in November of 1989, it worked well to protect my investment in the *Supercops* name during preproduction stages as I further developed the concept. I didn't feel comfortable waiting until after releasing the *Supercops* concept to decide if it was worthwhile to secure the trademark. It seemed to be too valuable a property to not protect immediately. For a few hundred dollars, I had my lawyer file an "intent to use" trademark registration. Then, in early 1990, a few months prior to my first issue's release, I came across an article about a new syndicated television show to be released that summer called *Super Cop*. I contacted the legal department of Viacom, the show's producers, and informed them of my recent registration of the name and title of *Supercops*. They were very surprised, but after a few correspondences between lawyers, they realized that my company owned the legal rights to the name and title of *Supercops*. (Note that the *name* and the *title* are two different things: the name is simply the term Supercops, as either one word or two, while the title is when the name is used as any title for actual merchandise, such as comic books, magazines, books, videos, or movies.)

Since the Viacom show involved a police officer with a superpowered exoskeleton and his adventures in crime fighting, Viacom asked to purchase the *Supercops* name and title outright. I asked for $500,000. One of the show's producers counter-offered with a $15,000 advance on 10 percent royalty of the gross profits from the show and its merchandising. After analyzing their show, production values, distribution, and list of licensees, I declined. Under the law, Viacom was required to change its concept name, which it did—to *Super Force*.

It would have been easy to predict the winner of a legal battle, had I not registered an "intent to use" *Supercops* trademark. Caputo Publishing would have been no match for a company like Viacom, with its financial resources and powerful legal representation. I would not have even made it to the battlefield, unless my company decided it was worth it (and feasible) to add a substantial increase in legal fees to the coming year's financial forecast. The few hundred dollars it cost me to legally protect the *Supercops* name, title, and concept paid for itself one thousand times over.

Initiating trademark registration (and, to a lesser extent, securing copyrights) is also important in solidifying your concepts, names, and titles as "intangible assets." Proprietary characters are considered by potential investors in, or purchasers of, your company. Without legal registration, your intellectual properties may not be viable and, therefore, not be considered assets to your company.

The Indicia

The indicia is the technical information that appears at the front of every publication. It indicates the volume, issue number, and date of the publication of the work, and tells the reader who the trademark and copyright holders are

MAIL IT TO YOURSELF

After developing a concept and a few visuals, mail the material to yourself in a sealed envelope. On receiving the package, don't open it—ever. Create a "Trademarks and Copyrights" file in your filing system, and file it there. That sealed envelop with a dated government postmark will go a long way in protecting your concept, name, and title in any court of law. A government postmark is dated and can be used as legal proof of the date of creation of your material. It will help protect your concept even if you don't hold the copyright or trademark.

and where the publication was manufactured. It doesn't have anything to do with actually protecting copyrights and trademarks but just informs the reader of who owns them. Note that the printing location is required to export your product to another country. A sample comic book indicia would look something like this:

> *Vespers,* Volume 1, No. 1, July 1995 is published monthly by Mars Comics, a division of Mars Media Group, P.O. Box 333, Oak Forest, IL 60452. *Vespers* TM and © copyright 1984, 1994 Anthony C. Caputo. *Vesper, Dyspro, The Mystifier, Kinesis,* and *Denizon*™ and copyright © 1984, 1994 Anthony C. Caputo. *Mirror*™ and copyright © 1994 Anthony C. Caputo. All contents copyright © Mars Media Group unless otherwise indicated. All Rights Reserved. Absolutely no reproduction of any kind is allowed without the written consent of the legal rights holder and an officer of the company. Printed in the USA.

Traditionally, the volume number is used for indicating the year (for example, Volume 1 would indicate that it's the first year of publication, Volume 5 would mean the fifth year of publication, etc.); you can also use it to indicate mini-series or series number. Note that the date should be about two months later than the actual on-sale period, to give the issue a longer shelf life.

COPYRIGHTS AND FREELANCE EMPLOYEES

When you hire employees on a freelance basis, have them sign "work-for-hire" contract agreements. An amendment to the copyright law, passed by Congress in 1989, gives artists the right to terminate the use of a graphic depiction of a trademark after 35 years. This means that without a signed agreement specifically indicating that the work done for you is "work-for-hire" with all rights assigned to your company, the original artists can reclaim the copyrights to their work after 35 years, and so you may find yourself handing the rights to a logo (or other work) back to the designer 35 years down the road. This "starving artist" amendment does not include full-time employees but, rather, freelancers and other outside sources, such as art studios and ad agencies. So, be sure that the artists working on your design are full-time employees, non-contractual "independent contractors," or "full-time freelancers" of the outside companies that you use.

Following is a sample independent contractor (or freelancer) agreement between a company (here referred to as Publisher) and an individual freelancer. You should use this contract with any freelancers you hire to work on any of your company's graphic designs or written design elements, for example logo designs, ad layouts, and copy writing. In this way, you'll be protected from the "starving artist" amendment. Note that certain details of the contract, such as the services listed in the Project Schedule, may change depending on what you hire a freelancer for. (See chapter 5 for more about contracts).

Note that "Its" stands for the appropriate company's title where applicable. Also, you should have a lawyer draw up all your contracts, rather than write them yourself.

WORK-FOR-HIRE FREELANCER AGREEMENT
(INDIVIDUAL FREELANCER)

This Agreement is made _____(date)_____, 19___, between ___(publisher name)___, located at _____(address)_____, and ___(freelancer name)_____, a freelancer residing at _____(address)_____.

   In consideration of the mutual covenants herein contained, the parties, referred to hereinafter as Publisher and Freelancer, hereby agree as follows:

   1. **Services.** Freelancer agrees to provide the services specified in any Project Schedule that shall, from time to time, be defined and executed by the parties. Such duties are hereinafter referred to as Services.

   2. **Terms and Termination.** This Agreement shall continue until terminated by either party upon _____ days after written notice.

   3. **Payment for Services.**

   (a) Charges. As full compensation for Services provided by Freelancer pursuant to any Project Schedule, Publisher agrees to pay Freelancer the charges as set forth and defined under Project Schedule below.

PROJECT SCHEDULE

Services

Overall design and production of promotional and advertising materials, ads, flyers, and comic books.

Charges

Freelancer will be paid $_____ an hour as an independent contractor. Payment will be every _____ weeks.

Term

The term of this agreement is _____ months (days, weeks), or _____ days after written notice by either party.

   (b) Reimbursement for expenses. Publisher shall reimburse Freelancer for reasonable out-of-pocket expenses incurred by Freelancer in the performance of Services only if specifically included on the applicable Project Schedule. Freelancer agrees to maintain appropriate records and to submit copies of all receipts necessary to support such expenses at the intervals and in the manner prescribed by Publisher.

   4. **Independent Contractor.** It is understood and agreed that Freelancer shall perform the Services as an independent contractor and freelance worker. Freelancer shall not be considered an employee of Publisher. Freelancer shall not be entitled to any benefits provided by Publisher to its employees, and Publisher will make no deductions from any payments due to Freelancer hereunder for state or federal tax purposes. Freelancer agrees to be personally responsible for any and all taxes and other payments due on moneys received from Publisher hereunder.

   5. **Warranty**

   (a) Original development. Freelancer represents and warrants that all work performed for, or on behalf of, Publisher and all work products produced thereby,

Sample independent contractor (or freelancer) agreement between a company (here referred to as Publisher) and an individual freelancer

will not knowingly infringe upon or violate any patent, copyright, trade secret, or other property rights of any former employer, client, or other third party.

(b) Warranty of expertise. Freelancer represents and warrants that he is highly skilled and experienced in providing the Services required under each Project Schedule entered into hereunder.

6. **Indemnification.** Freelancer shall indemnify Publisher from all claims, losses, and damages that may arise from the breach of any of his obligations under this Agreement.

7. **Protection of Confidential Information**

(a) Confidential information. For purposes of this Agreement, the term "confidential information" means all information that is not generally known and that: (i) is obtained by Freelancer from Publisher or is learned, discovered, developed, conceived, originated, or prepared by Freelancer during the process of providing Services to Publisher, and (ii) relates directly to the business or assets of Publisher. Confidential information shall include but not be limited to: inventions, discoveries, trade secrets, and know-how; computer software codes, designs, routines, algorithms, and structures; product information, research, and development information; lists of clients, sources, and other related information; financial data and business plans and processes; and any other information about Publisher that Publisher informs Freelancer, or that Freelancer should know by virtue of his position, is to be kept confidential.

(b) Obligation of nondisclosure. During the term of this Agreement and at all times thereafter, Freelancer agrees to not disclose to others, or otherwise appropriate or copy, any confidential information, whether or not developed by Freelancer, except as required in the lawful performance of obligations to Publisher hereunder. The obligations of Freelancer under this paragraph shall not apply to any information that becomes public knowledge through no fault of Freelancer.

8. **Rights to Work.**

(a) Disclosure. Freelancer agrees to promptly disclose to Publisher all work developed in whole or in part by Freelancer within the scope of this Agreement with Publisher including but not limited to: any literary works, artwork, graphics, or any concept, idea, or design relating thereto; and letters, pamphlets, drafts, memoranda, and other documents, writings, or tangible things of any kind relating thereto. Such material is hereinafter referred to as the Work.

(b) Ownership and assignment of rights. All Work created by Freelancer shall belong exclusively to Publisher and shall be considered a work made for hire for Publisher within the meaning of Title 17 of the United States Code. To the extent that Publisher does not own such Work as a work made for hire, Freelancer hereby assigns to Publisher all rights to such Work, including but not limited to all other patent rights, copyrights, and trade-secret rights. Freelancer agrees to execute all documents reasonably requested by Publisher to further evidence the foregoing assignment and to provide all reasonable assistance to Publisher in perfecting or protecting Publisher's rights to such Work.

Sample independent contractor agreement (continued)

9. **Duty Upon Termination.** Upon termination of this Agreement, for any reason or at any time upon request of Publisher, Freelancer agrees to deliver to Publisher all materials of any nature that are or contain confidential information or Work, or that are otherwise the property of Publisher or of any its customers and including but not limited to: writings, designs, documents, records, data, memoranda, tapes, and computer disks containing software, routines, file layouts, record layouts, system design information, models, manuals, documentation, and notes.

10. **Governing Law.** This contract will be governed by and construed in accordance with the laws of the state of _____(state name)_____.

11. **Entire Agreement.** This Agreement constitutes the complete and exclusive statement of the agreement between the parties with regard to the matters set forth herein and supersedes all other agreements, proposals, and representations, oral or written, express or implied, with regard thereto.

IN WITNESS WHEREOF, the parties have executed this Agreement as of the day and year set forth above.

FREELANCER

By: _____

Its: _____

PUBLISHER

By: _____

Its: _____

LICENSING ARRANGEMENTS

This is when you acquire the rights to publish a comic book based on an existing, highly recognized character, and this type of arrangement can have both disadvantages and advantages. The primary disadvantage is that trademark and copyright ownership reverts back to the licensor (the original rights holder). This means that the licensor will own every story line, artistic representation, and additional character you create. Another drawback is that you'll only have limited rights to publish the property; for example, if your contract is for two years with an option for another two, you have the rights only for four years. And, after the initial two years, the licensor may even choose to alter the contract so that it is more financially beneficial for them and less so for you. You have no rights to the material you produce or to the market you open up for that character. The many advantages include credibility, from publishing a highly recognized intellectual property; instant readership, since the property already has an established, immediate fan base; and, depending on the international recognition of the property, instant foreign reprint sales.

Within the past 10 years, some of the most successful comic books ever published were titles based on some of the most popular *licensed* properties in recent history. These properties are used by permission of the owners under licensing arrangement. Terms of each exclusive agreement differ, but typically, they require an advance against regular royalty payments, and some require minimum royalty payments over a specified period of time. The length and territories of these contracts can vary from two to four years for North American and/or worldwide rights.

If you only acquire the North American rights, you can still sell your reprint rights to foreign countries as long as the foreign purchaser has the legal rights from the licensor to publish in that territory. As a worldwide rights holder, you can sell to any publisher throughout the world as a sublicensor. Traditionally, it's required that the rights purchaser pay a larger advance to the licensor for worldwide rights. This is due to the potential foreign revenue that a popular licensed product may generate; comic books are more readily accepted and respected as literature, or a valid form of creative expression, in some foreign countries (such as Japan and England) than they are here, and so there is a chance that foreign revenue will be greater than domestic revenue.

If you sell the rights to translate and reprint a comic book series based on an internationally successful property to 60 countries, you can easily generate hundreds of thousands of dollars in foreign sales. So, if you obtain the rights to an international hit, you can make enormous profits even without legal ownership of the trademark or copyright. You only have the exclusive right to produce a product for a limited amount of time. Exploit that popularity, and assist in creating more interest, by exposing the licensed character to more overseas markets. Your comic book is a billboard for a licensor's trademark; whether you ship out 3,000 or 300,000 copies, you're increasing the awareness of the trademarked concept, name, and title. And, you pay the licensor for that privilege; it's a mutually beneficial venture with enormous financial potential.

In 1987, I acquired the exclusive North American comic book rights to *Speed Racer* for a $1,000 advance on a 5-percent-of-wholesale royalty rate; this agreement was for two years with an option for an additional two years at the same terms. *Speed Racer,* an animated cartoon produced in Japan that initially aired on North American television from 1967 through 1986, can now sometimes be seen on MTV. Columbia Pictures had no idea of the nostalgic popularity of *Speed Racer* or the surge of interest in Japanimation in the comic book industry. Had they known that *Speed Racer* was much more than a dead 1960s cartoon, they would have wanted a very different (larger) advance payment and royalty rate. I suspected that *Speed Racer* could be successful again, but I never projected that it would single-handedly catapult my company out of the Black-and-White Implosion quicksand of that year.

With a delicate balance of foresight, market analysis, research, determination, and capital, you can use the instant recognition of a licensed property as a powerful survival tactic, as well as a plain and simple money maker. If you find a rights holder whose property you're interested in, send a letter explaining your licensing interest. If you're not sure who the rights holder is, you'll have to do some research; for example, you could start by contacting the TV station that airs a particular cartoon that you're interested in. See Appendix, page 169, for more information on licensing resources.

COMIC BOOK CREATION

I look for quality, first and foremost. A book of high-quality production values will sell itself.

—John Stangeland
Owner, Atlas Comic Shop

Producing a high-quality comic book is not as easy as most veterans make it appear. It involves teamwork and talent and is usually a collaboration of creative individuals who all share a single, primary objective. Of course there are also those talented and experienced comic book masters who are proficient in every step of comic book production, and who independently create complete works of highly acclaimed material. Either way, comic books are an imaginative outlet for artistic expression.

Before you begin you should ask yourself the following: Am I producing this product solely as an expression of my own creativity or because I think it will be fun? Am I interested in building a profitable business? If you answered "yes" to these things, you're ready to build your own little creative empire and make it financially worthwhile. You should also step back and recognize your limits; once you've done this, you can devise and assess a game plan and go for it! There is always the chance that your concept will make you into the next comic book success story.

AN OVERVIEW OF COMIC BOOK PRODUCTION

The complexity of comic book production can be likened to that of motion picture or television show production. The similarities stem from the delicate balance between words and visual images. The different mediums also have almost identical formats for written scripts and all use the "storyboard" style layouts to guide the creation of striking visual expressions.

First, the writer scripts a story for a penciler to illustrate. (Detailed information on writing, penciling, lettering, inking, coloring, and on hiring freelance artists to these things follows later in this chapter.) To correctly illustrate a comic book story, the penciler must understand the comic book medium and the art of storytelling. On average, there are usually 22 pages of artwork in a standard 32-page comic book, and once penciled, the pages are given to a letterer, who hand letters in the dialogue, sound effects, and panel borders. After the letterer finishes, the pages go to an inker, who outlines or traces all the penciling with India ink, which enables the best possible reproduction of the black plate.

Spread from Vespers, #2
I wrote and penciled this page, and David Mowry inked it.

Page from *Vespers*, #2

Again, I wrote and penciled this image, which David Mowry then inked.

If the book is a black-and-white comic book, it is ready to be sent to the printer at this point. If, however, the entire book is in full color, production moves on to the blueline stage. A blueline is a reproduction of all the inked artwork at actual comic book size (6 x 9") in a light blue color (hence the term *blue*line). Bluelines are made either by the colorist or a production house, and are, traditionally, hand painted by the colorist. When hand colored, each blueline page is produced on high-quality art board to enable maximum support during painting. The light blue tints serve as a guide for colorists, enabling them to produce their best detailed colorwork.

The finished painted blueline pages are then laser scanned and made into pieces of film by a color separator, who then gives those films to the printer to print and produce the finished book. Sometimes, graylines are used instead of bluelines. These are similar to bluelines but are on photographic paper and tend to have a plastic-like surface, from which it is difficult to produce smooth, clean colors during printing.

Another form of coloring includes today's sophisticated computer technology. The inked pages are scanned into the computer, and colors are "filled" into the appropriate places using an Adobe Photoshop software program. This relatively new method of coloring has recently become much more common. With the power of the computer at their fingertips, colorists have the flexibility to produce outstanding quality and special effects. If you use computer coloring, you bypass the traditional blueline stage; instead, you send digital files of your pages on a disk to the printer, who uses this to produce film.

WRITING

The most important element of comic book writing is the ability to express and present a story visually. You may have a fantastic idea for a scene, but unless you can describe it visually, the penciler will draw his or her own interpretation. So, the technical quality of the actual script can have a direct effect on the final comic book outcome.

There are various ways to write a comic book, and you should choose the technique and format that is most comfortable for you. The most popular writing method is to produce a complete script. It is the more widely accepted format to use when submitting a story for the approval of editors or licensors. Technically, it's also quite similar to a movie script, in which the action is described in scenes, only in this case the action is separated into panels with the complete corresponding dialogue. (See example on the next page.)

KNOW YOUR CHARACTERS! ACCORDING TO MIKE BARON, CREATOR OF NEXUS AND BADGER, AN IMPORTANT ELEMENT OF STORY WRITING IS CHARACTER PERSONALITY; IF YOU REALLY KNOW YOUR CHARACTERS, YOUR COMIC BOOK WILL WRITE ITSELF.

Another script-writing method is to create a looser, less complete version of the script. This format includes a description of the action in a undetermined number of panels, along with a rough sample of dialogue. With this type of script, the writer finishes the dialogue after the penciler visually presents the story.

By Barry Daniel Petersen

Page 7

PANEL 1
Captain Rap Scallion is in heated battle with his archenemy
Blackrat. Scallion parries a thrust by Blackrat, who is
becoming weary from his opponent's efforts.

>   Blackrat: Fall down and die already!

>   Rap Scallion: Not bloody likely.

PANEL 2
Scallion jumps over the swing of a blade.

>   *Narration* (continued): . . . but being a simple and
>   quiet man . . .

PANEL 3
The cutlass is knocked out of Captain Rap Scallion's hand.

>   *Narration* (continued): . . . there was little time to
>   practice.

PANEL 4
An unarmed Scallion is surrounded by a small army of the
mutinous crew. There is no mercy on their faces. They know
they are victorious, with no reason to fear and all their
Captain's possessions and cargo to gain.

>   *Narration:* Besides, even the best swashbucklers would
>   be helpless against such odds.

>   Rap Scallion: Uh . . . guys!

PANEL 5
A silhouette of fists pounds on a broken Captain.

>   *Narration:* They were upon him. Within seconds,
>   Scallion was beaten . . .

PANEL 6
A close-up of the bound rat left leaning on a wooden barrel.

>   *Narration* (continued): . . . and bound.

Complete script page from Barry Daniel Petersen's *Piratz* comic book
*This page from a complete script describes the action in each panel and includes all the appropriate
dialogue. After each panel number is a brief explanation of the action that the penciler needs to represent,
followed by the corresponding dialogue or descriptive narration line to be penciled into the panel.*

Penciled page for *Piratz*
This is the corresponding finished penciled page based on Barry Daniel Petersen's scripted page shown opposite. The penciler read each panel description in the script and created an appropriate visual.

Sketched layout-scripted page from Vespers, #1
This type of script presents the dialogue and some loose visuals.

A PICTURE IS WORTH A THOUSAND WORDS! LENGTHY OR REPETITIVE COMIC BOOK DIALOGUE CAN BE OVERKILL. OFTEN, THE IMAGES SPEAK FOR THEMSELVES.

A more visual script-writing technique, as shown above and opposite, is to sketch each page's layout showing the panels, characters, and dialogue. This can work just as well as any traditional, complete script. Here, instead of writing a description of the action, panel to panel, you sketch out rough thumbnail layouts with handwritten dialogue. If you don't like the way a page or panel looks (or reads), simply change or redraw it. I would recommend using this scripting method when you have specific visual images in mind that you want to convey to the penciler.

Regardless of which script type is used, it's usually beneficial to the quality of any story for the writer to edit the dialogue before the finished penciled pages (sometimes also called "pencils") go to the letterer. This changing of dialogue to more closely fit the finished art simply helps fine-tune the overall flow

Sketched layout-scripted page from *Weird Melvin* by Marc Hansen
Another example of layout scripting, this page shows each panel with the comic book characters and their corresponding dialogue.

Finished art from *Weird Melvin* by Marc Hansen

This is the finished art based on the sketched script page shown on the previous page. By comparing the two pages, you can see how the script influences and guides the artist in creating the final output. The lettering has yet to be added here, but Marc Hansen uses computer-generated lettering to letter his books.

of the story. For example, in your script you might describe an action scene in which the hero opens fire on a villain with a sawed-off shotgun and the dialogue reads, "I'm going to blow your head off!" If the penciler actually draws the hero right as he is shooting the villain's head off, it's redundant to have him say, "I'm going to blow your head off!" because the penciler has already visually informed the reader as to what's happening. Therefore, you can tailor the dialogue and change it to something like, "You're all going to die!" Taking the time to edit the comic book is very important to the quality of the finished product. Using an outside editor, who can look at the work with a fresh eye, can be even more effective. An objective reader will sometimes notice things that you have missed.

PENCILING: THE ART OF STORYTELLING

Transforming a script into successfully drawn comic book pages involves a genuine understanding of the art of storytelling. The ability to communicate a story visually through penciling (but without the use of words) can be learned and mastered with practice and guidance. A good page will *tell* readers who, what, where, how, and why, *before* they ever read any dialogue.

Regardless of your comic book's style, it's imperative that your storytelling be effective. Skillful penciling is, therefore, a necessity for any good comic book story. To check how successful your visual storytelling is, simply move from one panel to another and add, for example, the test caption, "Meanwhile, 10 miles away . . .". If this caption suits the scenes but isn't part of your scripted story, this may be an indication of poor storytelling, and as a result of this, your readers might get lost. Your images must help relate your story.

You also have to ensure that the story flows clearly from one image to the next, and you can do this by giving the reader continuous visual hints about the characters, locations, and action. A visual hint might be something as simple as the lit elevator buttons in panels 1 and 2 of the example on the next page. This element immediately informs the reader that the two characters are in an elevator. Color (of clothes, the environment, etc.) can be another storytelling ingredient and visual hint. On pages 49 and 50 you can see the various stages in the creation of the colored version of the pencil on page 43. The color allows for additional clarity and excitement in the scene.

Penciling Quality

Creating a great penciled page involves more than fantastic storytelling and the ability to draw dynamic anatomy. It also requires crisp, tight penciling. This means that the penciled lines should be sharp and well defined. The pencil lead should produce lines that are clean enough to reproduce as they are, without being covered with ink. Sketchy penciled pages (those with unclear, undefined, soft lines) are difficult to ink over. The inker is supposed to ink directly over the penciling, and without crisp, sharp pencil lines, it is unclear which lines to ink. The final image, therefore, would end up being a mix of both the penciler's and the inker's images, and this rarely results in a satisfactory product.

To create the best possible penciled images, you'll need good tools: quality paper and pencils. Use Bristol paper, which you can find at your local art supply

Sketched layout-scripted page from *Vespers*, #1 (Elevator scene)

The visuals of this script page immediately show the reader the characters and the situation: a man walks into an elevator where he's impressed with a beautiful woman; he tries to pick up the woman, who is completely unimpressed with him; he gets a little too close when smelling her perfume, and she gets angry and begins to change form; he notices something unusual happening; and finally, he is shocked by the sudden transformation of the woman into a glowing reflection of himself. Each panel clearly indicates the location and actions of both characters.

COMIC BOOK CREATION

Finished penciled page from *Vespers*, #1 (Elevator scene)
The elevator buttons and control panel that appear in consecutive panels of the story are visual hints that tell readers the action is taking place in an elevator.

Finished pencil for the cover of *Vespers*, #1

This example shows good, clean penciling for the inker to work over. The lines are clear and sharp, ensuring that there is no confusion as to what should be inked. The inked version is shown opposite, and the final, colored image appears on the cover of this book; by comparing the three steps (pencil, ink, and color), you can see how comic book art arrives at its finished stage.

Inked cover art for *Vespers*, #1. Inked by Jeff Butler

Here, you see the finished inked stage of this cover image. Since the penciling was so crisp, the inker had no trouble following it, and the inked page successfully reflects the penciler's vision. Again, if you look at the cover of this book, you can see how the final, colored version of this image developed from the two previous stages.

store in 14 x 17" pads of 20 sheets. It comes in a vellum (slightly rough) or smooth finish. A vellum finish tends to absorb ink better, allowing for good solid black areas; it's the best choice for both full-color and black-and-white comic books. The standard size of original comic book art is 10 x 15", which is later reduced down (by the printer, color separator, or production house) to 61 percent of this for reproduction. You should work at this initial larger size, because it offers more space for detail.

Penciled and lettered page from *Vespers*, #2 (Sunglasses Scene)
*On this page you can see areas marked with **x**'s to indicate areas that are to be solid black. Note that some of the dialogue bubbles overlap x areas, but this is okay, as you can see in the inked version opposite.*

Which pencils you use depends on your individual preference. A 2H or 3H pencil has fairly hard lead, resulting in lighter pencil lines; this would be an excellent choice with which to start drawing your layouts. After executing your initial sketch, you can then go over the lines with an H or HB pencil, which has a softer, darker lead that makes more visible marks. This lets you "tighten" your original pencil sketching (or clean up your lines) to create the finished pencils. When penciling, don't use the pencil to fill in areas that are to be inked solid

Lettered and inked page from *Vespers*, #2 (Sunglasses Scene)
Here, the areas with x's have been inked in. Note that the dialogue bubbles are not covered by the ink. At this stage the art is ready to be colored. (The finished version appears on page 51.)

black. Instead, mark these spaces with a small *x*. This will not only keep your pages clean, but will make it easier for the letterer and inker to work with the black areas. This is because ink adheres far better to the actual original Bristol paper surface than it does to solid areas of pencil shading.

Creating quality penciled pages takes time. Good pencilers take about a day to draw just one outstanding page of comic book art. They must design a dynamic layout, research possible references (for which they can use anything from a photo in a magazine to an example in an artist's guidebook), tighten the figures, and add the dramatic black areas.

When creating a comic book, you should always concentrate on your strengths and let others work on the areas in which you are weaker. For example, if you're a good penciler, pencil the book, and do it completely; focus on finishing the pencils to the very best of your abilities. Then, once you finish the pages, leave the lettering and inking to someone who is better at these stages. The compilation of everyone's best work will generate a superior finished product.

LETTERING

Master lettering is the touch that gives your illustrated story that unmistakable comic book feel. It is an important part of the process in creating any high-quality comic book, and in fact, the dialogue balloon is such a universally recognized image that it continues to be widely used in the various advertising and entertainment media as a universal comic book symbol.

A letterer isn't just someone who can print neatly, although with some practice and the right tools, anyone with clean printed handwriting can learn to become a letterer. Letterers must have balance and uniformity in their lettering. They use precision instruments such as lettering guides (available at most art supply stores), technical pens (drafting pens), India ink, T-squares, and triangle. An experienced letterer should know the reading order of word balloons, which is from left to right and top to bottom. This format helps to ensure the smooth flow of dialogue and add extra dramatic emphasis to sound effects, word balloons, and free-standing words, all of which makes for an exciting read.

(text continues on page 57)

Sample comic book lettering
These are samples of quality comic book lettering in dialogue bubbles.

Partially colored page from *Vespers*, #1 (Elevator scene)

This page is in the process of being colored by computer. Here, the final box is still uncolored;
compare with the finished version on the next page.

Finished colored page from *Vespers*, #1 (Elevator scene)

Color adds interest and clarity to comic book art. The glowing elevator button (in the first box) and the paneling of the interior elevator wall (in the third box) work to inform the reader of the location. Compare this final colored version and the penciled stage of this scene on page 43 to see the difference.

Final computer-colored page from *Vespers*, #2 (Sunglasses scene)

Here, you can see how the color adds its own drama and excitement to the story. Compare with the penciled and lettered and inked stages on pages 46 and 47.

Hand painted blueline page

The blue tints on the blueline serve as a guide for the colorist. Note that the black areas and lettering are separate; they will be filled in by the printer using the same black negative film that was used to produce the blueline. If you compare this blueline with the image opposite, you can see how it will look with the black ink.

Hand painted blueline page with black film overlay.

In the printing process, the cyan, magenta, and yellow inks reproduce the images on your painted blueline, while the black areas and lettering come from the black (negative) film overlay. (See chapter 4 for more information on the four-color printing process.) This overlay guarantees rich solid blacks that are not diluted (or mixed) through a scanning process.

Hand painted blueline page

Another example of a hand painted blueline page without the black areas or lettering.

Completed comic book page

This is the final stage of creation for the comic book page illustrated on pages 38 and 61.

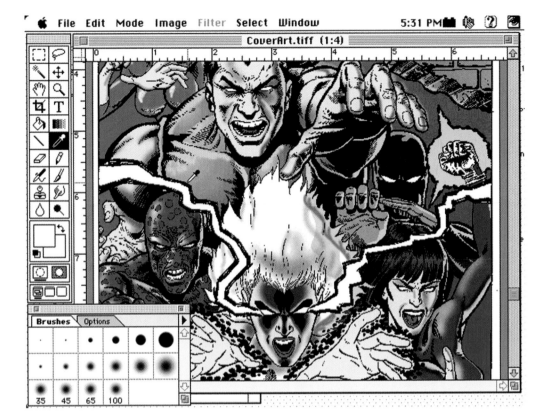

Photoshop screen with comic book art

Computer coloring equipment may be your best long-term investment. It produces the finest quality coloring available. This image is in the process of being colored on the Adobe Photoshop computer software program. You can see the finished version on the cover of this book.

Lettering can also be done with the help of your computer. There are many software applications with fonts that are similar, if not identical, to comic book lettering. Studio Daedalus (P.O. Box 11521, Campaign, IL 61826) offers a software package called Wizbang for $24.95. All you need is your computer and a laser printer. Once you print out the balloons with their dialogue, you just cut them out and paste them to your inked boards. You can either do this cutting and pasting manually, if you're producing a black-and-white or a hand painted color comic book, or by computer, if you've scanned your work into the computer to color. (See the Color Separators section in chapter 4 for more information.)

INKING

After the lettering is complete, the pages go to an inker, who inks over all the pencil lines of the drawings. Inkers are artists who have mastered the skill of

Inked comic book page
This completed inked page was lettered and inked by hand rather than on a computer.

applying India ink with a brush. They "ink" the penciled pages, giving them the best possible reproduction quality. A good inker is someone who can enhance the penciled images, rather than distort them. Smooth feathery lines should be crisp, sharp, and decisive, and there should be no shaky, wavering lines or disarray. Someone who can achieve these results has mastered the brush and pen to the point of technical perfection, and this type of proficiency will be reflected in the final product. Even with the greatest pencilers, any comic book that isn't created with a master inker will ultimately be an amateur product that garners only amateur sales.

Inked comic book page

Here is another example of a finished hand lettered and inked comic book page.

COLORING

Colorists have come a long way within the past 20 years. With today's scanning and computer technology, colorists are able to be more creative, thereby adding their own magic touch to the finished comic book pages. Colorists don't only bring additional life to the comic art, but also to the storytelling and overall plot continuity.

Experienced colorists are masters at adding their own dramatic input to a story. For example, they might visualize an explosion scene in the perfect blend of fire-engine reds, vibrant oranges, and bright yellows, rather than following the continuity of color coordinating (the idea that characters' outfits and sur-roundings shouldn't change from panel to panel), and this can enhance the dynamics of both the writer's and the penciler's vision. See how color does this in the finished example on page 51—the color adds intensity, vibrance, and a sense of anticipation to the scene. Comic book coloring can be accomplished either by hand or by computer, but either way, good colorists must also be good artists. They must understand the basics of tonal value and color to cre-ate extraordinary work. The mechanics of all comic book coloring today includes computer technology, but it's used at different steps of the process depending on whether your art is hand or computer colored.

Hand Coloring

If your comic book is being hand colored, a colorist will hand paint the blueline pages, which are then laser scanned by a color separator to produce the film that the printer prints from. As mentioned at the beginning of this chapter, a blueline is a reproduction of the completed inked comic book artwork. Blueline pages are usually the size of the final printed book pages (which are 61 percent of the original artwork size) but on a high-quality Crescent watercolor board. You can use other brands of watercolor board, but I think Crescent is by far the best. Painting on watercolor board works best because you can avoid the shrinkage that often occurs when you paint on plain paper. For your bluelines you should use a high-quality watercolor board, from which the watercolor-paper surface (the top layer of the board) can be "stripped" (or pulled off) by the colorist after coloring. This is done immediately prior to delivering the color art to the color separator so that the art is flexible enough for the separator to wrap around the laser drum used for scanning. (Note that sometimes the color separator, rather than the colorist, strips the top layer of paper off the board.) The final, scanning step produces the four-color film needed to print the comic book. (See chapter 4 for more details on the printing process.)

Most color separators can produce bluelines, which involves the production of a set of positive and negative films. The positive film is used as an overlay on the blueline as a guide for the colorist. The negative film is the actual black film, which shows only those areas of the pages that are to print black, and is sent to the printer to make your black plate for printing the black areas of the art-work. But, prior to that, it's used to make the blueline of your art so that the colorist can fill in the other three colors needed for four-color process printing. On pages 52, 53, and 54 you can see examples of hand painted bluelines both with and without the black film overlay.

You can produce your own bluelines by purchasing the film from a film or stat house. You can purchase the necessary Guidelines Sensitizer and Developer chemicals and watercolor boards from your local art supply store. Check the instructions carefully when purchasing any chemicals. You'll also need a special light bulb to activate the blueline chemicals to transfer them and your images onto the boards, and you can find this bulb at any hardware store. If you're planning to produce your own bluelines, you'll also need a heavy, flat piece of glass so that you can duplicate the Vacuum Frame, which is the piece of equipment professionals use that sandwiches the negative film between the watercolor board and the flat glass on top.

Computer Coloring

If your comic book is being colored on the computer, the art is scanned into the computer and a computer colorist fills in the color via a tint software program. The colorist then puts the finished colored art on a disk, which goes to the printer to use to generate the film from which the comic book is printed. This technique produces comic books that far exceed the quality of comics produced by the ancient "strip tint" method used for the first 50 years of comic book printing. (See chapter 4 for more on the strip tint technique.)

Computer coloring involves specific hardware, such as a Power Mac with an enormous amount of memory, a scanner, and software, such as Adobe Photoshop. If you're already familiar with this kind of sophisticated hardware and software, you're most likely aware of computer coloring's capabilities. If that's the case, you might want to build your own computer coloring station, if you intend to do the coloring yourself. You could then put your finished artwork onto a disk that you would simply give directly to your printer to use in making film. Keep in mind that electronics are ever-changing; new products, software programs, and opportunities are always just around the corner. Be sure to research the capabilities and cost of the next wave of hardware before investing in the current product; the greater speed of the upcoming equipment would cut coloring time in half and could greatly reduce the necessary investment.

If you have the funds, the best equipment for a computer coloring station is the following:

Hardware

Power Macintosh

40mg RAM (or more)

500mg hard drive (or more)

External SyQuest drive (200mg capacity)

Desktop scanner (600-1200dpi) with software

Color printer (for proofs), optional

Software

Adobe Photoshop 3.0+

Adobe Illustrator

Quark Xpress

This hardware alone will run you in the neighborhood of $15,000 but will allow you to do almost anything you can graphically imagine, except paint your house. It's a good, long-term investment—if you plan to publish just one full-color monthly, the equipment will pay for itself by the eighth issue. Adobe Photoshop is magical. That's the only way I can accurately describe this wonderful graphics tool. It's up there with the invention of the T-square. The image on page 56 shows you what a coloring software program looks like up on the computer screen.

Various stages of comic book art production
By comparing the different versions of this one page, you can see how comic book art develops. From the beginning, the steps are: rough layout script page (top left), penciled page (top right), lettered page (bottom left), inked page (bottom right), and, on page 55, the finished color page.

FREELANCERS AND CO-CREATORS

The creation of a high-quality comic book takes time—as a matter of fact, I think the only real difference between fine art and commercial art is a deadline—and, as I said at the start of this chapter, the collaboration of a team of enthusiastic creators who each can focus and concentrate on their strongest skills to reach the common goal of producing an outstanding book. So, for self-publishers who are not actually creating the artwork themselves, the key to making an exceptional comic book is to hire talented, dedicated freelance artists and co-creators to execute the various visual aspects of the comic book. The difference between freelancers and co-creators is simply that freelancers just produce a work-for-hire, while co-creators assist in the actual design and development of characters and concepts and usually get to share a piece of the profits.

If you're planning to publish a comic book of your written concept, yet have no artistic background or drawing ability, the freelance artists you choose to work with can either make or break your book. This holds true for every stage of production, from penciler to letterer to colorist. For example, to write an exceptional story and hire a superior penciler, but then have your Aunt Gertrude letter the book because you think she has nice handwriting, is sales suicide. One of the first things a potential buyer will notice is your comic book's lettering. If you hire an amateur letterer, the book will be seen as an amateur production, and the same is true for penciling, inking, and coloring, too. However, if you hire the right freelance talent, your book should have the same potential as any of you competitors' product.

Aside from providing artistic talent, freelancers can help you produce a high-quality comic book with limited, or no, financial resources. The comic book industry sees hundreds of newcomers who have dreams of breaking into the field. Most large comic book companies won't hire anyone without some kind of published history, so you can offer eager newcomers a chance to add to their writing or art portfolio at minimal cost to yourself. If you can't afford to pay your freelancers immediately, offer them a share of the profits or a small advance (say, $5 to $15 per page) against a percentage of the profits from sales. Of course, by accepting a percentage of profits as payment, they're also sharing in the risk; if the book doesn't make a profit, no one gets paid. This can destroy morale and affect the quality of any future work or collaborations, so you might want to think seriously about this payment option before you offer it to your freelancers.

No matter what the method of payment, always pay your freelancers on time. Nothing can destroy good professional relationships more than when your cash-flow problems become theirs. Late payments, and other cash-flow problems, can create a "domino effect" that affects everyone, but with a little foresight and money management, you can avoid, ease, or correct any glitches.

Page rates for creative talent within the comic book industry vary widely. For example, a new penciler may make as little as $10 per penciled book page, while a "hot" professional can take home up to $1,000 per page (including royalties). The following chart indicates actual rates paid (by myself and others in the business) for work. This chart is just a reference guide to give you an idea of possible prices, so rates may vary; costs are cost-per-page. Note that a finisher is an inker who is so talented that he or she can actually execute finished inkings right over the layouts, thereby bypassing the penciling stage.

	Newcomer	Seasoned Artist	Pro
Plot writer	$5–15	$15–40	$40 & up
Script writer	$5–15	$15–40	$40 & up
Complete writer (plot & script)	$10–30	$35–60	$60 & up
Layout artist	$10–30	$25–40	$50 & up
Penciler	$10–60	$50–120	$100 & up
Letterer	$5–10	$10–15	$15 & up
Inker	$10–25	$25–60	$60 & up
Finisher	$25–60	$75–100	$100 & up
Colorist	$5–20	$25–60	$60 & up
Cover penciler	$40–75	$100–200	$200 & up
Cover inker	$25–50	$75–100	$100 & up
Cover colorist	$75–250	$250–700	$1,000 & up

SCOUTING FOR TALENT

Finding and choosing a freelancer or co-creator takes effort and determination. A good place to start scouting for artists is a local comic book convention. This can be a gold mine for talent, because many writers and artists will bring in their material to have it reviewed by publishers attending the convention. As you become more experienced in seeking out freelancers, watch out for the "non-productives." These are artists who show the same work year after year. If a penciler has been showing the same samples for seven years, it's usually a sign that he's non-productive. If you're interested in an artist, but he isn't showing recent work, ask him to do a couple of sample pages and send you photocopies within a few weeks. If you receive the copies, you'll know you're dealing with an enthusiastic, deadline-oriented artist; if you don't receive anything, you'll see that the artist isn't reliable or doesn't really want the job.

Talent agents can also assist you in your search for freelance artists. These agents represent talented people in the creative community; their artists have already gone through a screening process, and the individuals they represent are usually seasoned artists and pros. You can often find agents at comic book conventions, and they work on commission, taking a percentage of the artist's pay. Two such talent agencies are Glass House Graphics (13 Hawk Court, North Park, Wheeling, WV 26003, phone and fax: 304-232-5641/attn: David Campiti) and Star*Reach Productions (P.O. Box 2328, Berkeley, CA 94702, ph: 510-644-1886/attn: Mike Friedrich).

WHOSE WORK IS THIS ANYWAY!?
UNFORTUNATELY, THE ONLY WAY TO GUARANTEE THAT ARTISTS ARE SHOWING YOU SAMPLES OF THEIR OWN WORK IS TO ASK THEM TO DO TEST SAMPLES FOR YOU. DON'T BE AFRAID TO ASK FOR THIS IF YOU'RE LEERY ABOUT A FREELANCER.

Artists

True artists are intensely emotional people, and their creativity is an expression and outlet for their feelings. By sharing their thoughts through their art, they will, intentionally or not, spark emotions in others; it's this ability to touch others through creativity that makes someone an artist. Talented actors make you experience what they are feeling; skilled writers express their thoughts so vividly in words that you, too, can feel them; and great painters and sculptors inspire your imagination and emotions with their visual representations. A great movie, book, song, or even a comic book, will kindle feelings inside and make you say, "Wow! That was good."

When dealing with any creative person, you must use a great deal of diplomacy and finesse. Coming from a creative background myself, I understand enough to know that art is an individual's creative expression, which is intensely personal and sparks strong emotions. Any industry that involves netting financial gain by using, or exploiting, an artist's creations, risks mixing business with emotions. This can be difficult for artists who refuse to accept the realities of the business world. However, you must keep in mind that your primary objective as a publisher is not to simply safeguard an artist's unedited personal vision; your concern is the bottom line and creating a product that will do well in the marketplace. This isn't conniving or deceitful—it's business. Still, artists often take a rejection of their creative expression as personal rejection, so be tactful.

The experienced freelancers and co-creators who can separate their personal feelings from public approval of their work will have more success using (and make a living off) their talents. Avoid hiring anyone who cannot take criticism, especially for a licensed title. There will most likely be changes, and you don't want to work with someone who takes everything personally. If you honestly critique a portfolio or writing sample, and the artist or author pulls a gun on you, you're obviously dealing with a loose cannon.

Try to hire freelancers who can put their egos aside and focus on creating their best work, and if you yourself are the writer (or penciler, letterer, inker, or colorist) for your comic, you should do the same. Concentrate on doing your best work, not on the size of your sales figures. If your writing or art doesn't sell a million copies of a book, so what? It's your book. You had the opportunity to express yourself in a colorful and imaginative way, and as long as you presented your best work, you can always do it again elsewhere on another project at another time.

The vast majority of the almost two thousand freelancers I've had the pleasure to work with were not only talented but very professional. The small percentage who created problems were those who slipped through my screening process. You can't avoid their reactions to rejection, but you can learn from the experiences and avoid other sticky situations: for example, never promise anything that you aren't absolutely positive you can deliver; use enthusiasm, not hype (save the hype for your advertisements), and always pay them on time.

Co-creators

If you choose to give creative partners co-creator status, offer them a piece of the secondary (or axillary) rights. Ten to 30 percent of any revenue derived from the licensing of a concept could translate into millions of dollars, if the comic becomes an entertainment phenomenon. Being a co-creator can be powerful motivation for producing outstanding work. (See chapter 5 for more information on contracts.)

PRINTERS AND COLOR SEPARATORS

Think of your printer as the magician who turns all your hard work into green-backs. Without a printer, you could find yourself with nothing but comic book art and bills. This is the supplier who transforms your months of work into dollars by giving you an actual product; without that, you have nothing to sell. Thus, the printer is the most important supplier for your business. Also important is the color separator, the production middle man who magically changes your artwork into digital film, which the printer needs to make the printing plates with which to print your comic book.

THE PRINTING PROCESS

The printing of a comic book is the same as any other publication. This universal procedure involves what is called the "four-color" process. The four standard colors associated with the four-color process are black (K), magenta (M), cyan (C), and yellow (Y). Using dot variations of 5 to 100 percent of each of these colors, the printer can achieve almost every color imaginable. The color separator has the technology to convert any art into screened dot variations of these four colors so that the printer can produce the printing plates that imbed (print) those variations on your choice of paper. A printing plate can be made of plastic or metal and is simply a three-dimensional version of those screened dot variations. Traditionally, art goes to the color separator, who makes the films, first and then to the printer for printing. However, because of computer technology, the printer often also does the job of the color separator, so the two stages are not as segregated anymore.

The presses used to print comic books vary depending on the desired product. Different presses are used to print anywhere from one to six colors at one time. The cost for the press set-up, or "make-ready" (the preparation of the press for printing), can determine your price structure. The make-ready cost for a one-color press is much less than it is for a six-color press, even if you're only planning to print a one-color book on the six-color press. When you compare the make-ready cost for printing a one-color book on a six-color press to the make-ready cost for printing that same job on a one-color press, you'll find that using the six-color press may be 1,000 percent more expensive than using the smaller, less complicated one-color press. Printers have been known to use six-color presses (if

USE A
"NEWSSTAND"
PRINTER FOR YOUR
NEWSSTAND TITLES
A NEWSSTAND PRINTER—ONE THAT
HAS ITS OWN IN-HOUSE NEWSSTAND
BULK-SHIPPING CAPABILITIES—
CAN SAVE YOU AS MUCH AS 60
PERCENT ON NEWSSTAND
SHIPPING COSTS!

they're available) for one-color jobs and then charge publishers for the use of the more expensive press, so watch out for this.

If you're producing a black-and-white comic book. You can print your interior pages on any press that can produce anywhere from one to six colors. But, a comic book with a full-color interior will need at least a four-color press to initiate the four-color printing process. (You could print a four-color comic book on a one-color press, but this would involve four times the make-ready cost and the time for running the paper through the press that many more times, once for each color.) The five- and six-color presses are traditionally used to print extraordinary colors, such as silver, gold, or a specific colored ink to match a tint exactly. For a low-run (a small print-run) black-and-white comic book, the set-up cost on four-, five-, or six-color presses can be expensive. These presses can be the length of an entire city block, and this means that their make-ready processes are more complex and they usually waste more paper. Instead, the best prices for a one-color comic book are generated from a one- or two-color press. These presses are smaller, requiring less time and effort for maintenance and make-ready. You can print your interior pages with very little effort on a one-color press, and you can print a four-color cover on the two-color press (it will go through the press twice). As you gather price quotes from printers, you'll find that for print runs of up to 10,000 copies, this is the most efficient and economical procedure.

GET IT IN WRITING

If a printer gives you a fantastic price quote, get it in writing. Many printers won't mention various fees to appear more competitive; then when they send you the bill, they've added various surprise charges. You should also get the approved ship date in writing, and if the printer needs film by a certain date to guarantee the shipment date, have them put that film date in writing, too.

Always review the printer's bill carefully on receipt. Some printers will add extra costs onto the bill that they accumulated in trying to make the promised ship date. However, it's not your financial responsibility if the printer runs into technical difficulties and delays during printing. This is when it helps to have the original quote and ship date in writing.

GOING ON PRESS

You can arrange to be at the printer at the time your comic book is printed. This is called going *on press.* If the printer is in your general area, I would recommend making an appearance at press time; printers produce better work when the person who's paying the bill is watching over their shoulder. Obviously, if the printer is across the country, it may not be economical for you to make the trip.

If your black-and-white comic book is a huge success with a print run of 375,000 copies, the cost of make-ready will be absorbed by the number of copies printed. You may also find that using a four-color press to print your cover and interior may be just as economical; the larger presses are faster than the smaller ones and can print a job in 16 hours, rather than 46.

Recently, the cost of paper has skyrocketed. This has made the cost of printing comic books double what it was about two years ago. You'll need to compensate for this increase in material costs by trimming your other production costs and increasing your retail price. For example, you could reduce the number of pages of art in your book from, say, 24 to 20; or, you could print the front and back inside covers in black-and-white, rather than color; or, you could do the coloring yourself on a computer, rather than hiring a hand colorist. While this paper price increase may only be a temporary condition, you still have to change your cost structure in order to minimize any effects on the bottom line.

FINDING A PRINTER

I've included a number of accomplished comic book printers for your reference (see Appendix, page 169), but don't exclude the possibility of seeking out a quote from a printer you may have some connection with. A monthly comic book is regular monthly income for any printer, and most printers love regular business, because all too often they are only working from job to job. This is why many printers offer better prices for publishers who can guarantee regular work.

When contacting printers, you'll need to furnish them with your comic book specifications (also called "specs"). You should also give the specs to your color separator. For a *black-and-white* comic book, the standard specs would be as follows:

COMIC BOOK: 32 pages, plus cover

INTERIORS: 1/1 *The symbol 1/1 means one color over one color throughout—one color on every page. This would be 4/4 for a full-color comic book.*

INTERIOR STOCK: 40lb. Mando or equivalent *Paper is measured in pounds. The standard interior comic book paper stock is anywhere from 35 to 50lbs., and is usually matte finish. The name "Mando" is simply a brand name, so always add "or equivalent" to your paper choice. If they happen to have a similar paper in stock and use this, it will be faster and cheaper than having to order Mando special from a mill.*

TRIM SIZE: 6⅝ x 10¼" standard *Any printed piece is always printed larger than the intended finished product and is then trimmed down to the correct size. This is to accommodate any bleeds, which are images that run off the edge of the pages. The larger printing size is also due to the fact that paper comes in standard sizes; for printers to offer you the best possible prices, they need to find a paper size that will fit your book with a minimal amount of waste. Note that you pay for any and all wasted paper that is trimmed off after printing.*

COVERS: 4/1 *The most economical full-color comic book cover has four colors on the outside front and back covers and only one color on the inside front and back covers—hence, it's 4/1. It's not necessary to add a second color to the inside cover or to print both sides of the cover in full color—unless you've sold the space as a full-color advertisement—because it can distract from your first black-and-white comic book page.*

COVER STOCK: 60lb. Escanaba or equivalent *Cover comic book stock is usually gloss finish and ranges from 50 to 80lbs. Again, Escanaba is simply a brand name; the printer may have an equivalent in stock that is more cost effective.*

THE DYLUX

Right before going on press, the printer should produce a *dylux* for you. Also called a *book blue* or *blue proof*, because of it's blue color, this is a one-color proof or prototype of your comic book's interior on which you can check pagination, text, and image registration. This is your last chance to catch any errors in details such as page layout and order, and trademark or copyright notices on advertisements. You should always examine a dylux, prior to going on press. Misplaced pages can be a common error. Don't rely on a color separator or printer to know the contents of your story and book.

BINDING: Saddle stitching *Pages are stapled together two or three times from the outside to the inside of the center fold. Magazines are often bound this way.*

PACKAGING FOR SHIPPING: Boxes of 200 copies (cardboard divider in between stacks of 100) *Always mention to any printer who is not familiar with comic books, that the product has to be packaged like gold. Unlike other periodicals or magazines, comics are instant collector's items, so they must be received in the best possible condition or the distributors will send them back for a refund.*

SHIPPING: Most cost-effective method *Whatever your shipping destination, instruct your printer to use the most cost-effective shipping method. It's more cost effective to use a truck shipper, rather than UPS. Unfortunately, truck ship-pers have a minimum amount of weight they'll deliver. Your printer can take care of this, though.*

Printers schedule *press time* months ahead. This is to guarantee that they receive and have the paper to produce and deliver a product on time. Printers will often be more than happy to give you a year's schedule, broken down by month, as a guarantee of annual revenue, and you should always request this. This way you'll have a guarantee of that specific press time, price, and ship date. The deadline for the receiving of film and the ship date for each month should be detailed in the annual schedule. See Appendix, page 169, for a list of a number of printers that I highly recommend. I've used them all, and they are the best.

COLOR SEPARATORS

As I mentioned earlier, due to changing computer technology, some printers also function as color separators, as well. The color stripping techniques used in producing comic books have also evolved over time. The oldest and now mostly obsolete method was the mechanical strip tint process. Using the four color printing process as the guide, these tints (which were on pieces of film) were manually cut into the shapes of the images in the illustrations and screened into dot variations using film and darkroom facilities.

Today, a similar technique uses sophisticated computer hardware and soft-ware. While the computer technology hasn't made it possible to produce the color any better using this method, it has made it more affordable. Basically, the finished inked artwork is scanned into a computer color software program on which a colorist (or a technician, following a colorist's guidelines) has filled in the appropriate colors electronically. Once a comic book is completely colored on disk by the colorist, the information is output into four-color film for the printer. Most color separators, or some printers, will do this for you at a nomi-nal cost. A computer (using special film output equipment) outputs the mater-ial onto the four-color process film used for printing. The film includes all the necessary elements the printer needs to create the printing plates and produce your comic book.

See Appendix, page 170, for a list of recommended color separators.

ALWAYS ASK FOR A "GANG" FILM SCAN

Scans are used to make the film that the printer prints from. Color separators will often spend too much time producing the highest quality (and most expensive) scans of your material as they possibly can, scanning each page individually. This would be fine for an ad agency that needs really incredible scans to satisfy a client, but it's not necessary for comic books. Make it clear that you're interested in a good scan at a *good price*. Depending on the size of their laser scanner drum, color separators may be able to fit as many as six pages onto one scan, which can reduce your (and their) costs dramatically. It will enable them to offer you a monthly rate of $35 (rather than $75) per page, and your readers won't even notice the slight quality difference.

In fact, the accuracy of electronic production makes for almost perfect registration of color during printing. Introduced to the mainstream comic book production process in the '80s, the laser scanner is a full-color scanning device that can instantly convert any full-color artwork into four sheets of four-color process film, which the printer uses for printing. This is the equipment, for use with bluelines, that's necessary to laser scan your painted artwork into film for printing. Although, computer technology has continued to evolve to produce higher quality desktop color scanners, the laser scanning system still offers the best reproduction.

Linescreens and Color Composition

The size of your dot screen pattern can effect the quality of your finished product. The dot screen pattern is the mass of almost microscopic dots that makes up your artwork on film. These dots are created in three dimension on printing plates, and hold the ink and press it into place on the paper in a variety of combinations; the dot mixtures produce thousands of colors from just the four process colors (black, magenta, cyan, and yellow). The dots vary in size so that they can print various amounts of each process color, thereby creating the desired final hues that match the colorists original artwork. The linescreen is the number of dots per inch. Linescreens for comics are traditionally 85, 100, 120, 133, 150, and 200. The smaller linescreen numbers indicate that a lesser amount of ink is used, while the larger numbers indicate that more ink is used. The finer 150- and 200-dot linescreens are only used for covers on a gloss fin-

Screened images
This photo was screened at 100 dots per inch. The detail above is enlarged 30 percent and you can see how the dots work together to create the image. I would recommend 100- or 120-dot linescreens for printing on high-grade comic book paper, such as 45 to 50lb. Mandobrite white. An 85 linescreen is your only choice for newsprint, as the ink tends to sink deep into the paper, leaving you little flexibility when deciding on screen.

ish paper, because a non-gloss finish, or "offset," stock is too porous to hold that much ink. If a linescreen is too fine (for example, 133, 150, or 200), the color dots may bleed together on certain papers, giving you a muddy looking book.

You should find out what number linescreens your printer has the capacity to print, then decide which linescreen you want to use, and then, if you're using a color separator to make film, pass this linescreen information on to your color separator. Below is a guideline for the best reproduction quality on various stocks.

Covers

50 to 80lb. gloss stock *Gloss papers are manufactured to handle finer screens. A 120- to 150-dot linescreen is the safest choice.*

Interiors

30 or 35lb. newsprint *When printing on newsprint, whether it's a full-color or tonal black-and-white (black-and-white with shades of gray) comic book, use an 85-dot linescreen. Newsprint is the cheapest, most porous paper, and so 85 is the best for linescreen for it. Note that you don't always want a very porous paper—certainly never with color, in which case a 100 or 120 linescreen on 40 or 45lb. paper is best.*

35 to 45lb. white Mando or equivalent offset *Offset means non-glossy finish. Also, if your book is full color, your printer is most likely using a* heatset web

press, which "bakes" the ink on top of the paper seconds after the ink impressions are made. (The term "web" simply indicates that the paper is fed into the press from a roll, rather than sheets.) This process allows you to use a 100, 120, or even a 133 linescreen (the finest possible screen for this paper) to produce the best possible depth of color and detail, which the heatset press bakes right into the paper.

50lb. white Mando or equivalent offset *If you're printing on a 50lb. offset sheet, your printer may be using a non-heatset web press. Ask your printer, but if you're not sure, choose a 100 or 120 linescreen to safeguard against a bad batch of paper. Remember, fewer dots means less ink, which means less blotchiness.*

Color composition refers to the combination of various percentages of the four process colors, which when mixed together result in the desired hues. (The computer colorist or color separator sets these percentages.) For example, a mix of 100 percent black, 50 percent cyan, 30 percent magenta, and 20 percent yellow results in a 200 percent color composition of a warm brownish-black color. When laser scanning or producing color film on a computer, "color composition" or "color saturation"—the maximum percent of the colors used to produce the desired hues—should be no more than 290 percent. Your color separator will understand what you mean when you say this. For the best reproduction, have the color separator or computer colorist always stay under 290 percent; this will guarantee that you don't print with too much ink for the paper to handle.

PRODUCING A DIRT CHEAP COLOR COVER

The most inexpensive way to produce a high-quality cover is by computer generation. If you know someone with the necessary equipment and software, you can produce film for a fantastic, full-color cover, with logos and all, for about $40. (Note that this price doesn't include the coloring work.) In this way, you would avoid having to use a color separator to generate the film. "Painting" on a computer always produces cleaner colors; you save your colored cover image on a disk, which you then give to your printer to output the cover film.

If you don't know anyone with fancy equipment, you can still produce film for a full-color cover for as little as $40. Upon receiving the inked, uncolored outside front cover artwork from the inker, go to a photocopy store and make the highest quality photocopies that you can at the same size as the art. The zoomer photocopy machine at a local Kinko's copy center is excellent (and about $3 per copy). Also design and make photocopies of your price, cover date, issue number, and any logos. Then, paste these elements onto the cover art photocopy. The final product should have everything you want to appear on the printed outside cover.

At this point, reduce the piece to a width of 6¾" and a height of 10½", using the high quality zoomer machine. Note that the extra, or "live," area between these dimensions and the eventual trim size of 6⅝ x 10¼" is to compensate for bleeding off the top, bottom, and right edges. Have the copy technician increase the darkness just enough to give you a dense black without any muddiness.

Now, color the photocopy with colored inks or markers, or whatever will give you nice clean colors without causing the black copy toner to run; Dr. Martin's Concentrated Water Color dyes are a good choice. Choose bright, primary colors and keep them clean. (Before coloring your actual cover copy, you may want to practice on a spare photocopy of your cover.) Once you're done, take the fully colored photocopy to a local color separator who services the publishing industry. Explain that you're producing a comic book and show them your cover image. Say something like, "If I let you hang onto this cover art for 30 days, do you think you could gang it onto another job? I can only afford $30 for a scan, and I don't need a color proof." What you're asking the color separator to do is to throw your job into the laser scanner while scanning another (paying) job so that both get scanned together and you save money.

The separator will most likely do it, and it will be a quality job. Color separators are always on tight deadlines, but still, one day they may have no work at all, and that's when they'll get to your job. If you can, have the color separator call you prior to scanning your artwork. At that time, ask him to "boost the black." This will result in a denser black for printing. (If the black is still faintly gray, have the printer boost the black at press time, as well.) You'll now have the full-color cover film for a mere fraction of the regular cost of hiring a color separator and not ganging it onto another job. You can also do the same for the back cover, and for the insides of the covers you can print them in black-and-white on a laser scanner or just give the printer a disk with the black-and-white files for printing.

5 CONTRACTS

A contract is a legally enforceable promise, or set of promises, between parties that have voluntarily entered into an agreement. For a promise to be considered a contract, it must include the following requirements:

An agreement on and acceptance of an offer

Voluntary acceptance of the contract terms by all parties

The capacity of all parties to enter into the contract

A legal act or acts (you are legally hiring someone)

Written evidence (the contract itself)

A contract is only as good as the two people who sign it. European companies have been known to take some time to get to know new business associates before signing contracts or agreements with them. This preliminary analysis enables them to discover the individual's values and personality. Unfortunately, smaller businesses usually don't have the time or the budget to spend on learning everything they need to know about the quality of their prospective contract partners. This is where references become almost as important as the agreement itself.

You don't want to waste time and money negotiating and producing a contract and marketing plan around an individual who won't deliver, for whatever reason. Always ask for a person's or company's references before doing any transaction. On contacting those references, be prepared with a list of questions regarding performance, attitude, and reliability. You can also ask these references if they know of any other possible references you could talk to. If you receive poor feedback from one out of, say, five people, you're most likely dealing with a simple difference of opinion or a personality conflict, rather than an unprofessional character. If, however, all five references offer only disparaging remarks, you may have a potential problem. You don't need a ticking time bomb.

CHECK MULTIPLE REFERENCES
WHENEVER ENTERING INTO AN AGREEMENT WITH ANY COMPANY OR INDIVIDUAL, ALWAYS ASK FOR A FEW REFERENCES. IT'S IMPORTANT TO KNOW THE PERSON OR COMPANY BEHIND THE AGREEMENT.

Contracts were created to protect the little guy from the big guy, and visa versa. If David sold Goliath a used car, and Goliath promised to pay for the car next month, how could David force Goliath to pay if he refuses? Or, how could Goliath get paid, if the tables were turned and David refused to pay? Obviously, Goliath could beat some sense into him, but what if he died? How would Goliath get reimbursed then? The law.

The Egyptians are said to be the first society to have had contracts enforced by governing laws. Many of the rules of contemporary contract law were first created in the 18th and 19th centuries. Over the decades, laws have changed, but the basic principles remain the same. Each contract or agreement should include the following important elements:

> **PUT EVERYTHING IN WRITING**
>
> WHEN DISCUSSING OFFERS, JOT DOWN NOTES ON THE NEGOTIATIONS AND THEN PUT THESE IN WRITING BEFORE MOVING FORWARD WITH THE DEAL. YOU'D BE SURPRISED HOW OFTEN PEOPLE FORGET WHAT THEY'VE PROMISED YOU, EVEN IN RECENT CONVERSATIONS.

Length of term

Territory (if applicable)

Services required

Compensation and/or payment terms

Liability

Ownership rights (if applicable)

Signatures of all involved parties

Date

If someone decides to breach your contract, you can legally file a lawsuit and wait until judgment is passed by the court. Of course, this could take years. Whether you decide it would be financially beneficial, or in the best interest of the company, to pursue a claim is another story. Always keep in mind that you have a business to run, and continue to run, without whatever party has breached the contract, so a time-consuming (and money-consuming) lawsuit may not necessarily be in your best interest.

LETTER OF INTENT

A *letter of intent* is a binding legal document in letter form, which describes all the terms of an agreement. Most business transactions will begin with a letter of intent while the final contract is being drafted by the legal department or law firm. It's just as binding as a 10-page contract, without all the legal costs involved in producing a more extensive agreement. (Note that you could draft a contract yourself—I don't really advise that you do this, but it is perfectly legal.)

Whenever doing any business transaction, always ask for a letter of intent upon the verbal approval of the agreed terms. If you don't receive this written documentation, write the letter yourself. Outline all the details discussed, and include the appropriate space for your partner's name, company name, title, business address, signature, and date; once they sign it, they can photocopy it and send the original back to you. (Or, you could send the letter in duplicate—

one copy for them to keep and one to return to you.) On some occasions, I've just used a letter of intent without following it up with a more extensive contract; it really just depends on the lengths and term of the arrangements.

The details are the most important ingredients in all aspects of business. This also holds true for any written documentation. In order to satisfy both parties and prompt them to move forward in planning their business project or strategies, the letter of intent can include every detail of a mutual agreement. The key to a successful business relationship and transaction is to get it in writing. You're both putting all your cards on the table and are moving forward with a clear understanding of what each party expects from the other. If any individuals, or companies, refuse to put their promises in writing, they're noncommittal and, therefore, unreliable.

ARTIST CONTRACT

As mentioned at the start of the chapter, a business contract should contain the following information: description of services, payment terms, ownership rights, length of agreement, liability, and the date. This holds true for contracts with any freelance artists or other workers that you hire, as well. As I mentioned earlier, you can draw up a contract yourself, but it's better to have a lawyer do it; you may miss something or not be aware of any recent changes in the law. When you send or present a contract for a freelance worker to sign, do so in duplicate; always send it *unsigned,* and have the freelancer keep one copy and sign the other copy and return it to you. On receiving this signed copy, sign it yourself, and then file it.

PAYMENT VOUCHER

This document, like an invoice, serves two primary purposes: 1) it simplifies and expedites the payment of freelancer, and 2) it requires freelancers to sign another work-for-hire release of the work upon delivery. After dealing with over a thousand freelancers in the course of a decade and receiving invoices on index cards (yes, index cards), mini-spiral notebook paper, and Bristol paper, using a payment voucher is much more sensible. You can make up a standard payment voucher form and then photocopy it for your freelancers to use. Whoever does your bookkeeping will love you for it.

SECURITY AGREEMENT

This is a document that can protect you and/or your family from losing your company, and your financial investment in it, in a hostile takeover. A hostile takeover could occur, for example, if an irate supplier or printer holds some of your valuable comic book film and artwork hostage and demands payment (or prepayment, which they shouldn't get) in exchange for producing your product or returning your film; the supplier or printer is suddenly in control of the future of your business, your cash flow, and your capital. A takeover could also happen if an investor snuck a loophole into your contract agreement that went unnoticed by an inept attorney.

To protect your, or your family's, investment from the inadequacies of many lawyers and the vicious attempts of desperate suppliers, you can offer your family the entire company (and its assets) as collateral to protect its investment. You do this with a *security agreement,* which is a document that signs over all the assets of the company to the secured party in the event of dissolution, merger, or consolidation. If the company is dissolved, for whatever reason, the secured party retains all the company's assets to collect on their financial investment. If you are negotiating with an investment interest for a merger or consolidation, this party will want the security interest, which will force your family to negotiate its interest and involvement. (See chapter 10 for more information on family investors.)

> **PROTECT YOUR FAMILY'S INVESTMENT**
> OFFER YOUR FAMILY PROTECTION ON ITS INVESTMENT IN YOUR BUSINESS BY GIVING THEM THE SECURITY INTEREST IN YOUR COMPANY'S ASSETS. KEEP THIS CONFIDENTIAL —TO GUARD AGAINST LAWSUITS — UNTIL THE TIME COMES FOR AN INVESTMENT INTEREST OR DISSOLUTION.

CONFIDENTIALITY AGREEMENT

Upon implementing discussions that may include confidential news or information, you should always insist on a *confidentiality agreement* between parties. If you're looking to hire a specific freelancer on a project or if you're exploring the idea of raising capital, you'll need to have any freelancer or involved parties sign a confidentiality or nondisclosure agreement. This will simply hold them, in writing, to secrecy and will protect your company's trade secrets, financial information, and marketing plans from the competition.

If a potential freelancer or collaborator is not willing to sign a confidentiality agreement, then you can safely assume one of following: 1) they're working on a potentially similar project and wish to protect their own plans; 2) they're considering stealing your ideas; or 3) they aren't serious about working with you. Don't be disappointed if someone refuses to sign a confidentiality agreement, and don't be too eager to move forward without it. It's there for your protection.

THE LIBRARY IS A VALUABLE RESOURCE

Your local library has many books on contracts and agreements of all kinds, with many examples of the different forms. It also never hurts to do research on any potential company or business associate, and the Internet is a valuable resource right at your fingertips. If you don't have your own computer, try the library for this, as well. Many branches have computer terminals that provide access to the Internet for free. All you need is your library card.

Jane Doe
1000 Main Street
Somewhere, IL 60000

January 1, 1995

Mr. John Doe
1000 Main Street
Somewhere, CA 90000
re: Penciling for the comic book *Spotman*

Dear Mr. Doe:

The following will set forth the terms of the agreement between you, John Doe, of Somewhere, CA, and myself, Jane Doe, of Somewhere, IL.

We have both agreed and confirmed that you will pencil the artwork for the comic book *Spotman* for six monthly issues at a page rate of $50 per page, which is to be paid upon publication, or no later than thirty (30) days after the scheduled ship date of July 31, 1995, and/or on completion and delivery of your artwork for each issue.

You understand that this work is produced as "work-for-hire" and that you have relinquished all rights to copyrights and trademarks forever. I, as the sole owner of said copyrights and trademarks, do understand that the physical artwork is your property and is to be returned to you no later than July 31, 1995.

In the event that any single issue (that you penciled) of the comic book *Spotman* sells above 25,000 copies, you will receive a royalty payment of an additional $20 per page. This royalty will be paid no later than sixty (60) days after the shipment of said issues.

In the event you do not finish the artwork for any given issue, for any reason, I am not obligated to pay you for any finished or unfinished pages you may have already produced for that issue.

I understand that your work will be completely original, and I will be left harmless to any cause of legal action that may arise otherwise. This agreement shall be governed by the laws of the State of Illinois.

If the foregoing correctly reflects your agreement with me, please so indicate by signing in the space provided below.

Very truly yours,

Jane Doe   Accepted and Agreed to by:
(company name)   John Doe

By: _____   Signature: _____

Its: _____   Date: _____

Sample letter of intent

FREELANCER AGREEMENT

This Agreement is between___(freelancer name)___(hereinafter referred to as Freelancer) of _____(freelancer address)_____ and ____(publisher's company name)____ (hereinafter referred to as Publisher) of _____(publisher address)_____.

1. Freelancer and Publisher desire to work together to produce the highest quality comic magazines and books. Freelancer shall be an independent contractor for Publisher.

Performance Requirement

2. Freelancer shall perform for Publisher the services listed in paragraph 3 (Services), for the period (Term), the publication (Title), and the compensation (Page Rate) listed in paragraph 3 of this agreement. Freelancer accepts said engagement and agrees to render said Services to the best of his talent.

Summary of Services

3. Artist Services: Layouts ___ Pencils ___ Inks ___ Finishes ___ other _____
    Writer Services: Plot ___ Script ___ Completed Script ___
    Term: _____ consecutive issues of 20–26 pages each
    Title: _____ Frequency: _____
    Page Rate: _____
    Payment: Within ____ business days of completion and delivery of artwork using payment voucher.

4. During the Term, Freelancer shall deliver the work for each issue (Work) to Publisher within 21 days of Publisher's delivery to Freelancer of plot, script, or pencils, (or other materials necessary for the job) unless another written agreed schedule is in effect. Freelancer further agrees to complete any reasonable revisions by any reasonable date requested by Publisher.

5. An editor, art director, or both, employed by Publisher, will be assigned to work with Freelancer to assist Freelancer's performance. Freelancer agrees to cooperate with said editor or art director and to comply with Publisher's standards for accepted work, including those involving artistic taste, judgment, and cooperation in correcting any scheduling.

6. Publisher may reject any Work it deems unsatisfactory and may employ others to complete the Work if delays caused by the Freelancer occur.

Confidentiality Clause

Freelancer agrees that all terms of this contract shall be kept in strict confidence and shall not be disclosed to any third parties. Failure to comply with this Paragraph shall constitute a noncurable loss of the Performance Bonus as defined in Paragraph 8 of this Agreement.

Compensation and Royalties

7. After approval of the Work for each issue, Publisher shall pay Freelancer the Page Rate, which includes payment for any revisions Publisher may have required.

8. If Freelancer has performed Services in a timely manner for the duration of the Term, and otherwise in accordance with this agreement, then at the end of the Term,

Sample freelance artist contract

Note that this is only a sample contract. I'm not an attorney, I just look like one in a three-piece suit.

Publisher shall pay Freelancer a Performance Bonus of _____.

9. Publisher agrees to pay Freelancer five (5) percent of cover price (per issue) for Work reprinted in any book or magazine published in the United States and Canada, provided such reprinting has been authorized by Publisher and Publisher has received payment.

Return of Artwork and Additional Copies

10. For comic book artwork, Publisher agrees to return the original Work to the Freelancers performing any portion of the Services involved in completing the Title. Between pencilers and inkers, distribution as follows: pencilers receive 70 percent of Work; inkers receive 30 percent of Work. Between layout artists and finishers, distribution as follows: layout artists receive 30 percent of Work; finishers receive 70 percent of Work. Publisher will divide Work in its sole discretion unless Freelancer sends to Publisher a notice signed by all Freelancers confirming a different distribution. Publisher agrees to return Work within six months after publication or cancellation of the feature for which Work was commissioned. If, after reasonable diligence, Publisher is unable to deliver the Work or if Freelancer refuses delivery, Publisher may retain, destroy, or otherwise dispose of Work without any liability to the Freelancer. If Publisher does not return Work, Publisher will reimburse Freelancer in the amount equal to the Page Rate paid to Freelancer pursuant to this Agreement.

11. Publisher will deliver to Freelancer, without charge, 10 copies of each installment of Freelancer's published work, which shall not be sold by Freelancer. Additional copies are not available from Publisher.

Ownership of Rights

12. Freelancer agrees that all Work has been specially commissioned by Publisher as work-for-hire under the United States Copyright Laws. In addition Freelancer assigns, transfers, and sets over to Publisher or its designee, and acknowledges that Publisher or its designee shall be the sole owner of, all rights existing in the Work, including all copyright and trademark in perpetual work, Publisher will reimburse Artist in the amount equal to the Page Rate paid to Artist pursuant to this Agreement.

Freelancer is not restricted from entering into this Agreement and has the right to grant all rights granted to Publisher. Except insofar as it may derive from the Title, all Work created by Freelancer will be wholly original, with Freelancer or in public domain, and shall not infringe on or violate any copyright, trademark, right of privacy or publicity, or any other right of any person or entity, or constitute libel or slander of any person or entity. Freelancer will indemnify Publisher against any and all damages, costs, and expenses, including attorney's fees, arising from any breach of these representations.

13. Publisher shall indemnify Freelancer against any damages, costs, and expenses, including attorneys fees, in connection with any claim or action based on material supplied to Freelancer by Publisher for incorporation into Freelancer's work, excluding any claim or action based on Freelancer's treatment of such material.

Sample freelance artist contract (continued)

Termination of Agreement

14. Time is of the essence for all delivery dates. Such dates may be postponed at Publisher's sole discretion.

15. If Freelancer does not comply with the Terms of this Agreement because of illness or disability (Incapacity), Publisher may suspend the Services, and if such Incapacity continues for more than three weeks, Publisher may terminate this Agreement by written notice to Freelancer at the address shown in this Agreement without any obligation except as to accepted Work. Publisher shall be entitled to all work in progress, subject to the payments provided in this Agreement.

16. If Freelancer fails to perform Freelancer obligations, and performance is not excused for any reason above, Publisher may terminate this Agreement by written notice to Freelancer at the address shown in this Agreement, such termination to be effective 10 days following Publisher's mailing of such notice, without further obligation or compensation to Freelancer. Publisher shall be entitled to all work in progress, subject to the payments provided in this Agreement.

17. If, prior to acceptance of the Work for any issue, Publisher shall cancel publication of the Title, then Publisher may terminate the Agreement by written notice to Freelancer at the address shown in this Agreement.

Complete Agreement and Waivers

18. The payment of Page Rates provided for in this Agreement shall constitute the primary consideration for the grant of rights made to Publisher. Freelancer's sole remedy for any failure by Publisher to make any payment due pursuant to this Agreement, in lieu of all other remedies at law or in equity, shall be an action at law to obtain such payments and under no circumstances shall any such failure entitle him to any reversion or termination of Publisher's rights under this Agreement.

19. This Agreement is the entire agreement of the parties, supersedes any prior or contemporaneous oral agreements, and can be modified only in a written document signed by Freelancer and an officer of the Publisher. A waiver of any provision of this Agreement shall not be deemed a future waiver of such provision.

20. This Agreement shall be governed by the laws of the state of Illinois. In the event any provision shall be declared invalid the remainder of this Agreement shall remain in effect.

(Publisher's name)   Agreed and Accepted:

By: _____ (your name) _____   _____ (Freelancer) _____

Title: _____ (your title) _____   Date: _____

Date: _____   Social Security or Employer Identification
                                           Number: _____

                                           Address: _____

                                           _____

                                           _____

                                           Telephone: _____

Sample freelance artist contract (continued)

PAYMENT VOUCHER

Name: _____

Address: _____

_____

Daytime telephone: _____

Evening telephone: _____

Social security/FEIN number: _____

TITLE:_____

ISSUE:_____

WORK PERFORMED

Book Interior:

plot ____ script ____ edits ____ layouts ____ pencils ____ lettering ____
inks ____ finishes ____

Page Rate: _____

Number of pages enclosed: ____

Total number of pencils due: ____

TOTAL DUE WITH VOUCHER: _____

Cover:

pencils ____ inks ____ pencils & inks ____ painting ____

Pay Rate:

TOTAL DUE WITH VOUCHER: _____

I, _____(Freelancer)_____, understand that the work for which I have been contracted
is a work-for-hire, as an independent contractor, and I relinquish all trademarks
and copyrights. I also acknowledge its originality and understand that I do own the
physical work, which will be returned to me upon completion of its reproduction.

_____   _____
Signature   Date

Sample freelance artist payment voucher

SECURITY AGREEMENT

_____(publisher name)_____, whose address is _____(address)_____, in the County of _____, State of _____ (hereinafter referred to as Party A) does hereby grant unto _____(name)_____, of _____(address)_____, (hereinafter referred to as Party B), a security interest in the following described property (hereinafter referred to as Collateral):

a. All inventory and work in process of Party A now owned

b. All accounts and accounts receivable of Party A now existing or hereafter created or arising

c. All contract and distribution rights of Party A now existing or hereafter arising

d. All furniture, equipment, and supplies of Party A now owned or hereafter acquired and used in connection with Party A business

e. All trademarks and copyrights owned or controlled by Party A

f. All other assets and properties of Party A

g. All proceeds and products of the foregoing to secure prompt payment to Party B of all sums presently due and payable, together with all other indebtedness owed by Party A to Party B due or to become due or that may be hereafter contracted or acquired and the performance by Party A of all of the terms and conditions of this Security Agreement (hereinafter referred to as Obligations)

Debtor shall be in default under this agreement upon the happening of any of the following events: (a) nonpayment, when due, of any amount payable on any of the Obligations or failure to observe or perform any term hereof; (b) Party A becomes insolvent or unable to pay debts as they mature or makes an assignment for the benefit of creditors, or any proceeding is instituted by or against Party A alleging that Party A is insolvent or unable to pay its debts as they mature; (c) entry of any judgment against Party A; (d) dissolution, merger, or consolidation by Party A, or transfer of a substantial part of the property of Party A.

In the event of a default: (a) Party B shall have the right, at its option and without demand or notice, to declare all or any part of the Obligations immediately due and payable; (b) Party B may exercise, in addition to the rights and remedies granted hereby, all of the rights and remedies of a Secured Party under the Uniform Commercial Code or any other applicable law; (c) Party A agrees to make the Collateral available to Party B at a place or places acceptable to Party B; and (d) Party A agrees to pay all costs and expenses of Party B, including reasonable attorney fees, in the collection of any of the Obligations or the enforcement of any of Party B's rights.

If any notification of intended disposition of any of the Collateral is required by law, such notification shall be deemed reasonably and properly given if mailed at least ten (10) days before such disposition, postage prepaid, addressed to Party A at the address shown herein.

Waiver of any default hereunder by Party B shall not be a waiver of any other default or of a same default on a later occasion. No delay or failure by Party B to exercise any right or remedy shall be a waiver of such right or remedy and no single or partial exercise by Party B of any right or remedy shall preclude other or further exercise thereof or the exercise of any other right or remedy at any other time.

This agreement and all rights and obligations hereunder, including matters of construction, validity, and performance, shall be governed by the laws of the State of _____ .
If any part of this contract shall be adjudged invalid, the remainder shall not thereby be invalidated.

Dated: _____

Party A
By: _____

Its:_____

Sample security agreement

CONFIDENTIALITY AGREEMENT

The undersigned requests that it be given access to certain Confidential Information that constitutes the proprietary property and knowledge of _____ (publisher name) _____, solely for the limited purpose of evaluating same, and in order to induce Publisher to disclose such Confidential Information, agrees that it will be bound by the following terms and conditions:

1. Confidential Information

The term "Confidential Information" means all information and data relating to Publisher and _____ (2nd party) _____ that is disclosed to the undersigned by Publisher (either orally or in a tangible form), including but not limited to inventions, discoveries, processes, and know-how; computer software codes, designs, routines, algorithms, and structures; product information; research and development information; information relating to actual and potential customers; financial data and information; business plans; marketing materials and strategies; and any other information regarding the foregoing that Publisher discloses to the undersigned hereunder. Failure to include a confidentiality notice on any materials disclosed to the undersigned shall not give rise to an inference that the information disclosed is not confidential.

Confidential Information shall not include information that the undersigned can establish (i) is generally known to the public (other than as a result of a breach of this Agreement); (ii) is independently developed by the undersigned; (iii) was lawfully obtained from a third party; or (iv) is later published or generally disclosed to the public by Publisher.

2. Protection and Use of Confidential Information and Data

Limited Use. The undersigned agrees to use the Confidential Information only for the limited time specified herein and solely for the purpose of evaluating Publisher's _____ (project/job description) _____ in order to determine whether to _____ (project/job goal) _____. The undersigned shall have no right to use the Confidential Information for production or commercial purposes without obtaining a license therefore from Publisher.

Protection. The undersigned hereby agrees to take all steps reasonably necessary to maintain and protect the Confidential Information in the strictest confidence for the benefit of Publisher and will not, at any time without the express written permission of Publisher, disclose the Confidential Information directly or indirectly to any third person, excepting employees of the undersigned who have expressly agreed in writing to be bound by the terms of this Agreement.

Term of Obligation. The undersigned's obligations with respect to the Confidential Information shall continue for the shorter of _____ (term length) _____ (#) year(s) from the date of its receipt of the Confidential Information, or until such information is subject to one of the exclusions set forth above.

3. Return of Confidential Information and Data

The undersigned acknowledges that its limited right to evaluate the Confidential Information shall expire _____ and agrees that all Confidential Information in a tangible form, including all copies thereof, will be returned to Publisher

Sample confidentiality agreement

at that time, or at such earlier time as Publisher may request. At such time, the undersigned also agrees to completely erase and destroy all copies of all portions of any software, comprising the Confidential Information, in its possession or under its responsibility, which may have been loaded onto the undersigned's computers.

4. Disclaimers

This Agreement does not require Publisher to disclose any Confidential Information. All Confidential Information disclosed by Publisher is disclosed on an "As Is" basis. Publisher will not be liable for any damages arising out of use of the Confidential Information, and the use of such Information is at the undersigned's own risk. Neither this Agreement nor the disclosure of any Confidential Information grants the undersigned any license under any patents, copyrights, or trade secrets.

5. Governing Law

This Agreement shall be governed by and construed in accordance with the laws of the State of _____ covering agreements made and to be performed in that State.

_____	_____
Firm name	Authorized signature
_____	_____
Address	Type or print name
_____	_____
City, State, Zip	Title
_____	_____
Date	Telephone number

6 COMIC BOOK DISTRIBUTION AND SALES

Any publisher is only as successful as his distribution. If you don't sell your product, you won't make any profits. Currently in the United States, comic books are sold through only a few channels: the direct market, newsstands, bookstores, discount distributors, and subscriptions. And then there are collectors and the foreign market, as well. Each market generates business and each requires the services of different distributors and wholesalers, and different sales strategies and tactics. The amount of distribution power you desire is based on your overall business plan and budget. (See chapters 7 and 9 for more information on strategies and budgets.)

THE DIRECT MARKET

This is the comic shop market and is serviced by what are called direct market distributors. It's called the direct market because the distributors sell on a non-returnable basis to the comic shops, which in turn sell directly to the comic book fans. The distributors sell titles from virtually all serious, credible comic book publishers to over 4,000 retail comic book shops, typically located in strip malls in suburban areas. These stores are frequented regularly by both new and veteran comic book fans between the ages of 11 and 29. Because of these demographics, the stores often sell other related items, such as magazines, games, T-shirts, and trading cards, which are also supplied to the direct market by the distributors.

The retail stores order the products from distributor catalogues approximately four months prior to the shipping date on a nonreturnable, guaranteed-sale basis; unlike traditional distribution, which has always been on a consignment basis, in this situation actual orders are actual sales. The standard industry discount from publisher to distributor is 60 percent off the retail price (35 to 55 percent off at the distributor to retailer level). You should bill distributors on shipping them their orders, with invoices to be paid within 30 days of the shipping date. Recently, more and more distributors require a "Printer's Shipping Completion Notice" to verify that the product has indeed been shipped from the printer. This notice is faxed to the appropriate individuals at each of the distributors' corporate offices, and can help clarify any miscommunication in regards to timely shipping.

This market is by far the most lucrative for any publisher. With the ability to have final sales (since sales are nonreturnable) over a month before going to press, it gives you the advantage of knowing your profits in advance. If you receive weak orders and calculate a $2,000 loss, you have a choice to either proceed with the project or cancel it, thereby cutting your losses at that point. In the direct market, you can always repackage a product and resolicit business at a different time and price; you don't have to publish a book that will lose money. It's the major blessing of this particular market—you can kill the dog before it kills you.

If you do choose to resolicit, always expect fewer orders. Traditionally any resolicitation generates less business because the retailers feel the anticipated customer has moved on to other products. Comic book buyers in the direct market can be very fickle; they often purchase one title on a regular basis until the latest hot title floods the market. This makes market shares in the direct market fluctuate greatly. Although Marvel Comics has traditionally dominated this arena, its market share has ranged from as high as 63 percent to as low as 27 percent over just the last three years (including month-to-month fluctuations of as much as 15 percentage points). DC Comics has traditionally ranked second, with a market share ranging from 35 to 16 percent over the same period. These figures were obtained from the distributor publications *Internal Correspondence* (from Capital City) and *Diamond Dialogue* (from Diamond Comic Distributors) and don't include reorders. (For the addresses of these publications, see Appendix, page 170.)

TIMING IS EVERYTHING!

Always promote your product at the time of solicitation—about three months prior to shipping. You need to *sell* the distributor and retailer on your comic books, otherwise your product won't make it to the store shelves or, most importantly, the customers.

Save your promoting and PR for when the product is available for purchase; you don't want to waste any free press coverage on a product that won't be available for three months. Customers are bombarded with thousands of products every day, and they will forget about your comic book if they don't see it soon after you publicize it. (See chapters 7 and 8 for more on sales and marketing, and promotions and public relations.)

Reorders (of any amount) are also less common for smaller publishers for a number of reasons. With the large number of titles being released (about 200 to 700 per month), the retailer can only focus on a complete turnover of new product. This, of course, leaves the customers who have missed a title to look elsewhere. If you do receive reorders, always ship them out immediately, within a day or two. Once the distributors and retailers realize that if they do reorder your product, they'll receive it within a week, they'll reorder more frequently and in larger quantities. With delivery time of more than about a week, they'll have lost the customer because the customer will have lost interest.

Whether making an initial shipment or shipping reorders, you should always strive to ship on time! There is no better form of advertising or promotion to both retailers and distributors than working with a credible, reliable publisher who produces product on a timely basis. Keep in mind that retailers have budgets, and with those limited dollars, they order their products for that month; if the product doesn't ship, they have nothing to sell (to generate the profits they need to pay the bills) and may not do business with you again. Shipping product late on a continuous basis will force buyers to cross you off their lists permanently and order elsewhere.

See Appendix, page 171, for addresses and contact names of current distributors. When dealing with distributors, be sure to gather as much information on their terms and procedures, such as the deadlines for inclusion in their sales catalogues.

NEWSSTAND DISTRIBUTION

The newsstand is significantly different from the direct market and is the traditional channel of distribution for comic books. The newsstand network is comprised of a few hundred wholesalers (like distributors, just in a different market) and about 100,000 outlets consisting of newsstands, book stores, convenience stores, and drug, variety, and grocery stores. In this market, comic books are distributed and displayed in much the same way as are magazines and newspapers.

A major newsstand distributor is assigned to handle the enormous distribution system through the wholesalers and retailers. Publishers sign an exclusive contract with this newsstand distributor who then assists the publisher in the promotion and marketing of all titles through their various channels. Much like the distributors in the direct market, newsstand distributors usually need four months to promote a new product. They solicit the wholesalers and retailers for an assigned allotment of books—normally five to 12 copies per rack in each store with rack space. Unsolicited titles are often returned to the wholesaler to be shredded. As in the direct market, it pays to offer newsstand distributor ample time to work the system.

Unlike magazines and newspapers, which have a discount structure of 40 percent off the cover price at the publisher to distributor level (with 25 to 35 percent off at the distributor to retailer level), comic books have a higher discount structure of 50 percent off (with 35 to 45 percent at the retail level). The major distributor also makes a commission of 3 to 9 percent off each copy sold. This can bring your total distributor discount up to 59 percent off the cover price.

The newsstand system works on a series of advances and settlements that are based on each title's "sell-through" percentage, which is the percentage that sold of the total order shipped to retailers on consignment. What's unique about this arrangement is that the publisher determines how many issues to print, and the distributor pays an advance of 10 percent of the wholesale value of all issues shipped. Typically, the publisher receives this advance within 10 days of shipping the books. The second advance is received about 60 days later, based on retailer information supplied to the distributor about how many books have sold to that point in time. In another 60 days, the publisher receives the final settlement, which is the final check paying on the balance of sales (less all the previously paid advances, of course); based on the actual sales, the settlement adjusts (or compensates for) the advance amount already paid. Unsold books are removed from the newsstand and shredded at the wholesaler level. Wholesalers are more than happy to show off their giant shredding machines. The settlement is the final check paying on the balance of sales. (For a list of comic book newsstand distributors, see Appendix, page 171.)

The newsstand system works entirely on a consignment basis. Although the risk of being left with unsold comic books is borne entirely by the publisher, the unit printing cost of each book is low enough that a sell-through of 20 percent of the print run can turn a profit. The idea is to minimize the number of unsold books while ensuring that no retail outlet runs out—each unsold copy is still a billboard, and so if there is a book on the stands, there is always the possibility of generating more interest and sales. The economics work because the allotment order (the allotted amount of copies ordered to ship to retailers) is traditionally 75,000 to 100,000 copies. With these numbers, you can print a comic book for about $.10, making it still profitable to shred 80 percent of the entire order (it costs about $.20 per copy to buy those books back).

You need capital to enter the newsstand distribution market. Don't, under any circumstances, enter this market without the appropriate capital investment. In the past, many publishers used their printers as their unofficial lenders. This worked well in the credit crazed 1980s, but credit terms of that magnitude aren't as welcome or popular in the '90s. Printers don't want to be your partner, just your supplier; they don't want to risk losing money. If you publish one title on a monthly basis with an allotment of 100,000 copies per issue, you'll accrue over $50,000 of printing (and shipping) costs in just four months. Add another $20,000 to $40,000 (depending on sales) on top of that for direct market printing, and you'll find yourself with a printing bill of about $90,000!

With only a 10 percent advance on a $1.95 cover price ($.80 wholesale), you're talking about receiving only about $32,000 from your wholesaler within the first four months. If the printer requires payment within 30 days, and your settlement comes in 180 days, this can cause a severe cash flow problem. In the newsstand market, you won't learn what the final sales amount is until 180 days later, and what happens if the product flops and your *final* sale is only 10 percent? (See chapter 9 for more on cash flow and budgets.)

The newsstand market requires a long term capital investment. As with direct market distribution, count on at least one year of shipping a product on time to the newsstand to achieve a substantial reader base. Whether you invest in one specific title or a few different titles, you need to establish that regular presence to build the credibility with wholesalers, distributors, and retailers.

If you do plan to distribute to the newsstand market, use a *newsstand printer* to print your comic books. These printers produce a larger number of mainstream publications and periodicals, and traditionally, they have their own newsstand shipping capabilities and services, which tend to be approximately 50 percent cheaper than those of outside sources. Always consider these potentially enormous savings when making a decision on which printer to use.

AN EXAMPLE OF THE NEWSSTAND DISTRIBUTION PAYMENT SYSTEM

On *The Green Hornet,* #1, Caputo Publishing, Inc., received a 10 percent advance on the total print run 10 days after the distributor, Warner Publisher Services, received the Printer's Shipping Completion Notice. In this case, for 125,000 copies with a retail cover price of $2.95 (this was a double issue), Caputo Publishing received 10 percent of the total wholesale value for the first advance. This came to $15,875, received within 10 days of shipping.

The second advance is paid 60 days after the "off sale" period. The "on sale" period for a monthly publication is 30 days, so the second advance is paid within 90 days after shipping. This amount is based on a percentage of projected sales as estimated by the percentage of returns received up to 60 days after "off sale." A reasonable estimated percentage of sales for this book was 40 percent of the total print run, which is 50,000 copies, with a wholesale value of $37,500. The second advance was estimated cautiously to cover the possibility of a previous overestimate. In this case, the second advance paid 75 percent of the estimated sales minus the original $15,875 advance of the wholesale value of the 125,000 print run.

The final settlement, which is usually received within 150 days after shipping, is based on the final sale percentage,

CMAA

The Comics Magazine Association of America (CMAA) is an organization that was created 35 years ago to promote and market comic books in new newsstand outlets. The vast majority of all the comic book racks you see in mainstream stores are organized by the CMAA. The association also regulates the color coding system that appears on the top of the front cover of all newsstand comic book titles (see chart on page 92). This provides a quick and easy way for the drivers of distributor delivery trucks to replace old issues with new ones.

hich in this case was 47 percent (7 percent more than
e estimate of 40 percent) less the total previously paid
dvances.

OTAL ORDER = 125,000 copies

:TAIL COVER PRICE PER COPY = $2.95

OTAL ESTIMATED SALE (WHOLESALE) = 40% (50,000 copies)

rst advance
)% of total wholesale value = **$15,875**

:cond Advance
)% of print run less original 10% advance multiplied by 75%
37,500 – $15,875 = $21,625 x 75% = **$16,218.75**

ettlement
ised on the final sale percentage, which was 47% of total print
n, less the total previously paid advances

3,750 total copies sold

14,062.50 (total revenue on this amount) – $32,093.75 (previous
dvances) = **$11,968**

his process may seem complicated at first, but that's
:cause it *is* complicated. The whole system is monitored via
)mputer through your assigned UPC bar code. If you want
 enter this market, it's best to do extensive research and
re a consultant to take you through your first few years of
:gotiations. Magazine Communication Consultants (P.O.
)x 277, Tuckahoe, NY 10707/ph: 914-337-6822, fax: 914-337-
)55) is a highly respected consulting firm; I've used them
id they're very good. Address your queries to Irwin Billman
 Ralph Perricelli.

The CMAA also issues the Comics Code Authority rating, which is a mainstream, G-rated seal of approval. This rating system, complete with its own Comics Code Authority seal, has been in existence since the 1950s, when comic books were cited as the reason for juvenile delinquency and almost banned by legislation. This general hysteria was caused by the book *The Seduction of the Innocent* by Dr. Frederick Wertham; the public's reaction to this book, coupled with the overall paranoia of the '50s, has been one of the main causes of the continued struggle of comic books to become an acceptable form of entertainment. Originally, only general audience, Saturday-morning-cartoon types of comic books earned the Comics Code Authority seal, and comics that didn't earn this seal fared so poorly that their publishers went out of business.

Only in the past 10 years have we seen a turn for the better, as comics have become more mainstream. This was thanks in part to the direct market channel of distribution, which allowed more creative freedom and an inexpensive alternative to the massive newsstand distribution system. Nevertheless, today the Comics Code Authority seal is still used, and if you want to have the strongest penetration within the newsstand market, it's the seal of approval that gives wholesalers and retailers an immediate indication that the book they're putting in their family grocery store won't attract an uproarious crowd of disgruntled parents. It's sort of like a G rating at the movies.

Comics Code Authority seal
When initially created, the Authority seal guaranteed a G rating for comic book contents. This is even the case today, and some retail outlets still will not carry comic books that don't have this seal.

You can gain a lot of useful information from the CMAA about the quality, size, and history of the comic industry in America, and I found my membership on its Board of Directors to be very enlightening. They voted me on as a mainstream comic book publisher, and I served from 1988 to 1994. It isn't every day that you can sit at a conference table with high-level executives from the largest comic book companies in America and learn from their experience and knowledge—some members had been in the comic business since before I was born! For more information on the CMAA write to The Comics Magazine Association of America, 355 Lexington Avenue, New York, NY 10017. Their phone number is (212) 661-4261.

The UPC Bar Code

The most important part of your newsstand cover is the mandatory UPC bar code and cover date. The UPC code is what keeps track of your books via a giant computerized distribution system; it's the system's way of recognizing the book, the issue, the on-sale and off-sale dates, and the publisher (the one who gets the check!), and all of this information is encoded in the bar code stripes.

Your newsstand wholesaler can furnish you with the appropriate UPC bar code films, which you then pass along to your printer with the rest of your cover materials for printing.

Your wholesaler (or distribution professional) should give you a bar code with the same cover date that is being used by all other publishers for that specific on-sale period. If your cover date and UPC code end up being, for example, a month behind the other titles on the rack, your comic book may be mistakenly pulled off the shelf within a week or two as an outdated issue. You want to have the title on the stands for the full one-month period for maximum sell-through, so make sure you get the right date. It's also *very* important that the cover date printed on the actual comic book *always* match the date encoded in the UPC code. The newsstand system doesn't recognize issue numbers at all, so if you publish a comic book with the wrong UPC code and/or cover date, a large portion of your allotment could end up in the shredder before ever hitting the stands.

BOOKSTORE DISTRIBUTION

Bookstore distribution is very similar to newsstand distribution, as it also works on a consignment basis. The only major difference is the traditionally higher sell-through average often achieved in this market. Comics that sell 30 percent through the newsstand wholesaler system can sell up to 80 percent in the bookstores. The payment structure is also similar, but a settlement is paid within 90 days of shipping, as opposed to 150 days in newsstand distribution.

Waldenbooks is by far the best bookstore chain for comic book sales. With 1,200 outlets nationwide, average sales can be as high as 50 to 60 percent, double the newsstand average. Unfortunately, this is a very difficult market to infiltrate without the right connections (or a magazine distribution consultant) at the right time. Once an opportunity arises for space within a racking program, the cost can be quite expensive. The racking program refers to a standing floor rack used in bookstores to hold up to 96 individual titles a month, and space on it can cost up to $25,000 for three years. (See Appendix, page 171, for the name of a comic book bookstore distributor.)

DISCOUNT DISTRIBUTION

Discount distributors will purchase any remainders you may have in your inventory. They pay anywhere from $.05 to $.15 per copy at large quantities (say, 100,000 copies), repackage your comic book with two others in a polybag, and sell three to discount stores for anywhere from $.99 cents to $1.99. (See Appendix, page 172, for a list of a few discount distributors.)

When considering selling in this market, don't offer current titles to discount distributors. If you sell copies of a current issue to be polybagged with older comics at a discount, you'll decrease or lose all the perceived value of that book, and it can affect your sales through the regular channels.

SUBSCRIPTIONS

When thinking of the subscription market, I like to say, "If they can't find you, you find them!" Subscriptions, however, are not a large source of revenue for the industry as a whole. Traditionally, they account for less than 10 percent of annual comic book sales. I believe the reason for this is that the collectibility of comic books makes it unacceptable to receive a less than mint condition copy, which often happens when the books arrive through the mail.

The key to subscription success is maintaining a mainstream presence through newsstand distribution, promotions, and public relations. Historically, cross-promotional plans have been very successful in generating thousands of subscribers. A cross-promotion is a joint effort between two companies or parties to generate interest in their related products. For example, if you're publishing a comic book that has a character who rides a Harley Davidson motorcycle, you could approach the Harley Davidson company or any of its licensees or helmet companies. A manager in the marketing department at Harley Davidson might love your comic book and want to use it as a freebie at motorcycle trade shows. In this type of situation you would then make sure to run a centerspread reader subscription advertisement in that issue with a special introductory offer or rate. You could also offer to have a character in your comic book wear a specific helmet brand in exchange for an additional subscription coupon in their next special Harley Davidson supplement or brochure.

These kinds of deals require an enormous amount time and salesmanship, coupled with a delicate balance of persistence, perseverance, and finesse. If your comic book only sells 5,000 copies and their special supplement or brochure will ship out 10 million copies, it's highly unlikely that any amount of persistence will work. But perhaps if you have an option for a movie (with your comic book character), and it's currently in preproduction, and you inform Harley Davidson that you'll make its helmet a permanent facet of your character's costume, then maybe. . . . (See chapter 11 for more on movie options and secondary rights.)

> **SEEK OUT OPPORTUNITIES!**
> ALWAYS BE ON THE LOOKOUT FOR CROSS-ADVERTISING OR PROMOTIONAL OPPORTUNITIES. ANY OPPORTUNITY, NO MATTER HOW SMALL, CAN BE A STEPPING STONE TO LARGER, MORE LUCRATIVE CONCEPTS.

The possibilities are endless, so be creative. Licensed properties have more potential for cross-promotions. There are usually at least a couple of dozen other licensees out there with related products that they're eager to promote. I've done cross-promotions with Ralston Purina, Coca-Cola Foods, Fuji Film, and Columbia Pictures that generated over 10,000 subscriptions in a two-year period. It works if you work at it.

THE FOREIGN MARKET

The standard 6⅝ x 10¼", 32-page full-color comic book format that you've come to know and love is exclusive to the United States. Foreign publishers have many different formats (and also different content), which makes it difficult to sell American-made comic books overseas. Distribution of the product is very limited (military bases and international collector stores, for example) because of the varying format and price structure. The only way you can break into this market is if your material is hot internationally, such as *The Real*

Ghostbusters, Married . . . with Children, Aliens, Bugs Bunny, or *The Terminator.* These popular products can open doors for other material.

Foreign sales can become one of the most lucrative sources of revenue out there. A foreign publisher will purchase duplicates of your comic book film at a per-page reprint rate, along with the rights to publish (much like a licensee). These reprint rates vary from country to country based on circulation, but they traditionally average $50 US dollars per page (plus shipping). A 20-page comic book will only generate $1,000 in revenue, but this amount is only from one country. Multiply that figure by 10 countries, and you have $10,000. Multiply that by six issues (since foreign publishers usually buy in bulk), and you have $60,000!

KNOW THE CODES

TO CALL OR FAX A FOREIGN COUNTRY, YOU'LL NEED THE APPROPRIATE CITY AND COUNTRY CODES. CALL THE INTERNATIONAL OPERATOR FOR THAT INFORMATION OR CHECK YOUR LOCAL PHONE BOOK OR LIBRARY.

Short of exhibiting at both the Frankfurt Book Fair (the world's largest book fair held every year in Germany) and the Bologna Children's Book Fair in Italy, acquiring foreign sales isn't an easy task for a small comic book publisher. Even with exhibits at these international shows (where most people do speak English), the amount of material you may sell often doesn't even pay your travel and exhibit expenses. The most economical way of reaching the foreign market, then, is through a foreign sales representative. Foreign "reps" usually work continuously in the international market with a portfolio of numerous clients. They typically work on a commission basis, averaging about 20 percent of receipts. So, for no initial cost, you can have your product presented to foreign publishers on a regular basis. (See Appendix, page 172, for a list of foreign publishers, agents, and foreign sales representatives.) Produce at least six issues prior to approaching a foreign sales rep. This will show them that you can actually produce. If there are hungry foreign publishers out there, they'll sooner be enticed by a bulk package. Make sure you have substantial product to offer.

Before they commit to publishing a comic book, foreign publishers will, understandably, want to see samples of the comic book. The foreign companies I list on page 172 are credible, but when sending comic book samples to any potentially interested foreign publisher, it's always best to send only one sample for an initial response. Armed with today's technology, there are foreign publishers who will scan right off your actual book and then publish it in their country without paying for the rights. So, a single sample, possibly with an incomplete story line, should be enough give them a taste of your title without making it easy to pirate.

Once you make a deal with an interested foreign publisher, the best way to handle international monetary transactions is to work in US dollars only (since the exchange rates fluctuate daily) and through a bank transfer of funds. A foreign publisher can have its bank electronically transfer funds directly into your account in a matter of hours. Check with your commercial banker for details about this.

THINK GLOBALIZATION!

Prior to purchasing the worldwide rights to any licensed property, contact a foreign representative to help you assess the international potential of that property. You may be unsure of a licensed property's popularity here in the United States, but it may be a very popular character in 10 other countries. With the right budget and marketing plan you might be able to transform a book with weak domestic sales into a tremendously profitable book for the overseas market!

Also, you don't have to purchase the international rights to sell worldwide. Structure the licensing agreement for exclusive North American (United States and Canada) rights. Then, upon being approached by a foreign publisher, contact a foreign sales rep to help with the legal aspects of working with the licensor. Pass along the paperwork on that foreign interest to your rep so that they can sign a publishing agreement and sell the film for the average reprint rate. Purchasing the *exclusive* (always exclusive) North American rights (meaning that only your company has these rights) alone will greatly reduce the advance royalty payment you make to the licensor.

COLLECTORS AND BACK ISSUES

Comic books have been called the fourth most popular collectible in the United States. Traditionally, the first issue of any title is an immediate collector's issue. Does this mean that every first issue will be valuable in 20 years? No. It all depends on the fundamental supply-and-demand factor. A title that only sold very small numbers for years may become the hottest collectible a few years later when a successful motion picture is released. *Teenage Mutant Ninja Turtles, The Crow,* and even *Alias* had small initial orders, but now they are valuable collector's items!

So, you may ask, If it's autographed, will it be worth more? An autographed comic book is only worth as much as an interested collector is willing to pay for it. Fans will actually stand in line for hours at comic book conventions just to get a premiere issue autographed by one of the creators. Unfortunately, there are usually more autographed copies than collectors, thereby reducing or limiting the value of the comic.

Whether copies are autographed or not, consistency is one of the major factors in collectibility. If you consistently produce a high-quality, timely comic book, fans will keep coming back. Also, knowing your inventory and offering back issues for sale through your current comic books is another way to keep your fans collecting. It's not outrageous to ask 25 to 100 percent over the cover price for back issues, and you can easily receive at least cover price plus postage for them. Check the updated *Comics Buyer's Price Guide* (see Appendix, page 170), which lists the current market value of every title, and offer your readers those prices. First volumes are the most valuable back issues to collectors and can usually sell for double the cover price from an ad that you place inside consecutive issues of that title.

PAID ADVERTISING

This is ads from other companies (for their own products) inside your comic book. In order to generate a substantial amount of revenue from paid advertising, you need to have an impressive circulation. Oftentimes, publishers will have the Audit Bureau of Circulation or ABC (900 N. Meachan Road, Schaumburg, IL 60173/ph: 847-605-0909) audit their circulation to accurately determine and guarantee it. However, if you're shipping 11 monthly titles (on time, of course) through all distribution channels, you can easily attract advertisers without an expensive ABC audit of your circulation, because the mainstream exposure that the advertisers desire is clearly visible in this situation.

Ad prices vary; consider this comparison: With a circulation of 1.5 million copies per month, a comic book company might receive $4,500 per full-page advertisement and $8,500 for a back cover (this is premium space). Yet, a mainstream entertainment magazine with a circulation of 225,000 copies per month can charge as much as $30,000 for a single full-page advertisement and as much a $70,000 for a back cover. If you're self-publishing a title and want to sell the back cover to, say, a local store that might be interested in a national expo-

PAID ADVERTISING REPRESENTATIVES

If you have an impressive circulation of hundreds of thousands, or even millions, of copies, you can instantly obtain the services of a paid advertising representation firm to sell ad space for you. These representatives require a commission of up to 40 percent of your revenue, but their connections and experience can generate tens of thousands of dollars worth of business. One such firm, which I've used and so has DC Comics, is Print Advertising Representatives, Inc., 233 Park Avenue South, New York, NY 10003/ph: (212) 780-3500, fax: (212) 280-3555 (attn: Bernie Slotnick).

sure of 10,000 copies, the rate is completely up to you. You can charge from $100 to $1,000. It all depends on your ability to *sell the value of the space*.

This amazing price difference is based on many variables. First, a magazine's circulation is almost always audited, for guaranteed circulation. Smaller comic book companies may consider an audit too expensive a process, and far beyond their investment budget. Therefore, they cannot guarantee their circulation number and cannot charge as much for advertising space. Second, comics still have the stigma attached to them of being questionable literature, with children as their primary audience. Advertisers might feel, therefore, that the actual readership is too young to buy the products they would be advertising in the comic books. Third, an advertising agency might find it safer to place a client's ad for its product on a prestigious magazine rather than a comic book.

When presenting your comic book ad space to advertisers, be creative but realistic. It may seem like a perfectly logical and obvious idea to have an ad peddling the video release of a major motion picture that's related to your comic book story on the back of one of your issues, but can you sell the advertiser on the concept with a circulation of only 10,000 copies? The movie studio probably won't be interested, but what about your local video rental store? If you mention that you have an autographing session scheduled at a comic specialty shop in the area, the video store might consider a special coupon offer to attract more customers. The national distributor of the product can be sold as an added bonus.

Also keep in mind that a paid advertisement doesn't have to generate cash to be valuable. Swapping space is another alternative. For example, if you can trade ad space in your comic book for additional promotion at your local chain of comic shops, you may be getting much more value from the space than a flat fee. Consider approaching another comic book publisher or a comic news magazine, too, to swap space. With three ad swaps, you'll have three ads for your title in three other publications, promoting and exposing your title to new potential readers. And, this is all without spending a cent!

SELLING DIRECT

A surefire way of building your circulation is by servicing the retailers directly. You can furnish them with new titles yourself (eliminating the middleman—the distributor), or deliver reorders, which, if in small quantities (2 to 5 copies), will often be ignored by the distributors. By contacting retailers directly, you'll get more firsthand feedback about your titles. You may find that a comic shop in Dallas sells enormous quantities of one of your titles, while the store down the block is doing very poorly with that same book.

This information might then inspire you to initiate a special marketing effort. Call the store and offer an autograph signing by any local artists at no charge. In addition to this risk-free opportunity, you'll be bringing in 20 extra copies of each issue of the title, that the store can sell autographed at cover price. By extending those copies at no charge, the store generates otherwise unprojected revenue, and you just increased the interest of your titles in that store.

You should check back with the store in two to three months and ask how subsequent issues have sold. You may be surprised to learn that the local store now blows the Dallas store out of the water. When they call to reorder directly, offer them a standard 50 percent discount off the cover price with free freight and a minimum order of 3 copies. Always ship the product UPS (which requires a signature), and generally (especially with all new accounts), ship the product C.O.D. (cash on delivery). Don't offer instant credit. Unless you plan to write off a bunch of copies of your titles as promotional expenses, don't ship any product to any retailer on credit. If they're serious about supporting your product, they can also support you by paying C.O.D.

Always recommend to your creative staff (pencilers, inkers, colorists, etc.), whether they be full-time employees or freelancers, that they support the company's titles. If they live out of state, that's a wonderful opportunity to implement a national retail store autographing promotion. Offer to pay their local transportation (by car) at about $.25 per mile and reimburse the retailer for any lunch meal that may be provided. After all, a great way of getting comic book stores interested in supporting your product is to support them!

Once you've decided to do some direct retail selling, it's best to start by sending a letter and a sample copy of your titles to every retailer that you'd like to have carry your titles. This gives retailers an actual product to examine rather than a listing with only a picture, as in distributors' catalogues. You'd be surprised how many retailers won't even bother to initially try your product (whether you send them a sample or they see it in a distributor catalogue); you may find that less than one third of all the comic specialty retailers actually order your product for resale, with another one fifth simply ordering by special request (for customers on their store's special subscription list). Still, your goal in selling directly to retailers is to get them to support your company's titles by offering you their valuable shelf space; if you make that extra effort, they may

DON'T BUY THE "I'M-YOUR-BIGGEST-FAN!" ROUTINE

If a retailer calls and babbles about how well your product was doing in his store but says that his distributor doesn't carry it anymore or stiffed him on his copies, call his distributor first before doing business with him. You may find that he was "stiffed" because he owes the distributor payment for three months of comic books, and he's desperately trying to get product (any product) to sell to make money to pay the rent.

eventually break down and give you a try. Then, once you develop a strong business relationship with several or even more retailers, depending on how much time and energy you put into this, continue to offer them perks, such as free flyers and autographed comic art for them to put up in their stores, and add them to your press release mailing list. The more you support them, the more they'll support you.

The Appendix, page 173, includes the names, addresses, and phone numbers of over 300 domestic and international comic specialty shops that you can approach. Always follow up your mailings with phone calls; ask for the owner or manager, and inquire about their comments and thoughts on your package and comic books. Don't expect overwhelming enthusiasm, and don't be surprised if they don't know what your talking about—they're bombarded with mail promotions. Overall, you should get some important feedback, and at least one percent of the people you contact should either order, increase an order they've already placed, reorder, or ask for back issues. Note that English is taught as a second language in many countries, so this opens up the international market to your American comic book. Despite the fact that American comic books do have a unique size format, and depending on your comic's concept, you may still find interest overseas. Remember, when dealing with international transactions, always specify that the cost of the product is in US dollars only.

7 SALES AND MARKETING STRATEGIES

At this point, it's probably pretty safe to assume that you have a comic book title or concept in mind and are now interested in formulating a strategy to sell the greatest possible number of copies of your potential product. The previous chapter explored the many different channels of distribution and other sources of revenue. Now you have to put together a marketing plan of action to best infiltrate those markets.

Every successful entrepreneur is a master salesperson. You'll constantly be selling your products and your company to anyone and everyone. Any temporary setback or inadequacy should be viewed as a learning experience from which you have to immediately move on to continue your drive for success. It's your vision and your dream; no one else will be able to sell it like you.

What you your own best salesperson? Experience, desire, determination, and commitment, along with any other emotions associated with the spirit and risk of the entrepreneurial adventure. And, since your company is your baby, you'll nurture, protect, and feed it like no one else. Plus, your energy and determination can also become very contagious. From the moment you decide to become self-employed, you'll be convincing everyone, from yourself to your spouse to your banker, that "Hey, this is going to work!"

Selling doesn't start or end with any specific plan of action—you need to be "on" at all times. Your goal, in most cases, is to convince someone to do something they don't want to do. Persuading employees to work overtime, for example, or freelancers to produce work twice as fast to make a deadline requires as much salesmanship as getting a bank to lend you money or convincing a supplier to give you credit. And doing these things takes a master sales job, especially in an industry with a long track record of undesirables.

A lot of fly-by-night comic book publishers have left a scar on many suppliers, freelancers, retailers, and distributors by not paying them for their work or promising work that they never deliver. Whether intentional or unintentional, this scar runs long and deep. Anyone can publish a comic book thanks to the immediate availability of guaranteed distribution and the possibility of any one single comic book becoming the next *Teenage Mutant Ninja Turtles, The Mask, The Crow, The Tick,* or *Spawn,* and the longer the list, the greater the enthusiasm of people who want to enter the field. If anyone mentions their negative experience with a previous comic book publisher, simply reply, "That's not me. I don't believe it's fair to be judged and punished by some other, unrelated incident." It has worked.

Hearing the historical comic book success stories, such as those mentioned in the previous paragraph, it's easy to see the attraction in becoming a comic book entrepreneur. Comic books, although still having to endure the stigma of being questionable literature, nevertheless make up a fascinating and wonderfully creative industry. No one can foretell if your book will make you the next comic book millionaire; you won't know until you publish it. But by using the suggestions collected in this book and avoiding the universal errors many companies make in the course of learning the ropes, you'll be one step closer to becoming that super success story. And of course, I can't stress enough that to achieve your goal, you have to *sell, sell, sell!* Once you choose to become an entrepreneur, you should file any negative feedback as future reference and still continue to exert your determination, without hesitation. No one can influence your company's future like you can.

THE KEY ELEMENTS OF MARKETING SUCCESS

I often say that people don't fail, they give up, and while sheer determination is very helpful and necessary, you'll also need a marketing game plan to help in achieving your goals. *Marketing* has been defined as creating a public perception of your company and it's products. (The *public* being everyone, from a distributor to the consumer.) It involves public relations (also simply called PR), promotions, advertising, product development (your final product is still your best form of advertising), and the ability to recognize what works best for your desired target audience.

The key elements of a profitable business and a successful, organized marketing strategy are always as follows (in order of importance):

Always ship on time

Always offer consistent quality and talent

Generate maximum exposure and high recognition

Never, ever, let 'em see you sweat

Whether success with your comic book takes a few months or three years to develop depends largely on your concept and your promotional and public relations efforts. To begin developing a selling strategy, ask yourself the following questions: What about your title makes it unique? What qualities does your title have that make it similar to other products out there? What special ownership, title, or talent name recognition does your comic have that may add a spark of interest? Every singular and familiar nuance that your product has will be the fuel that enables you to market it to its full extent.

The following strategies and tactics have worked very well for a variety of different comic book companies. Although many may be big-budget strategies, you can scale them down and tailor them to your business, and then work up from there. Regardless of which market you're selling to, your primary objective is to maximize your company's profitability by building an international publishing, licensing, and merchandising organization, with your ultimate goal being to develop your business into an internationally recognized and accepted entertainment phenomenon with sales in the tens of millions of dollars.

DIRECT MARKET SALES STRATEGIES

The direct market, which consists of the comic specialty shops serviced by about 11 main distributors, will be your first distribution channel. In this section, I'll provide a number of useful sales approaches that you can try when dealing with this market. Note that distributors require solicitation information approximately four months prior to the time when you ship your comics to them. (Contact the distributors listed on page 171 for all initial solicitation information and requirements.) Also, all these tactics are very common in the direct market and work, up to a point. Keep in mind that everyone else is also promoting their product as the greatest thing since sliced bread. So, you should always be thinking of new creative and innovative ways to boost your product.

Creating Interest Among Distributors, Retailers, and Fans

The idea in this basic sales strategy involves using the name recognition of, for example, your successful, well-known comic book writer and/or the talent of even a new artistic talent that you've discovered to stir up a frenzy of interest from your distributors, retailers, and fans. The more interest you have, the more comic books you'll sell, and the better your business will do. You can use all of the following tactics to focus distributor, retailer, and consumer attention on your comic book and the talented artists who create it.

Press Releases and Convention Appearances

One good tactic for increasing audience interest would be to develop an aggressive public relations campaign using detailed press releases in all trade publications (they print press releases for free) and convention promotions (when you or your talent make appearances at shows) for maximum exposure. A press release (just like the sample news release in chapter 8, only more introductory) is a very powerful source for generating sales; the right angle, coupled with the right format, can give you free publicity in every trade publication in which it appears. In this case, you could focus your press release on your writers and artists and their well-known names. See chapter 8 for details on how to write the perfect news release. For convention promotions, always make appearances at these shows with a high impact display and an autograph session. (Trade show promotions are discussed in more detail a little later on in this chapter on page 106.)

Always make use of strong press releases and advertising. Whenever possible and appropriate, include testimonials from various "names" in the industry and Hollywood if you have any. An example might read something like this: "Wow! What have you been doing all these years?" —John Stangeland, Owner of Atlas Comic Shop, on his reaction to *Vespers*. (You would include this as part of the text—see sample release on page 125.) Always keep your eyes and ears open for any interesting content for additional press releases. You can never receive too much free publicity.

The Teaser Ad

A teaser ad can be something as simple as my 1988 promotion for *The Terminator* comic book. This was a full-page, all black flyer with the words "I'll Be Back . . ." in white. The stark black background attracted attention, and the phrase "I'll Be Back . . ." was instantly recognizable from the original movie. It generated enormous curiosity and positive word-of-mouth interest. You can also highlight your talent and use their name recognition in a teaser ad; I did one for my *Twilight Zone* title in which I just listed their names, and it worked really well.

Retail Telemarketing, Direct Mail, and Co-op Advertising Campaigns

Consider developing a comprehensive monthly telemarketing and direct mail campaign targeting the direct market retailers themselves. Direct contact reinforces the promotional listing of your comic books that appears in the distributors' catalogues. A current distributor catalogue can contain as many as 500 pages of product choices for the retailers to purchase; you need to get your comic book to stand out from the rest. A simple phone call or a promotional flyer can bring added attention to your product and generate more interest.

Telemarketing is most effective if you're a phone-friendly person—one who's comfortable on the phone. What you're trying to do is sell a highly visual product verbally. For example, you should mention who your writers, artists or co-creators are, especially if they're well-known, recognizable names. You'll have the most success with this when the retailers already have the distributor catalogues or your promotional flyer in front of them. Producing and mailing up to 5,000 printed flyers can be expensive, but very effective. If you have the capability within your budget, have someone produce the most professional-looking flyer you can afford. Remember, this promotional piece is representing your company and the quality of your products, so knock their socks off! You could include page samples, a plot synopsis, contact and copyright information, and artist names.

To purchase a list of the current retailers, contact Fandata, a database of comic book fans and retailers, at 7761 Astrella Court, Springfield, VA 22152-3133, ph: (703) 913-5575. The *Comics Buyer's Guide* weekly newspaper also lists many retailers (see Appendix, page 171, for an address). On page 173, I list over 100 domestic comic specialty shops for you to start with. With these tactics, note that the quality of your communication can be more valuable than the quantity; if, for example, you can convince only 50 stores to order 20 copies of your title, that's already an order of 1,000 copies.

As another sales technique, offer co-op advertising with select retailers. Co-op advertising is a cooperative venture between a publisher and retailer to generate more local interest in the publisher's titles. Ads can appear on television or radio, or in print. The retailer and publisher share the cost, and both their businesses are mentioned in the promotion. You should concentrate on local public awareness with retail outlets. Have regular autograph sessions. Work together on public relations and advertising through local newspapers and television stations; local television stations often charge as little as $30 for a 30-second spot airing during many cartoons or science-fiction related shows. A local comic store chain may even have an existing television commercial that they've already produced to which they can add (for a nominal cost) a plug for an autographing session for one of your comic books. To successfully use television to generate interest, you'd ideally air a handful of spots during the right programming; so for example, if your title is about ninjas, you'd advertise during a martial arts movie or cartoon to make the strongest impressions on the appropriate potential audience.

Trade Shows and Conventions

Comic book trade shows and exhibits provide great selling opportunities. They create a good atmosphere in which to pitch your company and stir up interest in your titles. You should definitely take advantage of exhibitions to create the kind of high visibility that reaches to both fans and retailers. The comic book trade shows have come a long way since 10 years ago when there were under 100 retail organizations represented. Now there are over a thousand! These shows provide a chance to meet, on a one-on-one basis, the retailers who order and sell your products, and your goal is to create the opportunity to increase retailer support.

At select trade shows and conventions, you might present a *start-up kit* to all retailers who approach your booth, and you could also offer it for sale regularly to retailers. This kit would include various collectibles, posters, trading cards, flyers, and other premiums, along with vital information on your company and its officers and directors. You could also mention the comic book artists in these materials to further promote your titles. A retailer start-up kit is a sure way to get the immediate attention you'll need from the market when first starting up your company.

"Marilyn Monroe"
and me at a trade show

Talk about an attention grabber at your booth! Is it . . . her? No, it can't be! Hiring actors to portray your comic book characters at conventions is a very effective promotion. Everyone will come up to your booth to find out who they are. If you have a valuable, well-known licensed property, such as Marilyn Monroe, your fans will instantly recognize it and gather at your booth to discover more.

King of the trade shows!

This was a real, live lion at the MGM/UA party at a past Licensing Show in New York. How many opportunities will you ever have to get your picture taken with a live lion? MGM/UA thought this would attract people, and they were right!

Trade show booth

This is an example of a giant photographic trade show booth display, behind comic book creators Ron Fortier (front), David Mowry, and Jeff Butler (back). Having your creative talent do autograph signings at shows can be a big draw.

Offering a seminar at select trade shows is another promotional technique; it builds respect for your company and its products via an informative, hands-on session. You can coordinate a small comic book writing or drawing seminar at any small or large comic show, and this will build credibility for your talents and give you and your product good exposure. Send a press release about the seminar (and its outcome and attendance) to the trade press.

Your exhibit booth space, presentation, and salesmanship will determine if buyers order your merchandise, so try to be as professional as possible. Be creative when designing your booth—your trade show space should be an attraction in itself. Skyline Displays offers an inexpensive, portable trade show display unit (check your business-to-business yellow pages for a sales office near you), but if this type of investment (about $1,000) is completely out of your immediate reach, there are other, less expensive techniques, such as making the booth yourself.

Your primary goal in producing a trade show booth is to create a backdrop that can be seen from 50 feet away but still be interesting up close at 10 feet. Use large images to attract the crowds from a distance, and have smaller images or creative talent signing autographs to keep any nearby crowds interested long enough for you to get a chance to talk to them. To keep retailer interest at your booth, give them autographed copies of your product as freebees—that autographed edition may end up being the only copy of your product on display at their store. Perhaps offer a drawing for giveaways, free premiums, etc.—be creative. Your objective at every trade show and convention is to get every single retailer and/or customer to approach your booth uttering those magic words, "Who are you?" Traffic at your booth gives you the opportunity to show potential buyers what your company is all about and why they should carry or purchase your books.

You can have your comic book artists produce the large, dramatic backdrop images for your booth or go to a local photographic specialty darkroom lab. Many large photographic labs service the exhibition industry with inexpensive photographic enlargements. You may be surprised to learn that a 40 x 60" mounted black-and-white enlargement of your cover art costs less than $100. Check your local business-to-business (or regular) yellow pages under the photographic services section. A place like Kinko's copy center also has the capability to produce 18 x 48" black-and-white enlargements for about $10 with its zoom photocopiers. And, you can easily color in an enlargement of your black-and-white cover art with acrylic paints to create an eye-catching display piece.

Another product that is an inexpensive material for creating outstanding displays is Foamcor. Foamcor is a lightweight board that can be purchased in widths of up to almost an inch thick. It usually comes in 4-x-8′ sheets and is also available with a Velcro surface so that you can attach artwork to it. A regular sheet of 4-x-8′ board costs about $25 at your local art supply store. You can use Foamcor as your booth's backdrop, hinging three or four sheets together with tape, or you can create life-size cutouts of your characters with it, or you can even construct a simple—but impressive looking—pylon with your company's logo on top. If you opt to try the latter, your logo eight feet off the ground will guarantee visibility above the crowd. When designing your booth, always keep in mind how you plan to transport or ship it.

Promotional Contests

Another sales method for generating interest in your comic book is to offer retailers a raffle contest in which one retailer will win an all-expense-paid trip to the San Diego Comic Book Convention to work the booth with the staff. Some of this staff could be your creative talent to further promote the book. You would promote the adventure by sending your press releases to all the trade publications (remember, they print press releases as ads for free). Contests are very helpful in attracting additional attention to your product. A contest prize could also involve the entrant winning a cameo appearance in your comic book. It all depends on your budget and capabilities, and you should, of course, always check with your lawyer for legal viability of the contest in your state.

Newsletters and General PR

You might consider generating a quarterly retailer newsletter and offering it to retailers at a minimal cost through the distributors' catalogues. To produce approximately 15,000 copies of even a single one-sided 8½ x 11" newsletter can be costly. Therefore, it might be a very impressive and more cost-efficient sales tool for an entire line of comics, rather than just one book. If you do, however, have the capability to produce a newsletter, it can be a valuable asset for a company that's just starting up. You can produce 25,000 two-sided 8½ x 11" black-and-white newsletters for approximately $756 from Fosterprints, a specialty printer (see Appendix, page 170, for their address). This is a per-piece cost of about $.03. You could offer a bulk newsletter package to your retailers of 100 copies for $7 ($.07 per piece). The distributors would take $1 or $2 of that $7, making your ultimate revenue about $5 per bulk package (or $.05 per piece).

An impressive, high-quality newsletter, complete with interviews, reviews, and exclusive information about any of your well-known comic book artists or writers, and any upcoming news and events, could entice 150 retailers to each order a bulk order as a store giveaway. You should design the newsletter to have adequate space in which they can stamp their store logos and information; this offers them the ability to promote their store as the only local source of this free newsletter. With bulk sales of 150 at a $5 wholesale value, you would generate $750 against the $756 cost of printing! So, your promotional expense would just be about $100 for shipping. You could use the remaining 10,000 flyers (remember, you printed 25,000 in this scenario) in the distributors' promotional packs, or you could also use them as an impressive giveaway at the next trade show or comic convention. That's quite an impressive promotional piece for a bottom-line cost of about $100.

Sending photocopies and video cassettes of all PR material to all distributors and select retailers also helps create interest in and enthusiasm for your comics. If you receive any type of press from newspaper or magazine articles, television shows, or radio programs always send copies to your direct market distributors and/or select retailer shops along with a press release. Constant communication about your growth and success produces and reinforces confidence in your company and its products. It isn't necessary to send these clippings individually; send a bunch of them, or send them with a solicitation package.

Discounts

To boost sales, extend to your distributors and retailers additional discounts for supporting your product line. This can be an added incentive to buy your comics. Just offering distributors an extra discount above and beyond the 60 percent standard, doesn't necessarily guarantee additional sales; nor does it guarantee that the distributor will pass the added discount on to the retailer. So, you should connect the discount to the selected discount group. Require that the distributors offer all retailers a 50 to 55 percent discount in order to receive their incentive discount of 62 percent off the cover price. You can easily verify that your distributor is passing the incentive discount along by your catalogue order form listing.

Autograph Promotions

As I mentioned previously, you can organize special autographing promotions at conventions. Comic conventions present your chance to greet the *public* one

Colorist Suzanne Dechnik at a comic convention
Signing autographs is a great promotional tactic to drum up business and increase popularity. (And, I guess a little prayer couldn't hurt your sales either.) Suzanne Dechnik has worked on such popular comic books as Ghostbusters II, Terminator, *and* Elfquest.

on one, as well as the retailer. Having a booth at these shows strengthens your credibility, and gives your fans the opportunity to talk to the creators of any one of your books. Meeting the creators and getting their autographs increases fans' enthusiasm and solidifies their loyalty.

You could also try offering signed and numbered editions of premiere issues that would be sold exclusively through one distributor who is willing to promote the title to its full potential. Product exclusivity is the wave of the future; as the industry becomes an increasingly bigger business, self-publishers will have to initiate more desperate actions to increase their sales and profits. Don't expect an enthusiastic response to an exclusive proposal at first; distributors desire titles to have track records of being best-sellers, otherwise they may feel it's not worth their time and energy. You should also realize that offering an exclusive edition through one distributor will dramatically increase that distributor's market share on that product and your company. So, don't expect the other distributors to appreciate their loss. Still, the marketplace is changing, and the successful businesses (and distributors) of the future are the ones that can master the management of change.

Another way to drum up interest might be to offer exclusive cover illustrations for each distributor catalogue. You'll know you have a hot title when the distributors are willing to let a promotional illustration grace their catalogue covers.

Use Past Successes
Develop an advertising campaign that revolves around all your past success stories. Make references to your previous popular titles in your newsletters and press releases. You could use phrases like, "From the creators of Spawn comes . . . ." or "The people who brought you *Vespers* and *The Real Ghostbusters* now give you . . . ." in your press releases, newsletters, or even print advertisements. And, you could also mention how many copies a previous popular title sold. Sales of 20,000 copies or more is a large enough quantity to boast about. And, as I mentioned above (under Press Releases and Convention Appearances), testimonials from outside sources in your advertisements are always an additional good selling tool; they reinforce what you believe about your product, but they come from an unbiased and possibly more recognizable name.

Also building on previous achievements, retain the services of any of your "hot" talents from past projects to create covers and spin-off series. And, even "guest" cover illustrations from highly recognized talents will generate more sales. This has been proven time and time again. Unfortunately, it's difficult to forecast if a hot talent's cover illustration will generate a profit above and beyond their fee. This requires a careful analysis of their sales history in other, similar situations. Still, the affiliation with any hot talent also increases credibility and awareness of your company and its products. While analyzing your sales forecast, ask yourself if you can afford to consider using hot talents simply as a marketing tactic, in the event that the project fails to sell enough copies to cover the talent's fee.

Ad Swapping
Develop cross-advertising plans with various trade publications and other small publishers; ad-swapping is a fantastic way to increase public and retailer

awareness of your products. What it entails is you offering to run another company's ad in your comic book in exchange for them running one of your ads in their publication. Although most trade publications won't "swap" ad space, there are a few who may consider the prospect and many other publishers, similar to yourself, will certainly also consider the possibility. To approach another company, open communications by sending a photocopy of your advertisement, a cover letter explaining your request for ad-swapping, and a description of the ad space that you're offering. Note that the smaller trade publications and other self-publishers may be more accessible to the idea than the larger businesses.

The Monthly Comp List

Your complimentary copy list (or comp list) is a listing of all the individuals who get a free copy of your comic books when they're first published. On this list should be retailers, trade publication editors, distributors, press people, movie producers and directors, actors, artists, writers, and anyone else you can think of who needs to know you exist. It is usually the only means for business associates within the industry to know that you're shipping on a timely basis, or even actively publishing. After all, how many times will they visit a comic book store and see your product on the shelves? And, what guarantee do you have that the store they frequent even carries your product?

If, on the other hand, business associates receive the product every month and like it but never see it in their regular comic shops, they'll eventually ask the owners about it. Chances are, the store owner will start carrying your company's titles from that moment on! So by using a comp list, you've immediately created or increased interest in your product, and if you employ some well-known talents, you've also instantly informed everyone of that fact, as well.

You should also pick various affluent individuals for a monthly comp list. Pick 50 to 100 important individuals, from distributors to members of the trade press, and send them a copy of your book every month. You can have your printer add these names and addresses to the shipping manifest to guarantee consistency.

Building an Image of Affluence

This is the next sales strategy you should work with. Always keep in mind the key success elements, which, again, are always shipping on time, offering consistent quality and talent, generating maximum exposure and high recognition, and never, ever, letting them see you sweat. These elements will immediately build an image of affluence for your company.

Prompt Delivery

One of the key success elements—shipping *all* titles on time, to the day—is also an effective sales tactic. Your product is your best form of advertising, promotion, and PR. Nothing gets the word across to the distributors, retailers, and buyers that you are a credible, serious publisher like a timely product. And, if you adhere to schedules, you'll also create the image among your clients and consumers that your company is a successful, profitable, and reliable one, since you have no trouble delivering product on a regular basis.

Trade Publication Advertisements

You should advertise regularly in a variety of trade publications. In fact, regularity is more important than picking the publication with the highest circulation. The number of impressions that you make on a weekly basis with different advertisements can eventually convince even the most skeptical of readers to try your product. And, placing regular ads implies that you run a profitable business, that you're doing well, and have the money to spend on an advertising campaign.

Design an entire advertising campaign that displays some continuity in its overall visual presentation. If you use the same thick black border, background color, specific type style, or even the same concept in every ad, readers will immediately recognize the product as something from your company. Think of the Absolut vodka ads, which all use the same concept and the same typeface, or any Coca-Cola promotions, which always use the company's recognizable logo. In these cases, you always know what they're selling and who's selling it. Placement within a certain publication is another way of adding continuity. Always reserving the inside front cover of a magazine or a quarter-page ad on the editorial page of a trade newspaper gives readers an immediate and constant location to which they know they can always go for information on your products. (See chapter 8 for more information on advertising in the trade publications.)

Free Trade Show Promotional Premiums

At trade shows, offer retailers free promotional premiums that have a high *perceived* value (but are really inexpensive). One of the best inexpensive premiums for trade shows is the button. It can be pinned onto anyone, and you then have a small walking advertisement for your company and/or title. Nothing does more to promote a successful company image than having hundreds of people wearing a button for your product—it translates to hundred of people saying, "I like this." That's quite an endorsement!

You can produce 5,000 1¼"-diameter buttons for about a dime. You must furnish the button manufacturer with the printed material to insert in the button, but you can generate that yourself for free! Check with your printer for what size paper they're using to print the covers of your comic books; chances are, they have some extra ("dead") space on the paper, alongside the covers. All you have to do is add the artwork for your promotional buttons in this space, and you'll have an endless supply of printed sheets for buttons. The button image is like part of the cover mechanical that you give to the printer, who just runs it off with the covers. Just make sure you tell the printer not to throw that extra paper away and to give it to you.

You can produce as many buttons (from 50 to 50,000) as your budget can handle at any given time, but the smaller the amount, the higher the per-unit cost. I've used buttons many times and recommend that you give them a try. One button manufacturer you can contact is Filo Enterprises/Promotional Buttons, P.O. Box 11484, Milwaukee, WI 53211/ph: (414) 332-5612 (attn: Susan Filo).

T-Shirts, Sweatshirts, and Jackets

Consider providing a limited number of T-shirts, sweatshirts, and jackets for you and your staff to wear at each convention and trade show. You can produce a handful of T-shirts with your characters or company's logo on them for about

Mars promotional button
A promotional button is a simple and inexpensive premium that you can give away to retailers at the trade shows you attend. On this button I just chose to feature my company name, but you could just as easily promote a comic book title or character, too.

$10 per piece at your local T-shirt screen printer. This is always a good way to build an image of affluence because it says to people, "We support our products. Look! Aren't they great? You should support them, too!"

Don't think of these as mere T-shirts, but rather as walking billboards for your comic book and/or company. A large dynamic illustration and logo will attract the attention of every single individual who walks by you and your booth. It will make and leave an impression in their minds of your company's existence, and if they like what they see, you'll have another reader and potential fan. (Note: You could also produce T-shirts, etc., to sell to retailers and distributors, but this is very expensive—usually about $5 per quality shirt for a minimum order of about 500.)

Trade Show Schmoozing

Promote all unique relationships and convention trips with exuberance. For example, if you're planning on traveling to various trade shows and conventions, let business contacts know and always schedule time to meet with any business associates who are also going to be there. Whether you meet for lunch, dinner, or a cup of coffee, personal attention to a business relationship cements that alliance. Making your out-of-town business associates feel important by taking the time out of your busy schedule to meet really does work.

Licensor Promotional Materials

Take advantage of all promotional materials available from licensors and licensees. At the 1990 Capital City Conference (a comic book trade show that's no longer in existence), my company offered free, full-color *Married . . . with Children* T-shirts to the first 250 retailers who came by my booth. Since this is one of my comic book titles, I obtained the T-shirts in exchange for promoting and listing the shirts and their manufacturing company in the direct market catalogues and at trade shows. There was no money exchanged, and the winning premium item created excitement, increased the perceived value of my company, and generated and solidified interest in my company's products!

If you're publishing a licensed title, there are probably up to 100 other licensees of that same character. Contact them to open cross-promotional discussions. They may be willing to cooperate with exciting results. Giving away $15 T-shirts sends the message that you're so successful you've got money to burn. And, who better to give them to than the retailers?

Credibility and Name Recognition

You should try to promote your entire business as a credible entertainment publishing entity. Whenever possible, push your company name; you want to establish yourself as a reputable comic book publishing outfit. The odds are your company will outlast your titles, so take advantage of any recognition you may receive from all the current titles you publish to establish a professional business identity.

If, out of the blue, one of your titles is singled out for massive publicity, you want to be sure your company name and/or your other titles are mentioned along with it in any articles, advertising, or reviews. The highlighted title might not be everyone's cup of tea, but any other titles you name might generate additional interest and buyers. And, as your company name and comic book titles become more recognizable, your business associates and the public will perceive your image as being one of success and affluence.

Developing Licensing and Merchandising Opportunities

This strategy involves developing your own comic characters and/or other intellectual properties for exploitation in licensing and merchandising to derive revenues. Once you've published a comic book series, your possibilities for introducing new characters is only as limited as your imagination. You may introduce a character in issue #4 who may generate new exciting reactions from your readers, and who now creates an instant readership for immediate sales recognition. You're actually one step further than when you first introduced the title.

Cultivating your characters for licensing opportunities involves using the four key elements of success that I mentioned earlier in the chapter, but you should especially concentrate on *generating maximum exposure and high recognition,* and on creating a product with a *consistent level of quality and talent.* Of course, timely shipping and maintaining a cool, collected attitude are still important, too, but focusing on getting the maximum exposure of your product will lead to more sales and, more importantly, will attract the attention of people who are interested in purchasing "secondary rights" for the development of, for example, toys, television shows, cartoons, or major motion pictures. If your title sells hundreds of thousands of copies per month (due to good exposure), selling your concept as a successful entertainment phenomenon will be much easier.

High recognition is also important and can be accomplished simply by having a highly acclaimed talent work on your project. If you hire a respected talent, you'll attract the right people immediately. Well-known, well-respected creative talents have fans in high places. Even with minimal sales, the quality of the work can make it a shoo-in for larger success in another entertainment medium, such as a movie. Another example of high recognition is the credibility of your company image. If you have a reputation for producing high-quality, popular licensed titles, the introduction of your own intellectual property will be immediately noticed (and possibly more readily accepted) by those licensors who respect the product you are producing for them or others.

As far as consistency of quality and talent is concerned, I'd like to be able to say that it will guarantee you a movie deal, but quality isn't always what makes concepts successful. Sometimes, it's the name, the concept itself, or the current tastes or fads of the moment that influence which titles become marketing miracles. Still, a high-quality product does have a better chance of being an infinitely successful comic book at various levels. And, keeping your character concepts in the public eye on a consistent basis will also make it consistently available for any future licensing possibilities.

As I said, timely (and reliable) shipping is still important to any licensing or merchandising deal. A potential movie production can take three to five years; keeping the comic book available maintains public interest, which contributes to the future success of any movie release. And you should also keep your cool (never, ever, let 'em see you sweat) when it comes to negotiating any licensing rights. Hire a reputable entertainment attorney to handle the deal. Potential licensees will have one fighting for their side, so you'll need one, too. (See chapter 11 for more information on secondary rights.)

Establishing Foreign Publishing Relationships

Working toward a future goal of unlimited foreign sales, you should try to establish as many relationships with foreign publishers as you can. Your goal is to expand your product line in order to increase your sales, profitability, and credibility. Consider purchasing worldwide rights to "hot" licenses and hiring an international agent.

As far as good sales tactics are concerned, I'd recommend annually presenting your products at both the Children's Book Fair in Bologna, Italy, and the Frankfurt Book Fair in Germany. This will help you establish a presence on the foreign market. Using a foreign sales representative, set up scheduled meetings with various foreign publishers to show them your projects and to examine theirs. Purchase foreign material at low reprint rates for translation and publication in the United States and Canada. Experienced foreign sales reps can be a big help here; they set up and attend meetings with foreign publishers and regularly go to all the international shows for many clients. They really know the business.

Another way of opening up the foreign market for your material is to show that you have interest in globalization and international trade. If you purchase foreign material to publish in the United States, you'll attract the attention of other foreign publishers. Once you have their attention, you can introduce your titles to them. You should also add all foreign publishers and trade publications to a regular promotional materials and PR list. Everyone likes to ride on a successful person's coattails. Keeping the international market aware of your company's growth is keeping them aware of your existence, and eventually, they may see a popular and profitable product of yours that they like, and you'll have opened your business up to a whole new market.

Acquiring Intellectual Properties

Selectively purchasing intellectual properties, produced by other creators, that you can develop and capitalize on is another way to increase your revenue. (This is becoming a licensee.) When you purchase a concept from another company or person, offer them a percentage of future profits. A 10 to 50 percent royalty on revenue (depending on the property's current success) derived from "secondary rights" not only offers an incentive for people to produce great work, but also helps you avoid any potential future legal battles that the original creators might otherwise think about waging if their concept does become a huge international hit (and they want to see some of those profits). And, this obvious logic works both ways—a percentage of something big is, after all, much more financially beneficial than owning 100 percent of something small.

When considering which properties to acquire, seek out the lost rights of highly recognized characters, concepts, and trademarks. Frequent estate and bankruptcy sales, which you can learn about by word of mouth or in the legal section of newspaper classifieds. Keep your eye on poorly managed properties, and examine foreign publications; look for stories that may work well in the American market.

Using National Publicity to Increase Sales

You can generate a frenzy of sales by riding the tidal wave of national publicity that comics often receive. What do the comics *Teenage Mutant Ninja Turtles, Image Comics, Batman: The Dark Knight,* and *The Death of Superman* all have in common? They received maximum exposure through highly successful public relations campaigns. If you can get news stories about your product on every television station and in almost every magazine and newspaper, you're going to sell a lot of copies because the more people who know, the more people who buy.

With a "hook" (a creative marketing angle) and a list of the news syndicates to send the perfect press release to, you can generate enormous publicity, as with the products listed above. (See chapter 8 for more detailed public relations information.)

Surviving the Glut

In 1993, the direct market included some 700 titles from nearly 100 publishers, all competing for the attention of the distributors, retailers, and buyers. This overflow of product into the market is commonly referred to as a "glut." This type of situation has occurred a few times in the past, although not as severely as it did in 1993.

In 1986, there was the Black-and-White Glut, when everyone thought they could publish the next *Teenage Mutant Ninja Turtles* comic book. This was a successful black-and-white comic, and when it came out, everyone then rushed to publish their own black-and-white comics. In 1989–90, there was the *Batman* movie glut, when the direct market distributor warehouses and their retail stores were full of *Batman* movie merchandise. During these historic occasions enormous amounts of products were introduced onto the market, and the results were usually disastrous, because there was just too much stuff out there that was junk.

For example, after the Black-and-White Glut of 1986, Glenwood Distributors filed for bankruptcy. Up until then, Glenwood had been one of the largest, if not *the* largest, direct market distributors. Two other distributors soon followed suit. All the other distributors asked for over 30-day credit terms because there weren't enough buyers for all the products that were out there. A large number of products were delivered in questionable quality and were rejected by the public.

Basically, what happens during a glut is that all retailers now have to order, let's say, double the amount of product within their same budgeted resources. They also have to find the display space in their stores. This results in a reduction of orders across the whole industry (because everyone is ordering more, so they're trying to sell what they've already ordered), which in turn affects everyone's bottom line—especially if the ordered products ship late.

Not shipping your products (or shipping them late) during a glut is suicide. Remember, this is a glut—an enormous amount of products are being made available to the retailers and customers at one time. If they can't find your product, direct market retailers will buy something else. They *need* products. Without products on their shelves, they have fewer opportunities to sell, make a profit, and pay their overhead. In any highly competitive market, retailers will find other products; its their scheduled source of revenue.

Be aware that retailers also have the almost impossible task of ordering hundreds of titles on a nonreturnable basis, so they have to estimate how many copies of each book will sell. If they order five copies of a title and only two sell, they have three copies in inventory. Multiply that by 500 other miscalculations and it'll eat up all your profit very quickly.

As a small comic book publisher, the only way to survive a glut is to bite the bullet and cut your expenses in order to maximize your profits as your sales drop. If you're producing an entire line of products, introduce a hot title with an expectation of half the initial estimated orders. You'll have built credibility as well as attracted attention by introducing another popular title but not getting lost within the mass of new product. Without that product to keep your head above water, you may be one of the many publishers that retailers delete from their outlets to make room for the latest hot item. In the past, fighting fire with fire has always worked effectively.

The same key elements of success hold true, especially during a glut and its aftermath. You'll have a better chance of surviving the next glut if you have an exceptional shipping record—if you've shipped promptly for three years, retailers will remember and support you. But, if your latest issues have been late, for whatever reason, that will be the last impression retailers will have of you. Your lateness will be noticed and remembered. In "Little Hollywood" (the nickname for the comic industry inspired by the long lines of autograph-seeking fans) you're only as good as your last issue. Retailers want to be able to rely on you, the sure thing, in a time of chaos.

Also helpful during a glut is having high recognition. A hot licensed property or creative team can literally keep your head above water during the flood of products. If I had to give you one reason why my company (in it's first year of business) survived the 1986–87 Black-and-White Glut while a few other hundred other organizations disappeared, I would have to give the credit to my

1987 introduction of the *Speed Racer* comic book. It was a highly recognizable example of Japanese animation (which was also a big fad at the time) with all new stories, good creative talent, and timely shipping.

NEWSSTANDS AND BOOKSTORES: THE MASS MARKET

All the sales strategies outlined for the direct market are applicable when selling to newsstands and bookstores, as well—with a few exceptions. The mass market is generally unaware of any talent name recognition. Buyers in this market are driven by title, quality of art, and/or incentives (see Increasing Newsstand Sales through Innovative Techniques below), and they are, traditionally, impulsive buyers. So, what you need is a product that stands out from the rack, whether it's a nostalgic or contemporary licensed property, a special premium or cover enhancement, or an interesting and completely unique style or concept.

For example, the *Ralph Snart Adventures* comic books by Marc Hansen are a very good example of a successful newsstand title. The initial series was a constant best-seller; the title was unique, with humor and stylized artwork. And, it was known for consistent quality and prompt shipping. Marc Hansen drew all 26 issues and shipped them on time to the day for two years. Issue #24 (shipped May 1990) was a three-dimensional version, polybagged with 3-D glasses for a enormous newsstand price of $2.95 (US dollars). This unique incentive (3-D!) made it stand out from the other titles on the rack. The sales for that issue were almost double his regular sales figures (even with the huge cover price), with a permanent increase of about 5 percent on sales of subsequent regular *Ralph Snart* titles.

The newsstand market is a very expensive but very powerful marketing tool in and of itself. Direct market comic shops, because of their nonreturnable terms, have to be more conservative in the sizes of their orders. Therefore, if they only order five copies of your title and sell all of them in one weekend, for the rest of the month your title doesn't exist for most of their customers. At newsstands or bookstores, however, you'll usually ship out an allotment of about 10 copies to each store. So, if you sell three or five and you have a hit, the remaining copies are still visible on the shelves for the rest of the month, every month, promoting your title and company as an existing comic book publishing entity.

As a result, the newsstand and bookstore market is where you can recruit new readers and build your fan base. It's more amenable to new products, companies, and ideas than the direct market. You should note, however, that newsstand wholesalers and distributors do have more regimented rules on format than direct market distributors; their preferred comic book format is full color and at least 32 pages, and they will usually reject other formats, although there are a few exceptions, such as the 3-D format, which is only two-color. Below are some strategies that you can try using to generate sales in the mass market.

Increasing Newsstand Sales through Innovative Techniques

Your goal here is to increase sell-through and wholesaler support using innovative sales techniques. Historically, any premium item polybagged or inserted within the comic book has worked phenomenally to increase sales. Called a "cracker jack" prize after the surprise in Cracker Jack candy, it's an added incentive to consumers to purchase the product. Even with a higher cover price, if you offer something more that gives your product a higher perceived value, it will attract the buyer's attention. Remember, you're not the only comic book on the rack.

Another technique is to create instant recognition and sales through the use of your licensed properties. These properties have the most success in the mass market. The instant recognition and admiration of an already established character offers immediate sales potential, and the exclusivity of a license agreement makes for a powerful magnet for new readers.

THINGS TO AVOID

Entering any unique market, such as the comic book industry, there are certain tactics that almost every new publisher attempts with unsatisfactory results. As in most entertainment markets, you base your success on public acceptance. In this case, you should think of your distributor as the public, because you have to convince the distributor (and then the retailer) to carry and support your product before the consumer even sees it.

Learning about (and, ideally, avoiding) the costly mistakes and miscalculations that have been made by countless others before you usually takes years of experience. Hopefully, though, you can save yourself some money and avoid unnecessary stress by using the information provided here.

Over-Printing

Printing a huge quantity (over-printing) on the second issue of a comic book series just because the first issue sold out in two weeks is a financially dangerous risk. Often, a first issue sells out for a number of reasons, which are usually only unique to first issues. The most likely is the simple fact that it's a first issue, not that you have a hot title. If you print 30,000 copies of issue #2 expecting to sell out, you may find yourself with an unnecessary $7,000 added to your printing bill, whether or not you sell the books.

If the title's first issue is hot, plan and solicit a second printing—an inventory of 10 to 15 percent of the first issue is adequate. You'll eventually sell your entire inventory of issue #1 but not of consecutive issues, unless that issue also becomes hot. Unsold inventory is a profit-eating risk that you should avoid at all costs.

Dog Is a Dog Is a Dog

Let's say you're publishing another title in a series in which the first issue sold 30,000 copies, but by issue #5, the sales have dropped to 5,000 copies. This may not be a successful, profitable comic book series anymore, and if it's not profitable, it's a dog. The chances that you'll be able to turn the title around with, say, different editorial direction, creative teams, or logos is remote. Smaller publishers usually can't afford to invest additional resources into a title, for any length of time, hoping it will turn around. Cancel it immediately. You can more wisely spend your capital elsewhere, and you can always reintroduce the concept again in a new series.

Using Unlimited Story Lines

When writing a new series, limit the development of initial story line to the first through the third issues. Dragging anything out for more than three issues stretches the reader's interest too far, and your audience will get bored. Concentrate on creating a strong story line in the early issues to hook readers into the series; extending the story line on through eight issues will certainly bore them.

Replacing a Vanishing Creative Team

When hiring a creative team to produce a series, sign them up for at least one year's worth of product. As I mentioned earlier in this chapter, consistency in quality and talent is important for success. What will happen if your creative team suddenly disappears off the face of the Earth after the first or second issue?

If the title is successful, and you can't find an *exact match* in talent, cancel the title. You're probably thinking, "Hey, wait a minute! You also said to always ship on time. What gives?" To try to save a successful series by creating consecutive issues that have a different look or style will instantly kill the series' popularity. It's better to cancel the title while it's on top, find another talented (and committed) creative team, and start over. The popularity of the initial, unfinished series will generate more interest in the new subsequent series.

Bankruptcy

In the entertainment industry, image is everything. Any strategy that an investor may recommend to you that involves shipping delays and/or bankruptcy will have a dramatically negative effect on the credibility you've struggled to achieve. The word "bankruptcy" is a powerfully derogatory term that sends the wrong signals to any future business associates. Even though it's a common occurrence in big business—as with Marvel Comics or the candy company that filed bankruptcy eight times before becoming the chocolate king (Hershey's)—you should steer clear of any tactics that involve declaring bankruptcy.

For example, an investor may recommend a Chapter 11 reorganization or a Chapter 7 liquidation to avoid investing in the company's existing debits. Don't fool yourself into thinking that most companies are never in debt and that you shouldn't be either; if you borrowed $10,000 from Aunt Gertrude to start your publishing venture, you're in debt. If Aunt Gertrude decides to retire to Florida and wants her money back, you'll most likely need to find another investor to replace that capital investment. This is normal. That $10,000 has turned into "working capital," which is the funds necessary to keep your business in business. (See chapter 10 for more information on capital, investors, and lawyers.)

Inexperienced Business Partners

Any individual or organization that you introduce as a partner, or with whom you develop an investment interest, needs to understand the entertainment industry. The entertainment industry involves eccentricities that many normal (or conservative) businesspeople don't understand or fail to accept. When dealing with the colorful personalities of some artistic talents and the "slick" attitude of most entertainment professionals, ordinary businesspeople may find them illogical, greedy, or flaky. So, you should try to look for business partners who have a respect for creative people and their environment, because this will enable them to understand the blood of any entertainment field.

For inexperienced businesspeople, the fact that most of the production process is out of their control and in the hands of individuals who may be a bit eccentric can inspire feelings of chaos and panic. You want to work with people who will analyze any potential problems and research possible solutions. No one businessperson has the power to come into an entertainment industry and, even with extensive professional experience and accomplishments, change the world or control everything. So, ideally, you want to hire flexible people who can adapt to and manage stressful situations. After all, things can't always be done by the book (unless, of course, you're talking about this book).

The Dead Months

Traditionally, January, February, and sometimes even March are the weakest months for most businesses. This also holds true for the comic book industry. Introducing new products during these months will generate weak orders. Unless you have a continuing hit, and introduce a companion series or receive a massive amount of exposure through public relations, your sales may be weaker than you anticipated. Still, although your sales may falter during these months, with the right marketing plan you can bring them back up in April. Plan any special issues (special editions with hot guest artists, double issues, etc.) during these months. Be very careful that you've thought these added attractions through financially. If they cost more that the sales figures can accommodate, you'll be losing money and may find yourself in worse shape than originally planned. Expect the worst, then if it's still financially feasible, move forward.

8 PROMOTIONS, ADVERTISING, AND PUBLIC RELATIONS

Successful self-promotion in the entertainment industry involves a great deal of image finessing, skill, creativity, and money. Your goal is to spark the interest of your target audience. If you're generating potential buyers through public relations campaigns or advertising, you need to grab their attention. The general public must be aware of your product's availability in order for you to achieve good sales revenue. If no one knows, no one buys.

Your promotion begins with the various distribution channels. They are the public's link to your most important form of promotion—your actual product. Nothing will spark an instant sale of your comic book faster than its immediate availability. This holds for the wholesalers and retail outlets, too. In this chapter, I'll cover all the basic promotional items, but for starters, you could begin by offering an introductory packet to be sent to all distributors and select prominent retail outlets. This would include a preview of your company, its products, talents, and corporate information, all on your new, suave business stationery; you should also include a news release detailing your initial goals. This is your one chance to make a good first impression, so make it count. You're only as successful as you look. If it's within your projected budget, use a custom presentation folder as an outstanding example of your company's high production values. If you spark interest with this introductory packet, clients will examine all your other materials. Your goal is to convince them that your products will sell many copies and make them enormous amounts of money.

NEWS RELEASES

Your primary objective in using a news release is to persuade your readers (in this case, news media editors) to publish it in their newspapers and magazines or air it on their radio and television shows. The release should also encourage their readers (the public) to choose your product. The news release included in the introductory packet that I mentioned above will be your first news release and should include pertinent information targeting the distributors, retailers, and consumer. At no time should you ever include any confidential information within a news release, since this is a document you'll be offering for publication in various distributor periodicals and catalogues.

Below are all the elements of a good news release, listed in the order that they should appear in the release. I suggest that you really make an extra effort to produce the perfect news release about your company and product. It can be worth thousands of dollars in free advertising.

RELEASE TITLE *Always write your title in the present tense, and include the major benefits of your product. For example, you might lead with a heading that reads, "The most fantastic comic book ever ships May 30th!" If your news release is targeted to the distribution channels, try to express in your title how your product can make money for the distributors. For example, potentially beneficial and profitable aspects of your comic could include its title or talent recognition, or your guarantee of timely shipping. Assistance (from fellow comic enthusiasts, co-creators, friends, etc.) in analyzing your product for a news release can help you open your eyes to what consumers might find attractive.*

LEAD PARAGRAPH *This first paragraph needs to grab your readers' attention in a matter of seconds. So, after using the release title head to do this first, draw them in here with any factual or intriguing information. Keep in mind that you want them to read on.*

SECOND PARAGRAPH *This paragraph should include your solutions for producing better comic books and/or some product descriptions.*

QUOTES *Comments from experts in the field should be intelligent and used in moderation. When using quotes from other people, always include their title of affiliation within the industry to add credibility. Also, intersperse the quotes throughout the release, rather than clump them all together.*

TRANSITIONAL SENTENCES *Since each new paragraph begins a new thought, you should immediately inform your readers where they're headed with the first sentence of each paragraph. This will provide a smooth transition from one point or idea to the next.*

HYPE PARAGRAPH *The hype paragraph should be the last paragraph in your news release. In it you should include a sales pitch for your company and/or products.*

SPECIFICATIONS *These are all the descriptive details about your comic book, such as page count, price, shipping date, and whether or not it's a full-color title.*

It's standard news release format to use three number signs to indicate the end of the body of release information.

CALL TO ACTION *The end of the news release should include a complete "call to action," which is a listing of your name, company name, address, and phone number.*

Statistics indicate that only 24 percent of all generated news releases are ever published. To make yours part of this select group, you must write concise and exciting text. And, always use double line spacing in your releases to allow for easier editing by your readers; in this way, they'll have the option of reducing copy to create a small plug within their news features.

If your first attempt at a news release goes unnoticed, try another angle. Don't stop writing about any intriguing details of your business or product. To reach the general public you may need to write another news release—one with a new hook or angle. Examine your news release from the general public's point of view, and ask yourself the following: Would the public find my release interesting? Is it targeted for a select niche market? You might want to create different news releases geared to different audiences. Keep at it, and remember, as I said before, each news release can generate thousands of dollars worth of free advertising.

THE NEWS MEDIA

The vast majority of Americans don't buy comic books. Many have forgotten they even exist. Your product will need a hook to reel them into buying a comic book—maybe for the first time in their lives. The catch could be as simple as a story line paralleling today's headlines or maybe a catchy title. If your product includes the resurrection of a dormant intellectual property, such as *Speed Racer* or *The Green Hornet,* for example, you'll have an instant hook for massive publicity.

No matter what your angle, to reach the general public, you need to meet the press. However you plan your public relations strategy, always concentrate regularly on your local press. Hometown papers are always interested in what locals are doing. Your community library should have a collection of directories listing media contacts to which you can send news releases. The *Bacon Books* directories (published by Bacon Books) are the most widely used and useful for obtaining contact names, addresses, and phone and fax numbers of all newspapers, magazines, and television and radio stations throughout North America. These books also include a list of news syndicates, which can also serve as a source that distributes news releases to many media outlets.

You can also inquire about a mailing list of these news syndicates through a local direct mailing service. You can purchase a list of approximately 150 news syndicates for about $100, and this price includes pressure-adhesive labels. Check your local yellow pages under "Mailing Lists" or "Direct Mail."

PUBLIC RELATIONS FIRMS

An experienced public relations (or PR) firm can handle all your news releases and media contacts for you for either a monthly retainer or on an hourly basis. Stay away from any PR firm that says it can handle your business *and* guarantee having hundreds of articles published about you and your company *and* get you a spot on Late Show with David Letterman if you pay for an eight-city media tour. You don't need this stuff. You won't get it. And you'll still have to pay for it.

As I've mentioned throughout this book, comic books have a limited, unique audience. The majority of the public still thinks children are the primary readers, yet a recent survey determined the average age of the American comic

News from MARS™ . . .

For Immediate Release!

TONY CAPUTO'S FIRST SELF-PUBLISHED EFFORT—*VESPERS*

The comic book industry has grown from a $160 million business in 1986 to one of almost $1.5 billion in just seven years. This enormous growth was partially sparked by such self-published mega-blockbusters as *The Crow, The Mask, Tick, Spawn, Speed Racer, Teenage Mutant Ninja Turtles, Bone,* and *Youngblood.* All these concepts began as small independently produced comic book titles, then exploded into international entertainment phenomenons. It's apparent that as the larger comic book companies continue to expand the market through change and consolidation, success becomes more attainable for the self-publisher. This is the industry's best-kept secret.

Tony Caputo is a 10-year comic book publishing veteran. He has published such hits as *The Green Hornet, The Twilight Zone, Speed Racer, Supercops, Married . . . with Children,* and *Mr. T & the T-Force.* He also created the comic book *Alias,* which was purchased by Universal Pictures for $100,000. Beginning in 1986, he initiated and managed his own comic book company's explosive growth, which developed from $110,000 to $3.5 million annually in just four years. He has been interviewed regularly by the media, including for over 40 television and radio shows, and articles detailing his accomplishments have appeared in such publications as *Entrepreneur, Advertising Age, Crain's Chicago Business, The Los Angeles Times,* and *The Chicago Tribune.* His knowledge is an accumulation of experience from a decade of producing almost **1,000** international comic publications and home video releases. He has written comic book stories for *The Terminator, Fright Night, Speed Racer,* and the award-winning *Rust,* and his artistic endeavors include coloring and cover painting for *The Terminator, Fright Night, Syphons, Speed Racer, and Vector* comic books. He now focuses his talents on the creation and self-publishing of *Vespers,* a full-color comic book.

"My new comic book is the very first one that I've created, written, and illustrated completely on my own," explains Caputo. "I think many people will be surprised." And on seeing Caputo's first self-published creation, John Stangeland, owner of Atlas Comic Shop in Norridge, Illinois, said, "Wow! What have you been doing all these years!?"

Vespers is the story of several superheroes who live in the real world—a world of religion, decay, starvation, greed, hatred, and prejudice. It is a comprehensive tale about characters with extraordinary powers and deformities who band together to give each other support, friendship, and love—the three humanistic needs that the rest of mankind has refused, out of fear, to offer them, leaving them alone and angry; sometimes, dangerously angry.

"My goal is to produce a comic book with real-life characters," states Caputo. "Let's face up to the truth; if a deformed monstrosity walks down the street toward you, you won't care if he can fly or that he just saved the world—you'll run away to hide."

Vespers, a 32-page full-color comic book, is available at the finest comic shops or directly from Mars Media Group for $2.50.

# # #

For more information, contact Tony Caputo at Mars Media Group, ph: (708) 802-1242 or e-mail: MarsMedia@aol.com

Sample news release

book buyer to be 21.5 years—definitely *not* children. If you hire a splashy PR and marketing firm that decides to promote products to children, or to people who think they're for children, you'll generate some publicity but not nearly enough to make it worth the expense.

The most attractive feature about public relations is the magnitude of articles, interviews, plugs, and publicity that you can receive for your dollar; you'll spend a mere fraction of the advertising equivalent for comparable ad space in magazines, TV shows, or newspapers. For example, let's say you'd like to reach 1.2 million music lovers because of your new music-related comic book, so you decide to buy advertising space in *Rolling Stone* magazine. That'll cost you about $30,000 for one full-page advertisement. But you could instead hire a small but experienced public relations and marketing firm for three months, on a monthly retainer of $1,000, and you could invest maybe another $1,000 for a professional press/presentation kit for them to use with their news release. They'll be able to reach music lovers by sending press kits to hundreds of music magazines—not just *Rolling Stone*. Out of these hundreds, 30 smaller music magazines might decide to run an article about your music-related comic book and, with an average paid circulation of 100,000 copies each, that would be a total reach of 3 million music readers. I've found that Top Dog Marketing is really the only effective PR firm out there that specializes in promoting comic books; contact them at 400 Silver Cedar Court, Suite 220, Chapel Hill, NC, 27514/ph: (919) 933-4700; fax: (919) 933-3555; e-mail: topdogm@aol.com; attn: George White III. Also, see Appendix, page 181 for a list of potential media contacts, and page 170 for a list of contacts at industry distributor and trade publications.

TRADE SHOW AND CONVENTION PROMOTIONS

Throughout this book I've included many suggestions for comic book promotions, and the success of your promotions is limited only by your financial resources and creativity. Distributor and industry trade shows and consumer conventions offer the most potential for any promotional concepts. These shows attract the media, and media coverage will always add more value to your promotions. Many trade show and convention coordinators look for sponsors for breakfasts, luncheons, dinners, breaks, and cocktail parties. Show sponsorships offer an opportunity for you (as the sponsor) to provide a meal for your potential retailers at which time you can discuss your company and products with them; the advantage to this situation is that you'll have your audience's undivided attention. The cost for sponsorships vary with every organization and can become very expensive. Smaller sponsorships, such as those for a break or a cocktail party, can be a group effort with other companies that may want to participate but have a limited budget.

Having your creative talent give autographs is also a very common but very effective show promotion. Since the majority of all businesspeople in the industry are either past or present comic book fans, there's always interest in autographs and conversation with a creator. There is also the possibility that autographs on trading cards, posters, comic books, or even convention program books will increase the value of those items. A free promotional *Green Hornet*

**Highly acclaimed author and screenwriter
Harlan Ellison**

*This was at San Diego's Comic Book Trade Show, where Ellison (center)
was signing autographs and promoting the release of* The Twilight Zone,
*a comic book that he wrote for my company. That's me on the left and
Ellison's wife, Susan, on the right.*

**Legendary comic book artist
Neal Adams**

*Adams signing autographs and giving up-and-
coming artists some solid advice at the San Diego
Comic Convention, where he was promoting the
premier issue of* The Twilight Zone, *which he
produced for me with Harlan Ellison. A master
penciler, inker, and colorist, Adams is best known for
his award-winning work on* Batman, Green Arrow-
Green Lantern, *and* Ms. Mystic *titles. In the late
1960s, he was instrumental in effecting the change
in production policy that enabled artists to have
their artwork returned to them after a comic book
was printed. Standing behind him is comic book
artist Dell Barras*

Terry Gilliam and myself

*Monty Python writer and animator Terry Gilliam (*Time Bandits,
Jabberwocky, *and* Brazil *are some of his movie credits) and myself
discussing the comic book adaptation of the movie* The Adventures of
Baron Munchausen, *which he directed and co-produced.*

poster, signed by artist Jeff Butler, was reportedly selling for $40 at various retail outlets. It's this kind of reaction to creative promotions that can add value to your company and its products. How many others will now seek out your trade show booth to grab your next promotional piece? Any way that you can bring those retailers or consumers to your booth gives you an opportunity to make a positive impression for long-lasting sales. (For a list of trade shows and conventions, see Appendix, page 169.)

Working with highly recognized creators creates instant credibility, attracts customers, and increases sales. Just as the highly recognized licensed properties that you purchase have an established following, great creative talents also have an instant audience that they may bring to your product. Although a popular licensed property is more recognizable than the name and work of a highly successful comic book creator, you're still hitting a bull's-eye straight into the comic book market by using known talents. After all, just because a licensed property generates a famous television show, video game, and toy line doesn't guarantee comic book success.

The mobs these talents have generated at trade show and convention booths present to all in attendance an image of success. Curiosity will then bring them to your booth. Take advantage of this by offering information about them, or at least a button (or even a promotional T-shirt) that they can wear at your booth.

Your talent doesn't have to have superstar status to attract a crowd. Having most or all of the creative team that worked on a series present gives a booth the prospect of accomplishing a promotional effort that few self-publishers ever achieve—generating copies of your product autographed by all the talents involved in the creation process. Because creators don't all live in the same area of the country, the chances of your fans meeting everyone—with a copy of your product on hand—is very slim. Here you've given them the opportunity to receive a true collector's item, whether it be free to a retailer at a trade show or sold to a fan at a convention. The complete creative team could also make

Holly Sansfilippo, well-known comic book colorist extraordinaire
While signing autographs at the Chicago ComicCon convention, Sansfilippo serves as a walking billboard for my Speed Racer *comic book.*

Ron Fortier and David Mowry
Green Hornet *comic book writer Ron Fortier and inker David Mowry at a Green Hornet Convention in Baltimore in 1989. Note the promotional T-shirts.*

a scheduled appearance at a panel discussion at the show. Panel discussions are formal talks organized by show coordinators; they take place during the shows and focus on a variety of issues related to the comic book industry.

Having live, costumed characters at your booth is a very popular and effective promotional strategy. You can have costumes created by a reliable costume manufacturer for about $200, depending on their complexity. Check your yellow pages under "Costumes." With the right contacts or friends, you can put together a model with costume and generate an enormous amount of free publicity.

The creative team for the *Married . . . with Children 2099* comic book
Left to right that's penciler Tom Richmond, inker Barb Kaalsberg, and writer Jim Caputo (What? You thought I was the only writer in the family?) all signing autographs and helping to promote the comic book series at a distributor trade show

Comic book creators Barry Petersen and Patrick Williams
Petersen and Williams were at a Chicago comic convention where they were promoting Petersen's comic book Mirrorwalker. Their presence at the show made a significant difference in the promotion and success of the title.

Peter Mosen in costume as a "Real Ghostbuster"
Mosen works as a part-time actor and part-time Ghostbuster (for special appearances). This photo was taken at the San Diego Comic Convention.

The "Real Ghostbuster" gang at a show
Peter Mosen and his group of two other people were available to make public or private appearances as The Real Ghostbusters, one of my big titles. Their promotional package included a giant "Slimer" balloon (left) and a replica of the "Ecto-1" automobile (in the background). Promotions like this can really boost interest in your comics.

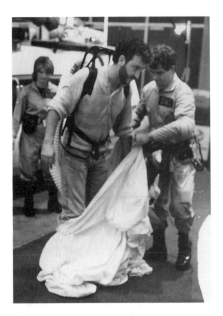

Me getting into the Staypuf Man costume

This is the amazing blow-up Staypuf Man costume, which I tried on at the San Diego Comic Convention. (It's one of The Real Ghostbusters promotional characters.) The things you've gotta do to make a buck!

Comic book writer Jim Bradshaw and myself with more characters at a show

From left to right, Susie Owens, as superheroine Flaxen (of Flaxen, a title from Golden Apple Comics), Jim Bradshaw (a co-creator of The Twilight Zone), Vampirella (the costumed vampire from Harris Comics), me, and "scream queen" actress Jewel Shepard (a scream queen is, typically, a pretty girl who screams a lot in B-movies). Having people portray characters from your titles is a sure way to increase traffic at your booth.

Gary Colabuono with Mr. T

Gary Colabuono, president of Classics International publishers, and the very recognizable Mr. T promoting Now Comics' best-selling title, Mr. T & the T-Force.

Me with Van Williams

Van Williams, star of The Green Hornet television show, with me at the giant Chicago Comic Show in 1989. He signed autographs and told the crowd stories about filming The Green Hornet for 1960s television with his sidekick character Kato, played by the one and only Bruce Lee. Note that I had the giant photographs in the background produced at Quantity Photo Chicago (ph: 312-644-8288) for only $65 each, and they made a fantastic impression!

Celebrities are an obvious people magnet. You want hundreds of potential buyers to come to your booth, and these kind of talents can bring them in—by the busload. They are, however, an expensive marketing tactic. Even if they waive their appearance fee (which, depending on the talent, can range anywhere from $1,500 to $25,000 for a three-hour appearance), you still have to furnish all transportation, lodging, and meals. Remember, whatever promotional tactics you create, always alert the media with a news release.

Speed Racer cartoon voices
Jim Rocknowski of Speed Racer Enterprises (center) with JoAnne Orr and Peter Fernandez, the voices of Trixie and Speed Racer, two of the Speed Racer cartoon characters.

Katie Segal holding a *Married . . . with Children* comic book
Married . . . with Children television-show star Katie Segal holding the comic book. What a fantastic PR photo! If you manage to have celebrities making promotional appearances for you, always try to get a picture of them either with you or holding your product. It can be an invaluable selling tool. (Photo courtesy Sony Pictures Merchandising.)

Chuck Dixon
Comic book writer Chuck Dixon gets a bang out of The Green Hornet at the Diamond Comic Distributor seminar in Atlanta.

Me with the Alien

The competition—eating everyone alive! This large alien worked well as a trade show attraction for Dark Horse Comics publishers.

An early trade show exhibit

For this trade show exhibit (in 1986), I made the backdrop myself from a heavy, black tarp material with painted letters. I rented the television for the entire week of the show from a local rent-to-own store for a fraction of the daily rate that the exhibit hall was charging. Another plus—the rental store delivered it and picked it up after the show.

Another trade show booth

The designers of this booth took advantage of the many recognizable licensed characters to attract the attention of retailers, dealers, and regular consumers. Seated in the booth ready for autographing are comic book artists and creators Brian Thomas (who has worked on such titles as Speed Racer, Astro Boy, *and* Fright Night*) and Marc Hansen (who currently self-publishes* Weird Melvin*).*

Point-of-purchase display

Like large, exciting backdrops and free autographs, point-of-purchase displays (or POPs) can also generate strong sales at the retail level and product interest within your booth space. I had the three-tier POP shown here made by a local corrugated cardboard box manufacturer for about $1.50 per unit (flattened—you have to assemble them), with a minimum order of 1,500. To find a box manufacturer, look in your yellow pages under "Boxes."

Stand-alone pylon display

As with a POP, a stand-alone pylon display like the one above will grab and hold the viewer's interest for an extended period of time, and the longer you keep someone in your exhibit booth, the more opportunities you'll have to make a sale.

Stand-alone display

Here you can see the stand-alone display from another angle inside the booth. Next to it is comic book writer and computer graphics master Jim Bradshaw, of The Green Hornet, Mr. T & the T-Force, The Twilight Zone, and The Adventures of Dirty Lyle & Squinty Daryl notoriety.

Promotional T-shirts in use

Here, comic book artists and creators Chris Ecker (EB'NN) and Marc Hansen (Ralph Snart, Weird Melvin) are dressed as walking billboards at a trade show. As I mentioned earlier, if you can afford them, T-shirts make a great promotional tool.

"The Green Hornet" at the 1992 San Diego Comic Convention

Sometimes, a T-shirt just isn't enough! Here, a comic book fan dressed up as the Green Hornet. It's not uncommon to see fans, as well as promoters, dressed in costume at trade shows and conventions; they often participate in promotional contests to see who can make the best costume.

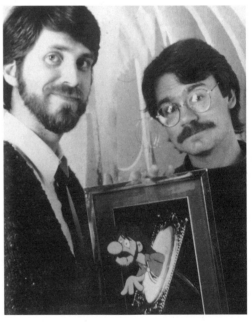

Promotional photograph

A high-quality promotional photo makes a serious statement about you, your company, and your products. Here, Barry Petersen and Erich Schrempp show their title Mirrorwalker.

PRINT ADVERTISING

Advertising savvy comes naturally to any true entrepreneur. Your primary goal with any advertisement is to convince the target audience to choose your company's product. You can spark curiosity with a printed teaser ad, creating a word-of-mouth campaign involving curious questions aimed at your target market. Also, an ad with a dynamic illustration, made by the same creative team that worked on your comic book, goes far in informing the reader of your product.

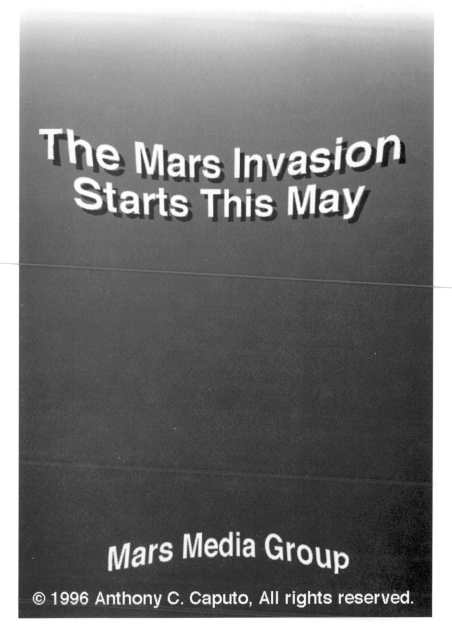

Sample teaser ad
Promoting the introduction of Mars Media Group as the "Mars Invasion" creates excitement and curiosity. A teaser ad can turn the introduction of a new company into a dramatic event.

In general, there are a few key factors that make up successful advertising: accuracy, quality, consistency, and hype. When the reader can believe that everything you say in your ads is true and *accurate,* your company, its advertisements, and its credibility will all thrive. If you print the on-sale date of your product in your ad, that's when the consumer will expect it. If it doesn't arrive, for whatever reason, chances are your next ad, and your company's credibility, will be

Print ad for *Vespers*

This advertisement for my Vespers comic book combines various advertising elements, formulas, and marketing tactics. The long illustration on the left immediately gives the reader an idea of content, style, and quality, and the word balloon sparks a bit of curiosity. The quote (or testimonial) at top right adds credibility and excitement. The cover and logo reproductions let the reader know what to look for when searching for the product. And finally, the body copy at bottom right provides more detailed information about what, who, and when. The credit line at the very bottom reads: VESPERS is TM and copyrighted 1984, 1994 Anthony C. Caputo. All Rights Reserved.

questioned. The *quality* or production value of your ads should be even better than that of your publications! This is a representation of your company and its products, so unless you want your ad to get lost among the pages of slick, professionally produced advertisements, you must make sure your ads are just as good. Advertising consistently in a few publications will generate regular interest in your company and products. Moving from one trade publication to anoth-

Mail-order ad

This mail-order advertisement for a video includes a coupon for easy ordering. When selling through mail order, you must include a charge for the appropriate sales tax in your state for its current residents. Out of state orders are tax free. Any periodicals (including comic books) are also tax free.

er will not be as effective as a *consistent* bombardment of the same select audience. Webster's dictionary defines the verb *hype* as "to promote or publicize extravagantly." To hype your company and its products is to take advantage of all avenues of promotion and to turn all your promotions into extravaganzas. Hype is not necessarily an exaggeration of the actual product, but simply a more dramatic representation of it. Remember, you're in the entertainment business—be melodramatic. And keep in mind that every promotion and ad, whenever possible, should describe an event in the making. You want your audience to feel as if they'll be missing something if they don't participate.

Be aware that in any advertisement or promotional piece, you must always indicate the trademark and copyright owners. This is to inform everyone of who possesses the legal rights to the property. (See chapter 2 for more information on trademarks and copyrights.) Also keep in mind that the amount of promotion and advertising you create is simply based on your budget; just plan how much you are able to spend, and choose the tactics that will work best for your company and its products.

THE INTERNET

I would encourage you to think of having a computer as having the world (Wide Web) at your fingertips. The Internet, which you can get on your computer, is a network linking thousands of smaller international networks together. The term "the Net," as the Internet is sometimes called, has become the latest buzzword. Information- and communication-hungry participants with modems stake a claim on the Internet and connect with universities, private companies, government agencies (such as copyright and trademark offices), and anyone else utilizing the Internet. As of January 1997, there were over 40 million Internet users in the United States and over 200 million worldwide with growth calculated at 14 percent per month.

The Internet is the framework that created the World Wide Web, which is simply a collection of commercial and personal pages and sites, each with their own address or URL (Uniform Resource Locator—the web address or location of a specific resource or site). These sites can be accessed by any one of the 200 million people worldwide. The result is instant globalization at a ridiculously low cost. Users gain a sense of power through the online world by gathering information, communicating with others, publishing their own pages, and advertising their own products. The real attraction is the delivery of information; users don't even have to leave their homes—they have instant access to practically whatever they're interested in. By way of improved technology and easy-to-use software, it's getting easier and easier to access both the Internet and the World Wide Web. "But I'm not online," you say? Well, get online! If you're not, you should be. It is, by far, the most important development in communication and entertainment technology since the introduction of the television.

The World Wide Web (WWW or "the web") is a hypertext page system (HTML—HyperText Markup Language) connected across the Internet that allows users to view information from thousands of sources primarily through text and pictures. Companies and individuals can advertise their services or products, or publish their works on the World Wide Web. There are close to one million commercial web sites. If you're not familiar with all the web lingo, don't worry about it—that will come in time. Many people, unfortunately, steer away from the Internet because they feel bombarded by strange phrases (such as URL, HTML, FTP, BPS, download, upload, etc.), but if you give yourself a little time, you'll get the hang of it.

All you need to go online is your computer, a modem, an Internet Service Provider (ISP), and a browser. The ISP gives you the access to the web, and the browser is the software that enables you to visit and browse the web. They're like your antenna and channel changer, respectively. When I first used a computer, back in the mid-80s, modem speeds were about 2400 bits per second, or bps. (Don't worry about what a "bit" is; just think of it like miles per hour.) This was considered fast, but today you can purchase a modem with 28,800bps (or 28.8bps) for about $200. That's well worth the cost when you're going online, because the more bits per second you have the faster your access to the web will be, including your downloading or uploading, which is any copying (downloading) graphics or software from a site or delivering (uploading) a copy to a site. When you're the master of your own web site, you'll thank me for the 28.8bps.

I've listed the addresses of a few of the more popular Internet Service Providers and browsers on page 182, and I'll also run through them here, as well. Due to an aggressive marketing campaign, American Online (AOL) is a widely recognized and used ISP. The company charges a monthly flat fee for unlimited use; it also offers you your own free web page with your own address and directory (in which to store your files). Earthlink Network is an excellent choice of an Internet access service for three reasons: 1) they offer a free copy of Netscape Navigator, currently the best and most popular browser software; 2) their Total Access program also provides unlimited access to the World Wide Web one monthly flat fee; and 3) they give you 2mgs (megabytes) of space for your own free personal web site! You can fit a considerable amount of web publishing files in two megabytes of space.

If you keep your eyes open, you may be able to locate a free copy of their access software on promotional disks in Internet magazines at your local newsstand. Once you're online, explore. There are literally hundreds of comic book related web pages and web sites on the Internet. Everything from virtual comic shops to your competition's web site. The Internet is the fastest tool for researching the market trends, releases, and anything else you need information on. As far as browser software, the Netscape browser currently has approximately 70 percent of the entire WWW market. They have consistently had the most advanced Internet access technology, although Microsoft Internet Explorer has caught up rather quickly.

If you're new to the web, here are a few web sites that I suggest you visit:

The Comic Book Depot
http://www.insv.com/comxdepo/
This site includes lots of great links to and information about the industry.

Wizard Press Online
http://www.wizardpress.com/
You guess it! This is the computer site of Wizard *magazine!*

Tony Caputo's WWW Site!
http://www.geocities.com/athens/3315
http://www.earthlink.net/~tonycaputo
Got any questions? Comments? You can e-mail me directly!

e-mail

Many Internet services also offer e-mail (or electronic mail). E-mail is an infor-
mal mode of communication (less formal than letters or faxes) that not only
alleviates the need for telephone conversations (and helps you avoid missed
calls, too) but also acts a form of electronic telecommunications that is consid-
erably cheaper than Ma Bell (a fact that she hates).

Why is e-mail so important for your company? Let me give you an example
of how it could have helped me in the past. In 1987, I negotiated the rights for
the Japanimation (a Japanese-made animation or cartoon) called *Astro Boy*. I
did this directly with the Japanese company that owned the property via fax
and telephone, but mostly by phone. Due to the different time zones Japan is
about 9½ hours ahead of the United States, so in order to talk to someone in

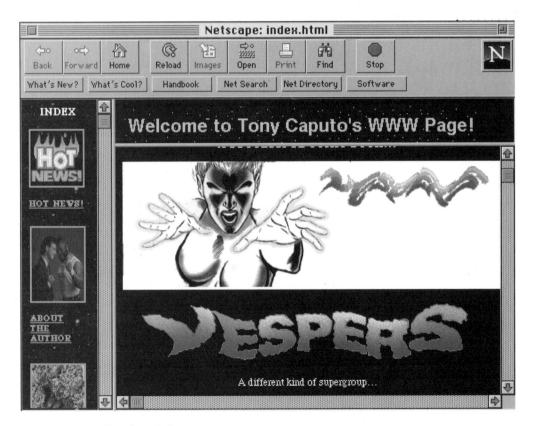

Sample web site
Comic book related web sites are some of the most colorful and fun places to visit on the Internet. This screen
shows one of the first versions of my web site promoting my comic book Vespers.

Japan at a reasonable time of day, I always had to make my calls at around midnight my time. By using e-mail, I would have been able to send transmissions via computer when it was more convenient for me, and my colleagues in Japan would have then been able to retrieve my messages from their computers whenever it was best for them. (Note that a detailed map of the world's time zones is available for review at http://tycho.usno.navy.mil/tzonemap.html—just another example of the value of the web as a resource.) So, e-mail can become your most important form of communication both internationally and domestically. It's easy, economical, and instantaneous. And, you never have to worry about having enough postage or the country and city telephone codes.

Setting Up Your Company's Own Web Page

Once you're signed on to either America Online or Earthlink, it's time to put up that promotional web page for your company on the free web space they offer to subscribers. Follow the directions that each company offers regarding your application for your free web space. After you've applied for the space, you'll receive your own web address. Keep in mind that many of these ISPs will automatically plug your "member name" into the URL, so when applying for the Internet access, use your company's name as the member name. In this way, you'll have an instant company web site; for example:

http://www.browser.com/spotman.

You now have an Internet presence! There is an endless supply of references out there that can help you set up a web site. Check your local computer store for books and CD-ROMs on setting up web pages and other aspects of web publishing. One good example is *Teach Yourself Web Publishing with HTML 3.0 in 14 Days* (SamsNet, 1996) by Laura Lemay. It's sold as both a book and a CD-ROM. Also available is Andy Shafran and Todd Staufer's CD-ROM, *Creating Your Own America Online Web Pages* (Que, 1996). *Web Page Essentials* by Paul Zimmerman (Que, 1996) is another CD-ROM. As for books, try *Home Sweet Home Page* by Robin Williams and Dave Mark (Peachpit Press, 1996) and *Creating Cool Web Pages with Word for Windows 95* by Rod Wodaski (IDG Books). Your local library is also a good source of information.

9 BUDGETS AND BOOKKEEPING

If you're not familiar with traditional accounting and bookkeeping procedures, your local public library has many books on the subject that are geared for small business. The Small Business Administration (SBA) also offers booklets with helpful hints on record keeping (ph: 800-U-ASK-SBA). If you have friends or relatives who have experience in bookkeeping or setting up bookkeeping departments, ask them for assistance. Establishing procedures is a very critical part of running an efficient business.

INVOICES AND SHIPPING MANIFESTS

Two of the most important elements of bookkeeping for publishers are the invoice and the shipping manifest. An invoice is the bill you send the distributor, which they pay you from. Since distributors handle hundreds of other titles, their bookkeeping departments won't know you exist without this form. Invoices are numbered and include all your company data, the address of where to send the payment, the name of the person to whom the check should be made out, the comic book title, and the agreed wholesale price. On receiving purchase orders (the actual written comic book orders, also referred to as P.O.s) from your direct market distributors, you should plug the quantities, address, P.O. number, etc., into a formal invoice, which you then use to bill that distributor for payment. Purchase orders also include all the information you need to fill out the shipping manifest (including quantities and drop-ship locations for your printer).

The shipping manifest is a form listing all the addresses to which a particular comic book is supposed to ship. It also specifies how many copies go to each address, and it is usually attached to the invoice. It's basically a simple description for your printer of your shipping needs. In it you should include the complete quantity and all the shipping locations; this would also include your own office copies, any complimentary copies (comp list), and inventory copies you store in your warehouse. Most printers will store any inventory overages for you (like a warehouse) for a nominal fee. No matter where you store your overage, I recommend always making sure you have easy access to it; in this way, if you find yourself receiving reorders, you'll have the ability to expedite shipments.

Of course, the key to receiving regular reorders is to ship books immediately on receipt of a purchase order. This will give the distributor and retailer the confidence to make the sale. If they reorder a title for their customers and the book doesn't arrive until four weeks later, their customers will have already purchased it elsewhere, and they'll be stuck with the unsold extra copies. You can bet they won't take that risk again. I would also suggest that, as the publisher,

ABC COMPANY

INVOICE

1000 Main Street

Somewhere, IL 60000

(708) 000-0000

FEIN: 000-00-0000

INVOICE #:

0000000

REFERENCE (title/issue #):

Spotman #1

DATE:

MM/DD/YY

PURCHASE ORDER #:

000-00-000

TERMS:

30 day net

TO:

(distributor address)

SHIP TO:

(attach copy of the shipping manifest)

[note: 10-copy drop ship minimum]

Quantity	Title/Issue Number	Cover Price	Discount	Per Unit	Total
20	Spotman #1	$2.50	60%	1.00	$20.00
Shipping:					$00.00
Total due on MM/DD/YY					$20.00

Please make checks payable to ABC Company

Thank you for your order!

Sample invoice

Invoices provide the written documentation with which you bill your distributor for the quantities of product they've ordered. To ensure that your invoice is processed and you get paid, ask your distributor to whom in their accounts payable department you should send the invoice. Of course, the information I've plugged in to this sample invoice is just an example, but you get the idea.

ABC COMPANY
1000 Main Street
Somewhere, IL 60000
(708) 000-0000

SHIPPING MANIFEST

TITLE:

Spotman #1

SHIP DATE:

MM/DD/YY

CUSTOMER:

ABC Distributors

PURCHASE ORDER

000-00-000

TOTAL COPIES:

70

30 (copies)
ABC Distributor
California Warehouse
100 North Elm Street
Somewhere, CA 00000

10
ABC Distributor
Boston Warehouse
1200 NW Briar Street
Somewhere, Boston 00000

10
ABC Distributor
San Diego Warehouse
100 South Tequila Avenue
San Diego, CA 00000

20
ABC Distributor
North California Warehouse
115 Eloston Avenue
Someplace, CA 00000

Sample shipping manifest

The shipping manifest provides a breakdown of your distributors and how many copies go to each. It goes to the distributor with your invoice. Here, I've just inserted dummy information to give you an idea of what your manifest should include.

you should always initiate a wholesale minimum order quantity for any shipment. You don't want to get stuck sending out one copy to various locations, because when you add on the shipping and handling charges, you'll be losing your shirt. Your minimum order requirement could be, for example, as little as five copies to any one drop-ship location, as long as it saves you from having to ship one copy at a time.

Remember that newsstand and bookstore distributors have different payment methods from direct market distributors. The newsstand payment method is based on an automated percentage of your shipped allotment, as stated on your printer's completion notice, and the newsstand wholesaler usually handles the shipping information out of a database. Bookstore distributors may ask you to invoice them for their estimated percentage of sale; this can be from 20 to 40 percent of the wholesale value of the entire allotment, paid within 60 days of the shipping date. Bookstore distributors require only a few drop-ship locations, as they handle the delivery of hundred of titles to only a few thousand locations; newsstand distributors, on the other hand, service up to 100,000 locations.

When selling your product directly to retailers, always send the shipment C.O.D. (Cash on Delivery). After you establish a reliable working relationship with them, you can then offer them credit. Never offer anyone (except an established distributor) instant credit—not even for five copies. You may never see that payment! Believe me, it happens. Also, when mailing these direct retail orders or reorders, always insert additional promotional materials into the package. Retailers appreciate any information that will assist them in selling more product.

KEEPING AND MONITORING YOUR FINANCIAL RECORDS

As the operator of a small business, you should prepare financial records on a regular basis. After all, after everything is said and done, the final analysis is the bottom line. This valuable information is important for producing reliable budget forecasts, capital management, sales projections, and to file an accurate tax return. You should plan regular meetings of your company's management and/or the board of directors so that they can provide a guiding force for ongoing financial control.

If you are your only employee, then you have all the control—and also all the responsibility—for making all financial decisions. The best way to handle this enormous workload is with modern technology—specifically, a computer with a fax/modem and Microsoft Office software. This program is the closest you'll get to having a diligent, robotic staff of accountants and executive assistants. How often you gather this financial material depends on the size of your enterprise, but overall, your financial records and data should include the following information:

Weekly (and/or monthly) income statements

Monthly balance sheets

Weekly (and/or monthly) cash-flow or application-of-funds statements

Quarterly market and sales forecasts

Monthly production and procurement plans

Monthly spending plans for promotion and expansion

Weekly (and/or monthly) capital improvement and additional expenditure projections

All this accumulated data will give you a view of your company's financial health, and it can give you the foresight to determine any future needs or visualize any future increase in profits, costs, or expenses. You can gather the data in income statements and spreadsheets. For example, if you speculate a 30-percent increase in profits within the next three months, you can guarantee payment for a special promotion during that time. On the other hand, if you forecast a 40-percent deficit, you'll be able to adjust your budget immediately to compensate for that loss or seek out the credit or capital to counterbalance the deficit with no effect on your production, your employees' salaries, or your own pocketbook. If you feel you need a little help with all these financial matters, your local library is a good source for more information and reference guides.

Income Statements

To generate an income statement like the one opposite, you'll have to look at your financial records, so you should always keep all receipts and clear records of all transactions. You'll find that these will go far in helping you when you're doing any financial analyses. Basic elements of the statement include a listing of revenue (where the money is coming in from), current year-to-date sales (YTD), and listings of production costs and operating expenses. An optional component is the percentages of all the YTD sales that go toward generating those corresponding income amounts; this calculation is an interesting addition on income statements for companies that deal with large numbers.

In the first line of the statement on page 148 (direct market YTD sales = $70,800), we can see that an average of 5,000 copies are selling monthly. The retail price is $2.95 with a direct distribution discount at the standard 60 percent off retail. The additional revenue includes minimal sales of back issues, mail order T-shirts, and 100 subscribers all within a 12-month period. Subscriptions for this type of title can be lucrative, as many retailers often stop carrying a title after the first few issues. The freelancer expenses may be for an inker or letterer; this estimate is for an average of 22 pages of story at $20 per page. The printing cost is at approximately $.40 cents per copy.

A single salary to a part-time assistant is paid as an independent contractor (freelancer). This person could even be a family member. Benefits might be your own annual health insurance premium, and outside services might be a telephone answering service. I estimated the legal and accounting fees for trademarks and financial statements. Note that, if you're working out of your house, deducting even a portion of your own home or apartment payments or rent as "office" rent on your taxes is said to raise eyebrows at the IRS. You can deduct a part of your home as office space as long as it's a completely separate office; if you do this, you're not even allowed to do your personal finances within that space.

INCOME STATEMENT	YEAR ENDING MM/DD/YY		ABC COMPANY		

Revenue	Current YTD	% of Sales	Revenue	Current YTD	% of Sales
SALES			Legal fees	19,728.76	00.43
Direct market	$1,049,630.42	37.00	Accounting fees	11,345.90	00.04
Back issues	3,115.82	00.10	Office rent & utilities	45,997.87	01.62
Newsstand	1,596,374.54	56.28	Telephones	6,373.52	00.22
Subscriptions	39,490.17	01.39	Office repair & maintenance	1,517.65	00.05
Mail order	24,050.39	00.84	Office supplies	13,923.71	00.49
Paid advertising	105,436.23	03.70	Computers	11,446.54	00.04
Foreign	18,061.55	00.63	Postage	4,150.80	00.14
TOTAL GROSS REVENUE	$2,836,159.12	100.00	Leased fax machine	457.70	00.01
Subscription refunds	(356.60)	00.00	Leased copier	1,272.37	00.04
			Leased telephones	1,380.97	00.04
TOTAL NET REVENUE	$2,835,802.52	99.98	Leased computers	995.03	00.03
			Equipment leasing— related postage	191.30	00.00
PRODUCTION COSTS			Business travel & lodging	9,126.26	00.32
Freelancers	397,290.05	14.00	Business meals	81.65	00.00
Typesetting	320.04	00.00	Business entertainment	22,166.83	00.78
Printing	1,286,001.75	45.37	Business car	3,582.93	00.12
Separations	112,042.60	03.94	Advertising	12,902.33	00.45
Shipping	99,151.27	03.49	Promotion	7,817.81	00.27
Postage	18,873.76	00.66	Trade show expenses	14,729.86	00.51
Messenger services	1,585.16	00.05	Dues & publications	4,569.69	00.16
Reference material	21.55	00.00	Bank service charges	181.48	00.00
Art supplies	1,467.98	00.05	Licenses & permits	633.88	00.02
Royalties	57,762.88	02.03	Depreciation— office equipment	1,389.75	00.04
TOTAL COSTS	$1,974,516.50	69.62	Depreciation—computers	3,166.67	00.11
TOTAL GROSS PROFIT	$861,286.00	30.36	Depreciation—darkroom	10,288.62	00.36
			Depreciation— show displays	1,637.12	00.05
OPERATING EXPENSES			TOTAL OPERATING EXPENSES	$481,007.97	
Officers'/owners' salaries	153,858.34	05.47			
Office salaries & wages	109,494.02	03.86	EARNINGS (LOSS) FROM OPERATIONS	$380,278.03	00.13
Payroll taxes	39,957.78	01.68	PROVISIONS FOR CORPORATE INCOME TAX	$114,083.40	
Payroll service fees	70.21	00.00			
Employee benefits	39,300.00	01.60	NET INCOME (LOSS)	$266,194.63	00.09
Outside service fees	26,841.52	00.94			

Sample income statement

This sample income statement is for a (fictional) company at the year ending 12/31. It shows the revenue and expenses for a comic book company that publishes an average of 11 full-color monthly titles with both licensed characters and proprietary ones (which are those owned by the company). It includes a column for the optional, percentage-of-YTD-sales data, and shows a net pretax profit of nine percent, or about $266,000. Numbers in parentheses indicate refunds or other losses. For a sample income statement of a smaller company, see the chart on the next page.

INCOME STATEMENT   YEAR ENDING MM/DD/YY   ABC COMPANY

Revenue	Current YTD	Revenue	Current YTD
SALES		Outside service fees	500
Direct market	$70,800	Legal fees	1,000
Back issues	2,000	Accounting fees	1,000
Newsstand	0	Office rent & utilities	0
Subscriptions	3,000	Telephone	1,200
Mail order	500	Office repairs & maintenance	100
Paid advertising	1,000	Office supplies	300
Foreign	2,000	Computers	0
TOTAL GROSS REVENUE	$79,300	Postage	600
Subscription refunds	0	Leased fax machine	0
		Leased copier	0
TOTAL NET REVENUE	$79,300	Leased telephones	0
		Leased computers	2,000
PRODUCTION COSTS		Equipment leasing—related postage	0
Freelancers	5,280	Business travel & lodging	500
Typesetting	100	Business meals	50
Printing	25,000	Business entertainment	50
Separations	2,650	Business car	0
Shipping	2,400	Advertising	2,000
Postage	500	Promotion	1,000
Messenger services	20	Trade show expenses	2,000
Reference materials	100	Dues & publications	0
Art supplies	300	Bank service charges	200
Royalties	0	Licenses & permits	0
TOTAL COSTS	$36,350		
TOTAL GROSS PROFIT	$42,950	TOTAL OVERHEAD EXPENSES	$19,850
OVERHEAD EXPENSES		TOTAL OPERATING EXPENSES	$56,200
Officers' salaries	0		
Office salaries & wages	5,000	EARNINGS (LOSS) FROM OPERATIONS	$23,100
Payroll taxes	0		
Payroll service fees	0	NET INCOME (LOSS)	$23,100
Employee benefits	2,400		

Sample income statement
This shows what an income statement for a profitable company producing a single, self-published black-and-white title might look like. (Year ending 12/31.) Note that this statement doesn't include the optional, percentage-of-YTD-sale data.

If you're operating as a sole proprietorship (the various types of businesses are covered in chapter 1), the net profits can be your income; you can pay yourself this entire amount, and then pay individual taxes (minus any deductions). If you reinvest any of the amount back into the business—for example, buying a company automobile—you don't have to pay taxes on that amount and can use a portion of the car's cost as a deduction. As a sole proprietorship, you also don't have to pay yourself a payroll check, thus avoiding the approximate 15 percent payroll taxes and the cost of additional benefits that companies are required to offer employees. However, you will have to pay the new 15 percent self-employment tax. This can bring your taxes to up to 40 percent of your income. The deductions become a very valuable asset to your annual revenue. Contact your local IRS offices or center for more information on home business taxes and deductions.

Spreadsheets

The spreadsheet is used to calculate and record detailed information for all projected revenue and expenses within any given time period. It assists you in establishing future budgets, managing cash, implementing marketing strategies, and planning any expansions. Again, Microsoft Office software (available for both PC and Mac computers) is a very helpful tool here. It includes several programs that are helpful to small businesses, the most useful of which is Microsoft Excel. This is by far the best financial spreadsheet software out there.

The spreadsheet on page 154 is an *accrual spreadsheet,* which is organized on an "accrual" basis. This simply means that all the income and expenses have been accumulated jointly to determine whether the product is profitable. This means that the costs are subtracted from revenue to show either a profit or a loss instantly. As a result, this type of spreadsheet doesn't show an accurate depiction of cash flow. It does, however, serve two important purposes: 1) it gives you an estimate of your gross profit, and 2) it offers a monthly estimate of income versus expenses for the year. You must figure your sales projections in some kind of spreadsheet form so that you gather all the critical information necessary to achieve the most accurate projection of your income and expenses for the next three months or three years (or whatever time frame you're using). This data is important, not only for making any business decisions, but also for finding investment interests. All potential investors will want to see how you plan to pay them back, or what kind of dividend they can expect from their investments in your company.

If you're proficient with any accounting software, creating spreadsheets can be much, much easier. Once you've formatted the entire spreadsheet with all the appropriate formulas, the accounting software enables you to simply change a single number and have the computer change all the other affected calculations accordingly. If you're not a computer accounting whiz, you can still produce a spreadsheet in one of three ways: 1) ask a friend to help (but creating a spreadsheet is a very time consuming process, even with computer software, so ask a really *good* friend); 2) pay an accountant to produce the information for you, which can be very expensive; or 3) break out your calculator, ledger pad, and a few sharp #2 pencils. Below, I've listed the various basic elements of a spreadsheet (in this case, a newsstand spreadsheet) so that you'll be better able to read one.

ASSUMPTIONS *These are various specifications listed at the top of the spreadsheet that indicate all the fixed costs, such as retail price, wholesale value, royalty rate (if applicable), and printing costs.*

MONTH *Under the months of the year are the number of copies projected to ship to each channel of distribution. The* wholesale retention, *when it's listed, is the percentage of the retail price to be received from the newsstand distributor (in other words, the wholesale price). The* prepayment percentage *is the number of distributors who will prepay for the product, in order to take advantage of an additional discount (usually of 2 percent).* Royalty to freelancer *is the royalty amount based on the number of copies sold, above and beyond a minimum number.*

SELL-THROUGH ESTIMATES *These three payment methods are for the newsstand market and are described in detail in chapter 6. They're the percentage of the newsstand order that is expected to sell.*

NEWSSTAND P & L *This is an immediate indication of your profit or loss (P & L) from newsstand sales. You need to keep a watchful eye on this. Any early indication of a dramatic drop in sales and profits can give you the foresight to save yourself tens of thousands of dollars.*

RETENTION *See chapter 6 for a complete explanation of the newsstand payment schedule.*

GROSS REVENUE *This denotes the total revenue from the newsstand three-payment method on an accrual basis. These payments are usually scheduled between 10 to 180 days after shipping.*

NEWSSTAND CASH FLOW *This section details the cash flow (or lack thereof) for newsstand distribution.*

DIRECT MARKET REVENUE *This shows what your orders look like in dollars.*

DIRECT MARKET CASH FLOW *This section of the spreadsheet is dramatically different from, and more attractive to investors than, the segment highlighting the traditional newsstand payment method, because the direct market pays 100 percent of the bill in 30 days. Note: A "net 30 days" payment term means payment is due within 30 days of shipping or receipt of invoice (depending on what you've indicated on the invoice).*

TITLE FINANCIAL PERFORMANCE *This section includes the detailed costs versus income, giving you a view of your profit (or loss).*

ADDITIONAL REVENUE *All your expected income derived from sources other than wholesale distribution, such as paid advertising, subscriptions, back orders, and foreign sales.*

GROSS PROFIT/(LOSS) *Your bottom line.*

You'll learn a number of very important things from a complete spreadsheet. With all this data at your fingertips, you'll have your publication schedule laid out in detail with all your monthly expenses. For example, your spreadsheet might indicate that you'll be giving your printer over $100,000 in business by the end of the year, and this can be a good selling point when negotiating your printing costs. Spreadsheets also give you an idea for a budget for overhead, which includes your own monthly income. In the spreadsheets that follow, I've included sections for both newsstand and bookstore distribution. Adding these two, more complicated channels of distribution makes a spreadsheet even more valuable.

Cash Flow

This is, simply, the amount of income versus expenses. As I mentioned earlier, an accrual spreadsheet, lines up all the receivables and payables nicely, making everything seem clear and simple. A spreadsheet showing a comic book's *real time* title cash flow performance, however, gives you a more accurate depiction of income and expenses, including the capital you'd need to start up any newsstand comic book title.

For an example of this, compare the charts that follow on pages 154 and 155. This is only one example of immediate cash flow; you may choose a different route depending on your goals and budget. Still, it gives you an idea of how cash flow works. Your wonderful net profits and healthy income begin to accumulate at the end of the first year; this is due to the fact that it will take about four to six months before you ever receive any revenue. In order to ship on a timely basis, you'll need to start working on the book months before, thus all the initial expenses for your freelancers, telephone, legal fees, your own medical insurance, postage, advertising, and promotion add up to what's called *working capital* (which is the money that funnels in and out of your business to keep it operating). In the spreadsheet on page 153, which details a successful direct-market-only, black-and-white title, you can see a need for about $6,000 in start-up capital, even with year-end receipts of over $100,000.

With all this information at your disposal, you can forecast a monthly budget for all your expenses. If you aren't able to acquire any capital or a loan, this data will enable you to plan a schedule for royalty payments to cocreators or part-time partners. If you do plan to hire workers and then pay them later, make sure that they're aware of the risk. Always update your data immediately upon receiving the actual numbers so that your spreadsheets will give you a head start on what the future may hold.

With a thought-out business plan (see chapter 10 for information on acquiring capital and investors) and detailed financial projections like those presented in the spreadsheets here, you'll be able to raise the capital or acquire a loan—with collateral. You can use your home equity, trust fund, car, or whatever you have that may be considered a *hard* asset. Note that your concept and trademark are *intangible* assets, and usually aren't solid enough to secure a loan or deal.

SPOTMAN (B&W) "A DOG"

MONTHLY ASSUMPTIONS

Retail Price	2.95	Shipping/issue	$300	Make-ready	$0
Wholesale (Direct)	1.18	Net 30 days	0.40	Print per copy	0.55
Royalty % (licensor)	0	Freelancer	$220	Separations	$300

MONTH	JAN	FEB	MAR	APR	MAY	JUN	JUL	AUG	SEP	OCT	NOV	DEC	TOTAL
Direct Market Order	0	0	0	5,000	4,500	3,000	2,700	2,500	2,200	2,000	1,800	1,500	25,200
Royalty to f/lancer	0	0	0	0	0	0	0	0	0	0	0	0	
DIRECT MARKET REVENUE	JAN	FEB	MAR	APR	MAY	JUN	JUL	AUG	SEP	OCT	NOV	DEC	TOTAL
Net 30 days	0	0	0	0	5,900	5,310	3,540	3,186	2,950	2,596	2,360	2,124	27,966
CASH FLOW TOTALS	JAN	FEB	MAR	APR	MAY	JUN	JUL	AUG	SEP	OCT	NOV	DEC	TOTAL
Revenue	0	0	0	0	5,900	3,540	3,186	2,950	2,596	2,360	2,124	1,770	24,426
Printing	0	0	0	0	2,750	2,475	1,650	1,485	1,375	1,210	1,100	990	13,035
Freelancers	0	220	220	220	220	220	220	220	220	0	0	0	3,520
Misc.(T-shirts)	0	0	0	0	0	0	0	0	0	300	0	0	300
Separation	0	0	0	0	300	300	300	300	300	300	300	300	2,400
Shipping	0	0	0	0	300	300	300	300	300	300	300	300	2,400
Royalty	0	0	0	0	0	0	0	0	0	0	0	0	0
PRODUCTION COSTS	0	440	440	440	3,570	3,295	2,470	2,305	2,195	2,110	1,700	1,590	21,655
GROSS P/L	0	-440	-440	-440	2,330	245	716	645	401	250	424	180	3,871
ADDITIONAL REVENUE	JAN	FEB	MAR	APR	MAY	JUN	JUL	AUG	SEP	OCT	NOV	DEC	TOTAL
Foreign Sales Revenue	0	0	0	0	0	0	0	0	0	0	1,000	1,000	2,000
Advertising Revenue	0	0	0	0	0	0	100	100	100	100	100	100	600
Subscription Revenue	0	0	0	0	450	300	150	210	300	150	450	150	2,160
Back Issue Sales	0	0	0	0	25	25	100	100	140	140	140	140	810
Mail Order/T-Shirts	0	0	0	0	0	45	45	150	150	150	150	150	840
ESTIMATED TOTALS	0	0	0	0	475	370	395	560	690	540	1,840	1,540	6,410
OVERHEAD	JAN	FEB	MAR	APR	MAY	JUN	JUL	AUG	SEP	OCT	NOV	DEC	TOTAL
Salaries/Wages	$0	0	0	0	417	417	417	417	417	417	417	417	3,333
Medical Benefits	200	200	200	200	200	200	200	200	200	200	200	200	2,400
Outside Service Fees	70	70	70	70	70	70	70	70	70	70	70	70	840
Legal Fees	500	0	0	0	0	0	500	0	0	0	0	0	1,000
Accounting Fees	0	0	0	0	500	0	500	0	0	0	0	0	1,000
Office Rent/Utilities	0	0	0	0	0	0	0	0	0	0	0	0	0
Office Telephone	100	100	100	100	100	100	100	100	100	100	100	100	1,200
Office Repair	0	50	0	0	0	50	0	0	0	0	0	0	100
Office Supplies	30	30	30	30	30	30	30	30	30	30	30	30	360
Office Postage	100	30	100	30	30	30	30	60	60	60	60	60	650
Computers Lease	160	160	160	160	160	160	160	160	160	160	160	160	1,920
Business Travel	0	0	0	0	200	0	300	0	0	0	0	0	500
Business Meals	0	0	25	0	0	0	25	0	0	0	0	0	50
Business Entertainment	0	0	25	0	0	0	25	0	0	0	0	0	50
Business Automobile	0	0	0	0	0	0	0	0	0	0	0	0	0
Business Advertising	0	0	0	0	300	0	300	400	0	0	0	0	1,000
Business Promotion	0	0	0	100	100	100	100	100	100	100	100	100	900
Bank Service Charges	15	15	15	15	15	15	15	15	15	15	15	15	180
TOTAL OVERHEAD:	1175	655	725	705	2122	1172	2772	1552	1152	1152	1152	1137	15,468
EARNINGS (LOSS)	-1,175	-1,535	-1,605	-1,585	-2,887	-3,852	-4,131	-2,652	-2,256	2,472	-588	-1,007	-25,742

Sample spreadsheet

Using a spreadsheet computer program, I created this detailed spreadsheet showing a forecast for Spotman, a monthly black-and-white comic book with a $2.95 cover price. In this example, Spotman is "a dog"—with average sales of about 2,500 copies, it will cost over $20,000 a year to publish. After you examine this information, compare it to the spreadsheet opposite, which presents an example of good cash flow. Note that most spreadsheets produced on specialized computer software will look something like this.

SPOTMAN (B&W)

MONTHLY ASSUMPTIONS

Retail Price	2.95	Shipping	$300	Make-ready	$0
Wholesale (Direct)	1.18	Net 30 days	0.40	Print per copy	0.25
Royalty % (licensor)	0	Freelancer	$220	Separations	$300

MONTH	JAN	FEB	MAR	APR	MAY	JUN	JUL	AUG	SEP	OCT	NOV	DEC	TOTAL
Direct Market Order	0	0	0	14,000	12,000	11,000	17,000	19,000	25,000	27,000	30,000	40,000	195,000
Royalty to f/lancer	0	0	0	0	0	0	0	0	0	900	900	900	
DIRECT MARKET REVENUE	JAN	FEB	MAR	APR	MAY	JUN	JUL	AUG	SEP	OCT	NOV	DEC	TOTAL
Net 30 days	0	0	0	0	16,520	14,160	12,980	20,060	22,420	29,500	31,860	35,400	182,900
CASH FLOW TOTALS	JAN	FEB	MAR	APR	MAY	JUN	JUL	AUG	SEP	OCT	NOV	DEC	TOTAL
Revenue	0	0	0	0	16,520	12,980	20,060	22,420	29,500	31,860	35,400	47,200	215,940
Printing	0	0	0	0	3,500	3,000	2,750	4,250	4,750	6,250	6,750	7,500	38,750
Freelancers	0	220	220	220	220	220	220	220	220	0	0	0	3,520
Misc.(T-shirts)	0	0	0	0	0	0	0	0	0	300	0	0	300
Separation	0	0	0	0	300	300	300	300	300	300	300	300	2,400
Shipping	0	0	0	0	300	300	300	300	300	300	300	300	2,400
Royalty	0	0	0	0	0	0	0	0	0	900	900	900	2,700
PRODUCTION COSTS	0	440	440	440	4,320	3,820	3,570	5,070	5,570	8,050	8,250	9,000	50,070
GROSS P/L	0	-440	-440	-440	12,200	9,160	16,490	17,350	23,930	23,810	27,150	38,200	166,970
ADDITIONAL REVENUE	JAN	FEB	MAR	APR	MAY	JUN	JUL	AUG	SEP	OCT	NOV	DEC	TOTAL
Foreign Sales Revenue	0	0	0	0	0	0	0	0	0	0	1,000	1,000	2,000
Advertising Revenue	0	0	0	0	0	0	100	100	100	100	100	100	600
Subscription Revenue	0	0	0	0	450	300	150	210	300	150	450	150	2,160
Back Issue Sales	0	0	0	0	25	25	100	100	140	140	140	140	810
Mail Order/T-Shirts	0	0	0	0	0	45	45	150	150	150	150	150	840
ESTIMATED TOTALS	0	0	0	0	475	370	395	560	690	540	1,840	1,540	6,410
OVERHEAD	JAN	FEB	MAR	APR	MAY	JUN	JUL	AUG	SEP	OCT	NOV	DEC	TOTAL
Salaries/Wages	$0	0	0	0	417	417	417	417	417	417	417	417	3,333
Medical Benefits	200	200	200	200	200	200	200	200	200	200	200	200	2,400
Outside Service Fees	70	70	70	70	70	70	70	70	70	70	70	70	840
Legal Fees	500	0	0	0	0	0	500	0	0	0	0	0	1,000
Accounting Fees	0	0	0	0	500	0	500	0	0	0	0	0	1,000
Office Rent/Utilities	0	0	0	0	0	0	0	0	0	0	0	0	0
Office Telephone	100	100	100	100	100	100	100	100	100	100	100	100	1,200
Office Repair	0	50	0	0	0	50	0	0	0	0	0	0	100
Office Supplies	30	30	30	30	30	30	30	30	30	30	30	30	360
Office Postage	100	30	100	30	30	30	30	60	60	60	60	60	650
Computers Lease	160	160	160	160	160	160	160	160	160	160	160	160	1,920
Business Travel	0	0	0	0	200	0	300	0	0	0	0	0	500
Business Meals	0	0	25	0	0	0	25	0	0	0	0	0	50
Business Entertainment	0	0	25	0	0	0	25	0	0	0	0	0	50
Business Automobile	0	0	0	0	0	0	0	0	0	0	0	0	0
Business Advertising	0	0	0	0	300	0	300	400	0	0	0	0	1,000
Business Promotion	0	0	0	100	100	100	100	100	100	100	100	100	900
Bank Service Charges	15	15	15	15	15	15	15	15	15	15	15	15	180
TOTAL OVERHEAD:	1175	655	725	705	2122	1172	2772	1552	1152	1152	1152	1137	15,468
EARNINGS (LOSS)	-1,175	-1,535	-1,605	-1,585	6,233	4,538	10,543	11,288	17,898	15,148	19,588	29,603	108,942

Sample spreadsheet

The spreadsheet above documents good cash flow. The Spotman comic book was thousands of dollars in debt by the time the second issue first hit the stands, but at year's end, its net income exceeded $100,000. By comparing this with the previous spreadsheet, you can see how a title that sells poorly can be a constant drain on cash flow.

HOT NEWSSTAND TITLE

ASSUMPTIONS

Retail Price	1.95	Prepayment retention	0	Miscellaneous Charges 100	Make-ready	2,500
Wholesale Newsstand	0.84	Net 30 days	0.40	Settlement chg. % 2	Print per copy	0.11
Royalty % (licensor)	6.00	Freelancer	4,950	Shipping 4,000	Separations	1,200

MONTH	JAN	FEB	MAR	APR	MAY	JUN	JUL	AUG	SEP	OCT	NOV	DEC	TOTAL
Newsstand print order	0	0	0	100000	100000	100000	125000	125000	125500	130000	150000	150000	1,105,500
Direct Market Order	0	0	0	15000	12000	11000	17000	20000	25000	40000	50000	60000	250,000
Cover/Misc.	0	0	0	200	200	200	200	200	200	200	200	200	1,800
Wholesale retention	0	0	0	0	0	0	0	0	0	0	0	0	
Prepayment Pct.	0.00	0.00	0.00	0.00	0.00	0.00	0.00	0.00	0.00	0.00	0.00	0.00	
Royalty to f/lancer	0	0	0	0	0	0	0	0	0	0	0	0	
SELL-THROUGH ESTIMATES													
First advance	0.00	0.00	0.00	0.15	0.20	0.20	0.20	0.20	0.20	0.20	0.20	0.20	
Second advance	0.00	0.00	0.00	0.20	0.20	0.20	0.20	0.20	0.20	0.20	0.20	0.20	
Settlement	0.00	0.00	0.00	0.56	0.45	0.50	0.51	0.47	0.40	0.37	0.37	0.35	
NEWSSTAND P&L													
Wholesale value	0	0	0	83850	83850	83850	104813	104813	105232	109005	125775	125775	
RETENTION	-	-	-	-	-	-	-	-	-	-	-	-	
First payment	0	0	0	0	0	0	0	0	0	0	0	0	
Second payment	0.60	0.60	0.60	0.75	0.75	0.75	0.75	0.75	0.75	0.75	0.75	0.75	
GROSS REVENUE	-	-	-										
First payment	0	0	0	7547	12578	12578	15722	15722	15785	16351	18866	18866	134,013
Second payment	0	0	0	5031	0	0	0	0	0	0	0	0	5,031
Settlement	0	0	0	34379	25155	29348	37733	33540	26308	23981	27671	25155	263,268
	0	0	0	46956	37733	41925	53454	49262	42093	40332	46537	44021	402,312
Misc. charges (1st)	0	0	0	100	100	100	100	100	100	100	100	100	900
Misc. charges (2nd)	0	0	0	100	0	0	0	0	0	0	0	0	100
Settlement Charges	0	0	0	688	503	587	755	671	526	480	553	503	5,265
NET REVENUE	0	0	0	46168	37129	41238	52600	48491	41467	39752	45883	43418	396,147

NEWSSTAND CASH FLOW	JAN	FEB	MAR	APR	MAY	JUN	JUL	AUG	SEP	OCT	NOV	DEC	TOTAL
First payment	0	0	0	0	7447	12478	12478	15622	15622	15685	16251	18766	114,347
Second payment	0	0	0	0	0	0	0	4931	0	0	0	0	4,931
Settlement	0	0	0	0	0	0	0	0	0	33691	24652	28761	87,103
NEWSSTAND RECEIPTS	0	0	0	0	7447	12478	12478	20553	15622	49376	40903	47527	206,381

D/ M REVENUE	JAN	FEB	MAR	APR	MAY	JUN	JUL	AUG	SEP	OCT	NOV	DEC	TOTAL
Prepayment	0	0	0	0	0	0	0	0	0	0	0	0	
Net 30 days	0	0	0	11700	9360	12980	13260	15600	19500	31200	39000	46800	199,400
NET REVENUE	0	0	0	11700	9360	12980	13260	15600	19500	31200	39000	46800	199,400
D/ M CASH FLOW	0	0	0	0	11700	9360	12980	13260	15600	19500	31200	39000	152,600

TITLE FINANCIAL PERFORMANCE

ACCRUAL TOTALS	JAN	FEB	MAR	APR	MAY	JUN	JUL	AUG	SEP	OCT	NOV	DEC	TOTAL
Revenue	0	0	0	57868	46489	54218	65860	64091	60967	70952	84883	90218	595,547
Printing	0	0	0	14538	14208	14098	17508	17838	18443	20588	23888	24988	166,097
Freelancers	0	0	0	4950	4950	4950	4950	4950	4950	4950	4950	4950	44,550
Misc.	0	0	0	200	200	200	200	200	200	200	200	200	1,800
Separation	0	0	0	1200	1200	1200	1200	1200	1200	1200	1200	1200	10,800
Shipping	0	0	0	4000	4000	4000	4000	4000	4000	4000	4000	4000	36,000
Royalty	0	0	0	3472	2789	3253	3952	3845	3658	4257	5093	5413	35,733
PRODUCTION COSTS	0	0	0	28360	27347	27701	31810	32033	32451	35195	39331	40751	294,980
PROFIT/(LOSS)	0	0	0	29508	19142	26517	34050	32058	28516	35757	45552	49467	300,567

ADDITIONAL REVENUE

	JAN	FEB	MAR	APR	MAY	JUN	JUL	AUG	SEP	OCT	NOV	DEC	TOTAL
Foreign Sales Revenue	0	0	1,000	1,000	1,000	1,000	1,000	1,000	5,000	5,000	10,000	10,000	36,000
Percentage/Ad Revenue	0	0	200	200	200	200	200	200	200	200	1,000	1,000	3,600
Subscription Revenue	0	0	100	100	100	100	100	200	500	1,000	2,000	2,000	6,200
Back Issue Sales	0	0	0	0	0	1,000	1,000	1,000	1,000	1,000	1,000	1,000	7,000
Re-Orders	0	0	0	0	10000	10000	10000	0	0	0	0	0	30,000
ACCRUAL TOTALS	0	0	1,300	1,300	11,300	12,300	12,300	2,400	6,700	7,200	14,000	14,000	82,800
PROFIT/(LOSS)	0	0	1300	30808	30442	38816	46350	34457	35215	42957	59552	63467	383,367

Sample spreadsheet for a newsstand title

This is an accrual spreadsheet detailing a best-selling, full-color, mass-market comic book. It ships an average of 150,000 copies every month, has an above average sell-through on newsstands, and even jumps to over 50,000 units in the comic specialty market. The bottom line shows a gross profit of about $300,000 in nine months, with total receipts of over half a million dollars. All in all, this could be considered a highly successful publication, but when you compare it to the cash flow performance opposite, you get a dose of reality.

HOT NEWSSTAND TITLE

TITLE CASH FLOW PERFORMANCE

CASH FLOW TOTALS	JAN	FEB	MAR	APR	MAY	JUN	JUL	AUG	SEP	OCT	NOV	DEC	TOTAL
Revenue	0	0	0	0	19147	21838	25458	33813	31222	68876	72103	86527	358981
Printing	0	0	0	0	14538	14208	14098	17508	17838	18443	20588	23888	141109
Freelancers	0	0	4950	4950	4950	4950	4950	4950	4950	4950	4950	4950	49500
Misc.	0	0	0	200	200	200	200	200	200	200	200	200	1800
Separation	0	0	0	0	1200	1200	1200	1200	1200	1200	1200	1200	9600
Shipping	0	0	0	0	4000	4000	4000	4000	4000	4000	4000	4000	32000
Royalty	0	0	0	0	1149	1310	1527	2029	1873	4133	4326	5192	21539
PRODUCTION COSTS	0	0	4950	5150	26037	25868	25975	29887	30061	32926	35264	39430	255548
PROFIT/(LOSS)	0	0	-4950	-5150	-6890	-4031	-518	3926	1161	35950	36838	47097	103434
ADDITIONAL REVENUE													
Foreign Sales Revenue	0	0	0	0	0	0	0	1000	1000	1000	10000	10000	23000
Percentage/Ad Revenue	0	0	0	0	0	0	0	0	0	200	1000	1000	2200
Subscription Revenue	0	0	0	0	0	0	100	200	500	1000	2000	2000	5800
Back Issue Sales	0	0	0	0	0	0	0	200	200	200	1000	1000	2600
Re-Orders	0	0	0	0	0	0	0	0	0	0	0	0	0
CASH FLOW TOTALS	0	0	0	0	0	0	100	1400	1700	2400	14000	14000	33600
PROFIT/(LOSS)	0	0	-4950	-5150	-6890	-4031	-418	5326	2861	38350	50838	61097	137034

Title cash flow performance

The title financial performance section in the spreadsheet on the facing page depicts a strong, highly profitable publication. That's because it is an accrual summary of financial performance and doesn't show the real flow of cash. Above is a title cash flow performance chart, which indicates that only one third of the estimated revenue will be paid within those first nine months, with the balance dwindling in the first six months of the following year. Why the long wait? Because newsstand sales are structured on a consignment basis; when you're dealing with 50,000 outlets on a consignment basis, you're dealing with time.

10 CAPITAL AND INVESTORS

> Whatever capital requirements you believe it'll take, get twice as much!
> —Dennis Mallonee
> President, Heroic Publishing

RAISING CAPITAL

In order to make money, you have to spend money. If you don't have the money on hand, you have to raise it somehow. Raising capital or gaining an investment interest in the publishing industry is difficult. The Small Business Administration (SBA) won't lend money to any publishers because it considers them to be high-risk ventures. And, it's true—what you're proposing to do by starting a publishing company is very risky. There are no guarantees, but then again, are there in any entrepreneurial venture?

Usually, when raising money, you'll have to offer something to the lender as collateral. For example, a hardware store has valuable inventory, a commercial printer has its equipment—all of which can be used as collateral for a business loan or investment interest. Expensive equipment, costly merchandise, or real estate are all considered *hard assets;* that is, something tangible that an investor can repossess and sell to regain any investment money if the venture goes sour. Even a graphic design studio or advertising agency with substantial debt can continue earning new or more capital by establishing multi-year contracts (with distinguished companies) that provide regular work and income. A new or young comic book publishing company, however, has only its *intangible assets,* such as the company logo trademarks and the intellectual properties, which are not always considered as substantial as material items. Still, these properties and your regular monthly receipts and profit statements are your best selling points for raising capital.

The SBA has stated that 75 percent of all new companies fail in their first five years. This is due partly to that fact that they have to "mark territory" from scratch; you're not only starting a new business, but building contacts, accounts, sales, and credibility all from ground zero. After all, it's not just what you know, but who you know that counts. The most important strategy in searching for capital or a financial partner is to use what you have in black-and-white—your financial statements and balance sheets will be the final analysis in acquiring capital. The second most important strategy or tool when looking for investors is your business plan, which we'll discuss in further detail below. This is a proposal presented to potential investors that includes the specifics on what you plan to do with any invested money and why, and more importantly, how you plan to pay it back. Your company's stage (whether you're in the start-up, expansion, or acquisition phase, for example) is also important in how you acquire capital and in what form of investment interest you attract.

A START-UP BUSINESS PLAN

When seeking capital for a start-up, which is a new company with no existing revenue, your business plan is your second most important element after your financial situation and statements. You may have had an enormously successful previous experience in publishing, but without a future plan of action, that's only history.

Your local library has an enormous selection of reference books on business plan and proposal writing, and business plan computer software is also available. One such program is *Success, Inc.: The Powerful Business Plan Writer*, which is available at your local software supply outlet. This special software package includes step-by-step instructions and examples for writing a complete business plan. You can also download templates for free from the World Wide Web! Once you're online, just type in "business plan template" in the "Net Search" feature. You'll be surprised at how much free information and help there is on the Internet.

Whether you use a computer program or not, a basic start-up business plan should contain the following elements in this order:

TITLE PAGE *Proposed company name, date, and your name and home address.*

EXECUTIVE SUMMARY *A short explanation detailing why you created this business plan. For example, "This business plan has been prepared to develop strategies and actions to be taken in creating a new entertainment publishing company specializing in comic books and related merchandise." This and the application and purpose statements should all appear on the same page.*

SHOULD I USE "I" OR "WE"? THERE ARE MIXED FEELINGS ABOUT WHETHER TO USE "I" OR "WE" IN A BUSINESS PLAN. A TRADITIONAL OPTION IS TO USE THIRD PERSON PHRASES SUCH AS "THE COMPANY."

APPLICATION *A statement of how much capital you're seeking and how you plan to pay it back. For example, "ABCD Company is requesting a $10,000 capital investment, to be repaid with interest at 1.5 percent over the prime rate, and/or equity partnership."*

PURPOSE *A short paragraph explaining why you plan on starting this new company. For example, "Jane Doe intends to use her experience and reputation* in the entertainment industry to create a successful entertainment company that will produce high-quality comic books and trade paperbacks featuring her new character, Spotman, and other original intellectual properties and will expand into related areas. In addition, the company plans to create and purchase original properties to license to motion picture and television producers for films and animation. Rights of original creations are also to be sold to merchandisers for games, toys, T-shirts, and other related products generating a total revenue in the tens of millions of dollars."

TABLE OF CONTENTS *Business plans can be run anywhere 20 to 200 pages long, so use your judgment as to whether a table of contents will make your plan more reader friendly. I usually include one.*

MARKET ANALYSIS *An analysis of the market, which gives your readers the information they might need to understand what the industry is all about. Depending on its length, the analysis could go on a page with the industry outlook (below).*

INDUSTRY OUTLOOK *A statement of your industry's outlook, as well as that of the industry's experts. Attach photocopies of relevant articles to further inform (and impress) potential investors. Considering the comic book market's current changes, investors will be bombarded with mixed reports from every end of the industry, so using positive articles can really help.*

DISTRIBUTION *An explanation of your channels of distribution.*

COMPETITIVE ANALYSIS *A description of the competition and why and how you'll be unique and/or similar. This should be about two pages.*

EXPLANATION OF COMPANY INFRASTRUCTURE *This description of what elements of production you have in place at the present time and what else you may need should go on its own page.*

SALARIED EMPLOYEES *An account of how many salaried employees you have or plan on having. You should list the planned positions by their titles and corresponding salaries. If these salaries are part of your original plan, you must include an additional 30 percent "fringe benefits" cost on top of the planned salaries amount; including insurance and payroll taxes, this is what it costs a company to have a full-time employee.*

STRATEGIES, GOALS, AND TACTICS *A declaration of how you plan to sell your products, and why you believe these strategies will generate sales.*

MONITORING OF GOALS *A statement explaining who will keep track of accounts receivable and payable.*

PROFESSIONAL OVERVIEW AND HISTORY *A short summary of your professional experiences (and those of any partners), followed by a detailed professional history that includes any and all accomplishments that have any link to your current plans. Note that without an existing company to sell, you are selling yourself. This isn't much different from a job resume, but you should keep the contents related to your future plans; nobody cares that you worked at McDonald's during college to make ends meet.*

PROFESSIONAL ASSOCIATIONS *If you were or are any part of an association that's related to your business, whether on salary or as a volunteer, list it.*

SIGNIFICANT ASPECTS OF OPERATION *A short summary of the comic book production process for potential investors who are not familiar with it.*

FINANCIAL PROJECTIONS OVERVIEW *A summary of financial projections. This should present all the important information from your financial records in an easy-to-read paragraph form. For example, "The following projections include all details of revenue derived from the sales of comic books through various channels. The majority of receipts will be from the sale of monthly comic books through wholesale distribution channels. We will produce a full-color monthly comic book and recognize revenue and expense on an accrual basis, although cash flow projections of newsstand and direct market receipts are included for comparison. The assessed start-up of the company is June 1995. In the first fiscal year, revenues are expected to reach $75,000 with a pretax profit of $26,000. This net sum includes the repayment of approximately $5,000 of the initial capital investment of $10,000. This goal will be achieved using the strategies listed in this plan; any deviation from these goals and strategies may affect the company's direction and financial planning. During the second fiscal year, revenues are expected to reach $125,000 with a pretax profit of $50,000. The third fiscal year shows the beginnings of nonpublishing revenue. . . ."*

DETAILED THREE-YEAR FINANCIAL PROJECTION *A declaration of where you plan to spend every single dime. This should include your estimated sales projections with the profit (or loss) and all overhead expenses in a separate summary for quick reference. If you're not familiar with finances, ask an accountant or knowledgeable friend for assistance. If you can't create a three-year projection, you should produce at least some kind of forecast. All investors will want to know that their money is going into a company with a future plan for success.*

Other pertinent information that you may want to have in your business plan includes market share information and documentation, lists of affiliated suppliers and industry services, a prototype of your comic book, significant articles and documentation of industry statistics, data on foreign markets, and references. Once you have your business plan together, you're ready to approach potential investors.

The Newborn

A newborn is a small company, less than a few years old, that generates revenue with a profit and is ready for expansion. If this description fits your com-

SELLING YOURSELF, AS WELL AS YOUR COMPANY

It's true that potential investors might find it unnerving to read how unexpendable you may be to the future of a new company, but you have to immediately notify them that you are part of the package. Most investors will look at a business plan in terms of dollar signs—that's their business, after all, to make money and, more importantly, protect it. Investors may wonder what will happen to the company, and any investments, should you disappear off the face of the Earth. Or, they may question whether you can be replaced if you're not doing your job.

If you're raising capital for a start-up, it is most likely that an investor will take a majority interest in the company and its assets (usually about 80 percent). The investor is investing in you and your future plans, but since slavery is illegal, the only collateral to protect an investment interest is the company itself. The only way to protect your job and your (potentially) minority interest is to instigate a "Pooling Agreement." This is an agreement signed by all the shareholders to initiate a unanimous vote on all vital decisions regarding the present or future plans of the company. In other words, if all the shareholders (with the exception of yourself) want to replace you, you need to *agree* to leave, too. You can't be kicked out. If investors refuse to sign a pooling agreement, they may be simply by looking at every possible avenue to protect their investment dollars, or they might just be greedy. (You should note that a minority shareholder position doesn't guarantee you a job with the company, nor does it guarantee any return on your shares. Minority shareholder's stock can be shrunk to almost nothing at a single board of director's meeting. It's not a safe or worthwhile position to be in, unless the company does well enough to generate dividends to all shareholders.)

pany, you should include audited (or unaudited) financial statements from a certified public accountant (CPA) in your business plan. If possible, you should produce monthly, quarterly, and annual financial statements to add to your plan; this will also reinforce the consistent focus on the bottom line.

Acquisition and Expansion

If your financial statements are strong, you can successfully obtain the capital to do almost anything using a business plan. A small- to mid-size company that is over a few years old and has achieved some success can accumulate its financial information into its business plan for use in further expansion goals or in the acquisition of another small- to mid-size company. Again, your business plan should describe the "what, how, and who" of the deal and give a financial forecast with existing financial statements.

Selling Your Company

You can sell your company at any time, provided you have an interested buyer. You'll need to show proof of revenue and profits via an audited financial statement, but you can actually receive from three to 10 times your annual revenue as a selling price. Usually, it is more financially beneficial to sell your company when approached by a serious buyer rather than to hold out and wait until you generate the equivalent of up to 10 times your annual sales in profits after taxes. If you're living comfortably on your own profitable company, you can live much more comfortably with three to 10 times your annual revenue *in the bank.*

Note that your business plan is very important when you have an interested buyer. It can be valuable selling tool, so you should update it or tailor it to appeal to a particular potential buyer.

INVESTORS

Investors come in all shapes and sizes. They can be individuals or huge companies. My personal experience with investment interests has included over a dozen different types of investors, from a major movie studio to a lawyer who wanted to find a job for his young son. I've had individuals declare that they were "swimming in money" (always a fishy statement), yet when they finally put their ideas in writing they simply proposed that I hire them to manage the company for a six-figure salary. Then, there was the accountant who wanted to find his comic book-fanatic son a job, so he offered $10,000 "capital infusion" for *half* of a $1.2 million-a-year company and, of course, a job for his son. These kind of investors don't consider comic books a serious enough business to make a serious offer. You'll meet with all kinds of possibilities; some may be absurd and others ridiculous, but with enough energy and determination, you'll find a comfortable, legitimate financial partner.

Investors' goals are to make a substantial return on their money. Usually, they prefer a short-term return (within a few years). In order to reduce their risk, they buy low and sell high. When trying to find investors or raise capital contact anyone and everyone, and network with endless determination within your pool of business contacts. Investors won't just appear at your door (although it

USE THE INTERNET

Check the Internet for even more investment possibilities. You have a worldwide opportunity for finding capital investment! Just go to your favorite search engine (Webcrawler, Yahoo!, Alta Vista, etc.) and type in the words "investors" or "capital resources." Examine each listing for any interest in publishing.

has happened), but eventually, you'll find an investor who fits your needs. I also advise that you don't discuss your plans for gaining investors or capital with the creative personalities in the business; they may not be well-versed in the money aspects of your company and may misinterpret your words as a sign of financial trouble. See Appendix, page 182, for a list of resources that can help you find and contact potential investors.

When dealing with investors, don't give up control of the ship. If you have a profitable existing business, there is absolutely no reason to give any investors anything more than a minority interest. They may go on and on about what a mess, or how risky, the business of publishing is, but your own profitable publishing company (even one with only one title) is uniquely successful. Keep the controlling interest at all costs. Eventually, you may find a person or company that will recognize the true value of your operation and be willing to pay for it!

Also, consider anything less than a "Let's meet!" from an investor to be a negative response. You have to meet one on one, face to face with a potential investment interest to really sell them on yourself and your company. It's your chance to greet them with enthusiasm, confidence, and professionalism; to show them that you know what you're doing; and to offer them a chance to join you in your new venture for success.

When meeting with possible investors always wear your best suit; this does wonders for a first impression. It makes a statement of confidence and success, and demands instant respect. Keep in mind that your enthusiasm for publishing a comic book may be fueled by your own creative accomplishments and a genuine knowledge of past success stories. Unfortunately, most of the rest of the world sees comic book publishing as a circus rather than a money-making opportunity; you must show them you can make it a profitable enterprise.

If you continue to discuss future possibilities via the telephone, yet the potential investors don't have the time to meet with you, they're not interested in investing, just in being educated about another industry.

LOVE MONEY:
BORROWING FROM FAMILY OR FRIENDS

Simply put, *love money* is money borrowed from your loved ones. Using love money to start up your business is the easiest and surest way to maintain full ownership of your company (or at least keep it in the family). Convincing a parent, sibling, or uncle to invest in your venture may give you the opportunity to create the newborn company that a more prominent investor might then consider acquiring. Everybody wins in this situation—your family gets a return on its investment and you have the ability to create a profitable company and then negotiate for a majority interest in it.

This is all well and good unless, of course, the company goes sour for whatever reason. It isn't pleasant to mix family feelings in a business environment. Money has the power to tarnish even the closest of relationships. So, if you're planning to start out using love money, always offer your family a security agreement (see chapter 5). Insist on this, even if they refuse; their love for you may cloud their business judgment. They may base their faith in you and the inevitability of your future success on feelings of pride they have for you. No matter how confident they are in you, the potential success or failure of your new enterprise is unsure, and the security agreement will give them (and you) some form of protection for their investment.

LAWYERS

If you were enlisted to fight a war, would you take a pencil with you, or would you bring the same heavy artillery that the enemy has at its disposal? You'd take the big guns, of course, and fight fire with fire! Lawyers are necessary in the world of business. All the investors you contact for negotiations will have their own attorneys looking out for their best interests, and you need to have one, too.

Research various attorneys or law firms through contacts and references. It's not necessary to hire an attorney who makes $300 per hour to get good legal representation; the United States is home to 70 percent of the world's lawyers. If you find a good lawyer who returns your calls, answers all your questions, and represents you and your best interests, retain his (or her) services. A good one is a rare breed. Keep this lawyer and pay him promptly; this is the best way to keep him working with you and for you. See Appendix, page 182, for a list of a few good lawyers for you to start with.

11 SECONDARY RIGHTS

Today, comic books are Hollywood's springboard for new and imaginative ideas. With super comic book success stories, such as *Teenage Mutant Ninja Turtles, The Crow, Speed Racer, Tales from the Crypt, The Mask, Youngblood, Spawn, The Rocketeer,* and *The Tick,* comic book characters are receiving much more respectability as an entertainment source. The similarity of comic book creation to film creation makes any comic book concept attractive to producers and directors. A comic doesn't require a multi-million dollar special effects budget to impart dramatic visuals to a "viewer." If viewers like what they see and read, that's solid enough preliminary market research to make a million-dollar movie deal transpire.

When you sell secondary rights to your comic book, this means that you are selling your comic book's intellectual property for exploitation in mediums other than comic books, such as movies, cartoons, toys, games, and T-shirts for example, and there's a lot of money to be made in this arena. Similarly, when you purchase licensed properties, meaning you buy the rights to develop someone else's hot characters into comic book properties, you can also turn a very nice profit.

SUCCESS WITH LICENSED PROPERTIES AND SECONDARY RIGHTS

If you're lucky (and also smart) you can achieve some major accomplishments using licensed properties. For example, the television cartoon *Speed Racer* had been lying dormant for 20 years when I purchased the rights to create a comic book based on it. Suddenly, the introduction of a this new comic book series brought the cartoon back from the dead and onto MTV, with an option for a live-action motion picture at Warner Bros., a new cartoon series, a home video, and games, toys, T-shirts, and the like. In 1993, Howell J. Malham, Jr., noted in the *Chicago Tribune* that I was "often credited with rescuing *Speed Racer* from obscurity."

The Green Hornet was another classic character that was lost in limbo with a seven-year option for a Saturday morning cartoon. After I introduced the new comic book series based on it in 1989, I started getting a flood of interest from many motion picture producers, directors, and actors. Deals were made with Leisure Concepts, Inc., and George Trendle, Jr. (the rights holders), and a wave of licensing followed as people expected a hot new movie to follow the comic book's success.

Hollywood has a reputation for taking its time when producing motion pictures. In most cases, it takes about five years for a project to hit the big screen (if ever). The first *Batman* movie, for example, was said to be in development for 10 years until Frank Miller's *Dark Knight* comic book generated a huge amount of press coverage and proved that there was still interest in the Caped Crusader.

Not all comic book success stories come from existing characters. Many of the titles that I mentioned at the start of the chapter earlier had very humble beginnings. The comic book *Alias,* which I created with Katherine Llewellyn and Chuck Dixon in 1990, sold poorly, yet the concept, creative team, timely shipping, and high visibility of the company (through hot licenses) made it attractive for an option. The rights to live action movie production were later purchased for $100,000.

Selling secondary (or ancillary) rights of your trademark marks your growth to a new and different position—that of a licensor. You're now the owner of a commodity that can generate revenue without any initial investment (except, of course, for the attorney fees for reviewing the contracts). For instance, you could sell the North American rights to put one of your characters on a T-shirt to a small apparel company. In this situation, you could give them these rights for two years with an option for another two at the same terms. You could also require a $3,000 advance on a 7-percent royalty rate, based on receipts. You can also retain all the power of approval for any artwork, advertising, and so on. On receiving your first quarterly royalty statement, you might just discover that the apparel company's sales have generated $10,000 in royalties, resulting in a $7,000 check for you! Now you're at a whole new level.

Die-cut buttons
Secondary rights deals come in all shapes and sizes, including a $1,000 advance on 10-percent royalties from these Great Shapes buttons. (Ralph Snart TM & copyright © NOW Entertainment.)

You can see how all the investment in your comic book title would begin to really pay off. And, your first licensee could turn into 50 with the right concept, salesmanship, and/or agent. Once you get the ball rolling in this arena, you may want to cultivate a list of licensees, which would in turn generate even more interest. To do this, offer potential licensors the rights at a reduced rate. It's worth it because having 10 licensees in your presentation package can show a growing level of interest within the licensing industry.

The Presentation Package

Used to entice potential licensees, your presentation package should be an attractive collection of print materials from your company. It should include full-color flyers, posters, and/or samples of your publications, as well as news releases, creator/artist bios, and photocopies of any and all press clippings. It should also contain synopses of all your comic book plots, any relevant business information, and your business card.

In the past 10 years, I've seen fantastic presentation packets, prototypes of toys, and film clips of many different concepts. All the people who created these presentation items, sometimes spending tens of thousands of dollars on their concepts, felt that comic books could be a springboard for entertainment success. Yet, it's not the money spent on a presentation that counts, but the product itself. Your comic book is not only a collectible and an enjoyable form of entertainment and art, but a billboard for your concept as well. Many of your readers who are waiting for your next issue to ship may be in high places. What other form of advertising do you know of that can actually generate income without creating any additional expenses or requiring you to produce more presentation items? A quality product can often do more than any pro-motion or presentation gimmicks.

SELLING AN OPTION

After viewing your comic book or presentation package, parties interested in secondary rights will want to purchase an "option." An option is an exclusive agreement for one or two years to freeze the motion picture/television and aux-iliary rights. This is like reserving those rights, thereby preventing anyone else from using the property. This agreement gives the purchaser time to develop the concept to pitch, and hopefully sell, it to a movie studio. An option can be purchased annually for about $5,000 and up. Then, on the sale of the concept to a studio, you could receive as much as $100,000 or more, plus royalties. (Hollywood bigwigs have paid as much as two million dollars, in some cases.)

On signing an agreement to relinquish the motion picture and television rights, *always* demand that your royalties be based on *gross*, not *net*, profits. Remember, gross profits are those made prior to the deduction of any operat-ing expenses, while net profits are what is left after all costs have been deduct-ed. You don't have any idea what a licensee's overhead and other expenses include, and so it's likely you might never see another dime. Also, when dealing with selling secondary rights, invest the time and money to find an outstanding entertainment lawyer; it will definitely pay off in the long run. If you're dealing with the big boys and their lawyers, you must ensure that you are adequately

OPTION AGREEMENT

For good and valuable consideration, receipt of which is acknowledged, ___(your company name)___ ("Assignor") grants to__Big Movie Company__ ("Assignee"), the exclusive and irrevocable option to purchase, exclusively, all motion picture, television and allied, ancillary, and subsidiary rights ("rights") in all languages and for the entire universe in perpetuity, in and to that certain comic book entitled ___(your comic book title)___, created by Assignor, and all adaptations, dramatizations, and translations thereof and all titles and themes thereof, all to be set forth in an Option and Purchase Agreement ("Agreement") between Assignor and Assignee to be agreed upon, no later than twelve (12) month period as of this___(day)___ day of ___(month)___, in the year _____(Initial Option Period), for a payment of ten thousand dollars ($10,000) due within ten (10) business days upon the full execution of this Option Agreement. Assignee has the right to extend the period during which said option may be exercised for an additional twelve (12) month period at the same terms set forth herein providing thirty (30) days notice and payment to Assignor for an additional ten thousand dollars ($10,000) at any time prior to the expiration of the Initial Option Period.

IN WITNESS WHEREOF, the undersigned has executed this inurement as of the __(day)__ day of __(month)__, 19___

(your company name)

By: _____

Its: _____

State of _____

County of _____

On this _(day)_ day of __(month)__, 19___, before me, ___(notary public's name)___, a Notary Public in and for the said County and State, personally appeared _____(your name)_____, known to me (or proved to me on the basis of satisfactory evidence) to be the person who executed the within instrument as the _____(Assignor's title)_____ of the company therein named, and acknowledged to me that such company executed the same pursuant to its bylaws or a resolution of its Board of Directors.

Witness my hand and official seal.

_____ Notary Public

My commission expires: _____

Sample short form option agreement

This is a sample of what an option agreement for a movie company might look like. Again, this is just an example, and I'd recommend that you have a lawyer draw up the real thing.

> ## LIMIT
> ## THE OPTION
> KEEP THE OPTION LENGTH FOR THE RIGHTS TO DEVELOP YOUR INTELLECTUAL PROPERTY INTO A MOVIE OR CARTOON, TO NO MORE THAN TWO YEARS FOR THE INITIAL FEE. IF LICENSEES WISH TO PURCHASE MORE TIME, ASK FOR MORE MONEY—ESPECIALLY IF YOU'VE HAD OTHER INTERESTED PARTIES.

represented, too. Remember, this is *your* concept you're trying to protect.

Of course, as I said before, the chances of your comic book making it to the big screen depends on your ability to produce an outstanding product. Kim Thompson, vice president of Fantagraphics Books, advises, "Don't loose your focus." Concentrate on producing the best quality comic book you can; if you follow the key elements for success, the audience and any prospective licensees will come to you. Your book might generate interest in a number of ways; it might have a catchy title, or it might have garnered maximum exposure and huge sales through a strong PR effort and a reputation for consistent shipping, or it might have a great concept or story line coupled with quality art. Of course, potential licensees might simply just be fans, although it never hurts to let them know you're around. Add a few agents and members of the Hollywood press to your comp list, and then let the product speak for itself.

I suggest, too, that you obtain the *Hollywood Reporter Blue Book*, which includes the names, addresses, and contacts for most of the producers, directors, and agents in Hollywood. Also look through licensing books and trade magazines (see Appendix, page 169) for intellectual property representatives. Many of these licensors, who represent big-name characters, also handle new properties. And don't forget to trademark and copyright all your work.

APPENDIX: RESOURCES

COMIC BOOK TRADE SHOWS AND CONVENTIONS

Trade Shows

Nepean Sportsplex
  Comic Book Show
Merz Productions
1701 Woodroffe Avenue
Nepean, Ontario
Canada
ph: (613)729-9398

San Diego Comic Book Expo
311 4th Avenue, Suite 512
San Diego, CA 92101
ph: (619) 544-9555
fax: (619) 544-0743

Conventions

Chicago ComicCon
6830 South Camden Road
Downers Grove, IL 60516
ph: (708) 852-2514
fax: (708) 852-2899

The Dallas Fantasy Fair
Bulldog Productions
P.O. Box 820488
Dallas, TX 75382
ph: (214) 350-4305

DragonCon & Atlanta Comics Expo
P.O. Box 47696
Atlanta, GA 30362
ph: (404) 925-0115

Game Manufacers
  Association/GAMA
9220 Lackland Road
St. Louis, MO 63114
ph: (314) 831-4510
fax: (314) 831-3811

The Great Eastern Conventions/
  New York & Philadelphia Shows
225 Everitts Road
Ringoes, NJ 08551
ph: (908) 788-6845
fax: (908) 806-8409
attn: Fred Greenberg

Heroes Convention
Heroes Aren't Hard to Find
1670 Highway 171
Charleston, SC 29407
ph: (803) 766-6611

Motor City Conventions
19785 West 12 Mile Road,
  Suite 231
Southfield, MI 48076
ph: (810) 426-8059 or
  (810) 350-2633

WonderCon
2831 Miller Street
San Leandro, CA 94577
ph: (510) 352-5841

TRADEMARK AND COPYRIGHT AGENCIES

The following is a list of various sources you can contact for more help and information on securing trademarks and copyrights for your concepts.

The Library of Congress
Copyright Division
Washington, D.C. 20559
Copyright information:
  (202) 707-3000
To request copyright forms:
  (202) 707-9100

McBride, Baker & Coles
500 West Madison Street, 40th floor
Chicago, IL 60661-2511
ph: (312) 715-5713
fax: (312) 993-9350
e-mail: arden@mbc.com
attn: Thomas P. Arden (trademark
  specialist)

Trademark Corporation of America
215 North Mountain Avenue
Montclair, NJ 07042
ph: (201) 744-7466
fax: (201) 744-7866
attn: Michael R. Peroff

United States Patent &
  Trademark Office
2021 Jefferson Davis Highway
Arlington, VA 22202
ph: (703) 557-4636
website: http://www.uspto.gov/web
Copyright registration:
  http://lcweb.loc.gov/copyright/
  reg.html
Copyright applications:
  http://lcweb.loc.gov/copyright/
  forms.html

LICENSING RESOURCES

The following magazines will give you more insight into the world of licensing. They list product names, the legal rights holders, and the agencies that represent them for licensing. They can also give you valuable hints as to what might be the next big craze.

The Hollywood Reporter
5065 Wilshire Boulevard
Los Angeles, CA 90036-4396
ph: (213) 525-2000
(fax): (213) 525-2150
Published weekly; lists all TV shows, animation, and movies in development, preproduction, and production; provides release dates every month in a special issue

The Licensing Book
The Toy Book
Adventure Publishing Group
264 West 40th Street
New York, NY 10018
ph: (212) 575-4510
fax: (212) 575-4521

Playthings Magazine
51 Madison Avenue
New York, NY 10010-1675
ph: (212) 689-4411
fax: (212) 683-7929

Toy & Hobby World
Licensing Today
41 Madison Avenue, 5th floor
New York, NY 10010
ph: (212) 594-4237
fax: (212) 563-1415

PRINTERS, COLOR SEPARATORS, AND COMPUTER COLORISTS

Printers

The following printers specialize in producing short-run black-and-white and full-color comic books. *Short-run* means that they only handle small print runs, which would be about 10,000 copies, but you'll find that these printers offer competitive prices for print-runs from as little as 1,000 to up to 30,000 copies.

Boyd Press
112 31st Street
    P.O. Box 6753
Wheeling, WV 26003
ph: (304) 232-2022
attn: Rex Metzger
Also handles trade paperbacks, graphic novels, trading cards, posters, and other related items, as well as comic books.

Brenner Printing Company
106 Braniff Avenue
San Antonio, TX 78216
ph: (210) 349-4024
fax: (210) 349-1501
attn: Gene Brenner or Buddy Ott
Also produces trading cards, trade paperbacks, magazines, posters, and other related products.

Port Publications
125 East Main Street
Port Washington, WI 53074
ph: (414) 284-3494
attn: Dennis Nemitz
Specializes in black-and-white comic books and trade paperbacks.

Small Publishers Co-op
2579 Clematis Street
Sarasota, FL 34239
ph: (941) 922-0844
attn: Scott McIntire

The following printers specialize in the production of full-color comic books with large print-runs of over 30,000 copies, but Transcontinental Printing also handles small print-runs of as little as 3,000 copies.

Sullivan Graphics, Inc.
187 Zimmerman Boulevard
Buffalo, NY 14223
ph: (716) 871-1077
fax: (716) 871-1108

Transcontinental Printing
395 Boulevard Lebeau
Saint Laurent H4N 1S2, Quebec
Canada
ph: (514) 337-8560
fax: (514) 334-1361
attn: Norman Tremlay
Also prints books, hardcover edition comic books, posters, trading cards, and other related items; the phone operator speaks English.

The following printers offer special formats, which include prestige formats (a popular 48-page, perfect-bound comic book format), graphic novels, and trade paperbacks, and distinctive production capabilities, such as the use of holograms, multi-dimensional techniques, and gold foil. Their print-runs vary widely.

Crown Roll Leaf
91 Illinois Avenue
Patterson, NJ 07503
ph: (201) 742-4000
fax: (201) 742-0219

Danner Press Corporation
1900 East Golf Road, Suite M100
Schaumburg, IL 60173-5011
ph: (708) 517-1611
fax: (708) 517-1709
attn: Joe Collier

Letterhead Press, Inc.
155 North 120th Street
Wauwatosa, WI 53226
ph: (414) 574-1717
fax: (414) 574-9687
attn: Marlo Newman

Quad Graphics
W224 N3322 Duplainville Road
Pewaukee, WI 53072
ph: (414) 691-9200
fax: (414) 691-5608
attn: Andrea Haley

Transcontinental Printing
395 Boulevard Lebeau
Saint Laurent H4N 1S2,
    Quebec, Canada
ph: (514) 337-8560
fax: (514) 334-1361
attn: Norman Tremlay
Also prints books, hardcover edition comic books, posters, trading cards, and other related items; the phone operator speaks English.

The promotional material printer listed below offers outstanding prices for low-run full-color (or black-and-white) flyers on high-quality gloss stock.

Fosterprints
4295 South Ohio Street
Michigan City, IN 46360
ph: (219) 879-8366 or
    (800) 382-0808
fax: (219) 874-2849

Color Separators
The following color separators are ones that I've used or that have come *highly* recommended.

Color Code, Inc.
1214 Market Avenue North
Canton, OH 44714
ph: (216) 452-7200 or
    (800) 262-8812
fax: (216) 452-1330
attn: Pete Goda

KGM Graphics
One IBM Plaza, Suite 2805
Chicago, IL 60611
ph: (312) 595-9900
fax: (312) 595-9910
attn: Michael Berk

Liberty Engraving Company
1112 South Wabash Avenue
Chicago, IL 60605-2384
ph: (312) 786-0600
attn: Richard Juckniess

Professional Graphics
4404 Boeing Drive
Rockford, IL 61109
ph: (800) 747-2741
fax: (815) 226-9830
attn: Pat Goley

Computer Colorists

Bear Byte Graphics
770 North Main Street
Orange, CA 92668
ph: (714) 771-7823
fax: (714) 639-3912
attn: Kevin Horn

Jamison Services
P.O. Box 943
West Plains, MO 65775
ph: (417) 256-7180
fax: (417) 256-3461
attn: Alan Jamison

KGM Graphics
One IBM Plaza,
    Suite 2805
Chicago, IL 60611
ph: (312) 595-9900
fax: (312) 595-9910
attn: Mike Berk or Mike Roberts

DISTRIBUTOR AND TRADE PUBLICATIONS

Distributor Publications

Diamond Dialogue
Diamond Dateline
Diamond Previews
Diamond Comic Distributors
1966 Greenspring Drive,
    Suite 300
Timonium, MD 21093
ph: (410) 560-7100
fax: (410) 560-7148

Internal Correspondence
Advance Comics
Capital City
2537 Daniels Street
Madison, WI 53704

Trade Publications

Comic Book Price Guide
Overstreet Publications
801 20th Street NW,
    Suite 3
Cleveland, TN 37311
attn: Gary Carter

Comics Buyer's Guide
Krause Publications
700 East State Street
Iola, WI 54990
ph: (715) 445-2214
fax: (715) 445-4087
attn: Maggie Thompson
Published weekly; has covered the comic book industry for over 25 years.

Comics Interview
Fictioneer Books
234 Fifth Avenue,
    Suite 301
New York, NY 10001
Presents interviews with today's top comic artists, plus other people involved in the various aspects of comics production, including writers, artists, editors, publishers, and celebrities.

Comics Journal
Fantagraphics Books, Inc.
7563 Lake City Way NE
Seattle, WA 98115
ph: (206) 524-1967
fax: (206) 524-2104
attn: Gary Groth

Comics Retailer
Krause Publications, Inc.
700 East State Street
Iola, WI 54990
ph: (715) 445-2214
fax: (715) 445-4087
attn: John Jackson Miller

Flux
Harris Publications
1115 Broadway
New York, NY 10010
ph: (212) 807-7100
attn: Jonathan Rheingold

Wizard: The Guide to Comics
Wizard Press
151 Wells Avenue
Congers, NY 10920
ph: (914) 268-2000
fax: (914) 268-0877
attn: Gareb Shamus

The Worlds of Westfield
8608 University Green
Middleton, WI 53562
attn: Joyce Greenholdt
This is a magazine/catalogue company.

DISTRIBUTORS

Direct Market Distributors

Diamond Comic Distributors
1966 Greenspring Drive, Suite 300
Timonium, MD 21093
ph: (410) 560-7100
fax: (410) 560-7148

Big O Amusements, Inc.
RD 1
Graniteville, VT 05654
ph: (802) 479 2383
attn: Gustave Osterberg

Big Picture Distributing
533 Ossington Avenue
Toronto M6G 3T3,
    Ontario
Canada
ph: (800) 895-6936
fax: (416) 533-2595
attn: Robert Myre

Bud Plant Enterprises
P.O. Box 1689
Grass Valley, CA 95945
ph: (916) 273-0915
attn: Bud Plant

Cold Cut Distribution
5704 Calmor Avenue #1
San Jose, CA 95123
ph: (408) 293-6645
fax: (408) 293-6645
attn: Mark Thompson

Entertainment Distributors
7321 Gateway Center
Manassas, VA 22110
ph: (703) 361-9000
attn: Steve Milo

Hobbies Hawaii
4420 Lawehana Street, #3
Honolulu, HI 96818
ph: (808) 423-0265

Liberty Hobby Distributors
1627 Gary Road
Lakeland, FL 33801
ph: (800) 654-6229
fax: (813) 683-5730

Lone Star Comics
6312 Hulen Bend Boulevard
Fort Worth, TX 76132
attn: Buddy Saunders

MAD AL Distributors
2507 Fairbanks Street
Anchorage, AK 99503
ph: (907) 274-4115
fax: (907) 274-4114
attn: Randy Ramuglia

Mile High Comics
2151 West 56th Avenue
Denver, CO 80221

Orion Marketing
1807 Cold Springs Road
Liverpool, NY 13090
ph: (315) 451-0667
fax: (315) 461-9066
attn: Robert A. Canino

Raven Entertainment Distribution
641 Bavarian Lane SE
Olympia, WA 98521
ph: (206) 456-7850
fax: (206) 923-1849

S & A Hobby Distributors
1709 Highway 34
Farmingdale, NJ 07727
ph: (908) 919-0909
fax: (908) 919-7117

Newsstand Distributors

Atlantic Coast Independent
    Distributors Association
    (ACIDA)
4000 Coolidge Avenue
Baltimore, MD 21229
ph: (410) 525-3355
attn: Don Devito

Curtis Circulation Company
Continental Plaza, 7th floor
433 Hackensack Avenue
Hackensack, NJ 07601
ph: (201) 907-5500
fax: (201) 836-7622
attn: Robert Castardi

Kable News Company
11 West 42nd Street
New York, NY 10036
ph: (212) 768-1000
fax: (212) 768-1063
attn: Robert Browne

Mid-America Periodical Distributors
    Association (MAPDA)
Palmer News, Inc.
P.O. Box 1400
Topeka, KS 66601-1400
attn: Joseph H. Lumpkin

Periodical Marketers of Canada
    (PMC)
Metro Toronto News Company
120 Sinnott Road
Scarborough M1L 4N1, Ontario
Canada
ph: (416) 752-8720
fax: (416) 285-2056
attn: Alex Petraitis

Warner Publisher Services
1271 Sixth Avenue, 39th floor
New York, NY 10020
ph: (212) 522-8600
attn: Bob Mattheissen or Bruce
    Jones

Bookstore Distributor
In my experience, this is really the only good bookstore distributor out there.

Eastern News Distribution
The Hearst Corporation
250 West 55th Street
New York, NY 10019
ph: (212) 649-4484
fax: (212) 265-6239
attn: Lisa Scott

Discount Distributors

Nationwide Merchandise
   Warehouse
52 Carnation Avenue
Floral Park, NY 11001
ph: (516) 437-5570
fax: (516) 488-5411
attn: Sam Smith

Anthony Radhill Associates
S. Weiner, Limited
Swan House
20 New Wharf Road
Kings Cross
London N1 9SF
UK
ph: 44-171-833-4027
fax: 44-171-833-8224

FOREIGN PUBLISHERS, AGENTS, AND SALES REPRESENTATIVES

Whenever calling a foreign country, you must dial 011 before the number; this gets you an international line. Then, you have to dial the country and city phone codes for each location before dialing the actual phone number. I've included the country and city codes here with each phone number, but you can also find a list of these codes in the front of your telephone book, or you can call an international operator for assistance.

Foreign Publishers

Abril Jovem
Rua Bela Cintra, 299
01415-000 São Paulo
Brazil
ph: 55-11-2364063
fax: 55-11-2364123

Bastei-Verlag GMBH & Co.
5060 Bergisch Gladbach 2,
   Postfach 200180
Scheidtbachstrasse 23-31
Germany
ph: 49-22-02121275
fax: 49-22-0230000
attn: Gustav H. Lubbe

Comic Art s.r.l.
Publishing House
Via F. Domiziano 9
00145 Rome
Italy
ph: 39-6-5404813
fax: 39-6-5410775
attn: Rinaldo Tranini

Comics USA
17, rue Brezin
75014 Paris
France
ph: 33-14-5453435
attn: Fershid Bharucha

Condor Verlag GmbH & Co.
Karlsuher Strasse 31
D-76437 Rastatt
Germany
ph: 49-7222-13403
fax: 49-7222-13404

Dalgar Press
c/. Comerc, 64
08003 Barcelona
Spain
ph: 34-3-3100316
fax: 34-3-3106742
attn: Esteve Dalmau i Puigdevall

Dargaud Editeur
6, rue Gager Gabillot
75015 Paris
France
ph: 33-14-0453535
fax: 33-14-2501120

Distribution International
   Characters Dic2, s.r. l.
Piazza G. Resta 9
20010 Vittuone (MI)
Italy
C.F. e P. IVA 01755810155
ph: 39-2-9011131
fax: 39-2-9110044
attn: Gianfranco Mari

EDIEUROPE
7 Ter, Cour des Petites Ecuries
75010 Paris
France
ph: 33-14-7700091
fax: 33-14-7700308
attn: Luigi A. Fiore

Editoria Globo
Rua Domingos Sergio dos Anjos,
   277
05136-170 São Paulo
Brazil
ph: 55-11-8365237
fax: 55-11-8367098

Editorial Perfil S.A.
Sarmiento 1113
1041 Buenos Aires
Argentina
ph: 54-1-3822046
fax: 54-1-3823462

Editorial Planeta DE-Agostini, S.A.
Aribau, 185
08021 Barcelona
Spain
ph: 34-3-2098022
fax: 34-3-2003751

Editorial Vertice, s.r.l.
Lavalle 1994
1051 Buenos Aires
Argentina
ph: 54-1-9530604
fax: 54-1-9536521

Edizioni Jolly, s.r.l.
Via Anagnina 318
00040 Rome
Italy
ph: 39-6-29846390
fax: 39-6-29846914
attn: Mario Romano

Edizioni Play Press
Viale delle Milizie 34
00192 Rome
Italy
ph: 39-6-3701592
fax: 39-6-3701502

Egmont Publishing
Via A. Rizzoli 2
20132 Milan
Italy
ph: 39-2-67081224
fax: 39-2-67081217

GPA Gerd Plessl Agenturund
   Verlags GmbH
Linprunstrabe 38
8000 Munich 2
Germany
ph: 49-89-554084 or
   49-89-1235303
attn: Gerd J. Plessl

GPA Gerd Plessl Agenturund
   Verlags GmbH
ul. Zupana Vlatimira
YU-11000 Belgrade, Checzasylvina
Serbia
ph: 011661-085-661915
attn: Mira Jovicic

Hellas Press Service
103 Kefallinias Street
112 51 Athens
Greece
ph: 30-1-8655052
fax: 30-1-8655989
attn: George Sgouras

Interpress
Basin Ve Yayinclik A.S.
Buyukdere Cad.
Ali Kaya Sokak, No. 8
80720 Levent-Istanbul
Turkey
ph: 90-1-696680 (20 hat)
fax: 90-1-696699
attn: Yalvac Ural

Kodansha Ltd
12-21 Otoaw 2-Chome
Bunkyo-ku, Tokyo, 112
Japan
ph: 81-3-3946-6201
fax: 81-3-3944-9915

Marvel Comics UK
Panini House
Coach and Horses Passage
Pantiles, Tunbridge Wells
Kent TN2 5UJ
UK

Max Bunker Press
Via Fatebenefratelli
20121 Milan
Italy
ph: 39-2-6592969
fax: 39-2-6570226
attn: Riccardo Secchi

Plaything Merchandising
Wilson House, Rm. 901
19-27 Wyndham Street
Central Hong Kong
ph: 852-525-9222
fax: 852-525-9690

The Redan Company Ltd
29 St. John's Lane
London EC1M 4BJ
UK
ph: 44-171-490-8819
fax: 44-171-490-7320
attn: Robert W. Sutherland

Semic Nordisk Forlag AS
6320 etterstad-0604
Oslo 6
Norway
ph: 47-2-650090
fax: 47-2-646782
attn: Haakon W. Isachsen

Semic Press AB
Box 1074, Landsvagen 57
S-172 22 Sundbyberg
Sweden
ph: 46-8-7993110
fax: 46-8-7645764
attn: Lotta Fjelkegard

Agents

European Bookseller
29 Circus Road
London NW8 9JG
UK
ph: 44-171-586-5969
fax: 44-171-586-2429
attn: Mark Shashoua

Filbar's, Inc.
Import/Export, Retailer, Wholesaler,
   Distributor
Cynthia Marie Building,
6 New, Cubao
Quezon City, Philippines
ph: 63-2-7210821
fax: 63-2-72271115
attn: Filemon Barbasa III

London Editions Magazines
Publishers & Distributors
P.O. Box 111
Great Ducie Street
Manchester M60 3BL
UK
ph: 44-161-834-4746
fax: 44-161-834-0059
attn: Brian Clarke

Lyndsay Distributors (1977) Ltd.
Lyndis House
P.O. Box 12017
38 Stewart Street
Christchurch, New Zealand
ph: 64-3-797186
fax: 64-3-793864
attn: A. L. McIvor

Foreign Sales Representative

As far as foreign reps go, I've found Jayne Rockmill to be the best; she's been selling my products to foreign publishers since 1989.

Jayne Rockmill
Rockmill & Company
235 West 75th Street
New York, NY 10023
ph: (212) 769-0609
fax: (212) 769-0609

DOMESTIC AND FOREIGN COMIC SPECIALTY SHOPS

Domestic Shops

I've listed the following domestic shops because I've found them to be friendly to self-publishers, but you could also try approaching any other comic specialty stores that you know of. Note that Canadian stores appear here under the domestic listing.

Amazing Book Store
3718 Richfield Road
Flint, MI 48506
ph: (810) 736-3025

Amazing Heros
1300 Stuyvesant Avenue
Union, NJ 07083
ph: (908) 687-4338

Another World Comics
1615 Colorado Boulevard
Los Angeles, CA 90041
ph: (213) 257-7757

A-1 Comics
5800 Madison Avenue W
Sacramento, CA 95841
ph: (916) 331-8203

B & D Comic Shop
802 Elm Avenue SW
Roanoke, VA 24016
ph: (703) 342-6642

B & L Comics, Cards & Nostalgia
5591 Ridge Road
Parma, OH 44129
ph: (216) 886-3077

Bailey's Comics
386 New York Avenue
Huntington, NY 11743
ph: (516) 427-5929

Bailey's of Babylon
167 Deer Park
Babylon, NY 11702
ph: (516) 321-7047

Best Comics Distribution Center
252-01 Northern Boulevard
Little Neck, NY 11362
ph: (718) 279-2099

Best Comics Gallery
38 Glen Cove Road
Greenvale, NY 11545
ph: (516) 621-2099

The Book Stop
226 East Meadow Avenue
East Meadow, NY 11554
ph: (516) 794-9129

Brave New Worlds
300 Old York Road
Jenkintown, PA 19046
ph: (215) 887-3335

Bruce's Comics
2432 Cerrillos Road
Santa Fe, NM 87505
ph: (505) 474-0494

Bullet Proof Comics
2178 Norstrand Avenue
Brooklyn, NY 11219
ph: (718) 434-8512

Captain Blue Hen Comics & Cards
280 East Main Street
Newark, DE 19711
ph: (302) 737-3434

Captain Blue Hen Comics & Cards
Talleyville Shopping Center
Wilmington, DE 19810
ph: (302) 479-5242

Card & Comic Supply of NY
7 Washington Avenue
Bayshore, NY 11706
ph: (516) 242-5904

Chameleon Comics & Cards
36-59 Main Street
Flushing, NY 11354
ph: (718) 461-4675

Chameleon Comics & Cards
5 Coenties Slip
New York, NY 10008
ph: (212) 809-1600

Chameleon Comics & Cards
3 Maiden Lane
New York, NY 10038
ph: (212) 587-3411

Chicago ComicCon
6830 South Camden Road
Downers Grove, IL 60516
ph: (708) 852-2514

Claude's Comics
39 South York Road
Hatboro, PA 19040
ph: (215) 672-6642

Clay's Comics
1018 "B" Street
Hayward, CA 94541
ph: (510) 733-9633

Collector's Comics
3247 Sunrise Highway
Wantagh, NY 11793
ph: (516) 783-8700

Collector's Corner
8109 Flatlands Avenue
Brooklyn, NY 11236
ph: (718) 531-6415

Collector's Corner
153 Gill Street
Frederictown, New Brunswick
Canada
ph: (506) 472-4135

Comic & Gaming Exchange
8432 West Oakland Park Blvd.
Sunrise, FL 33351
ph: (305) 742-0777

Comicards
8110 Bustleton Avenue
Philadelphia, PA 19152
ph: (215) 742-3611

Comic Art Gallery
940 Third Avenue
New York, NY 10022
ph: (212) 759-6255

Comic Book Emporium
5201 Nicholson Drive
Baton Rouge, LA 70820
ph: (504) 767-1227

Comic Book Week
225 Everitts Road
Ringoes, NJ 08551

Comic Cavalcade
502 E. John Street
Champaign, IL 61820
ph: (217) 384-2211

Comic Collection
931 Bustleton Pike
Feasterville, PA 19053
ph: (215) 357-3332

Comic Cubicle
5251-50 John Tyler Highway
Williamsburg, VA 23185
ph: (804) 229-5299

Comic Heros
1300 Stuyvesant
Union, NJ 07083
ph: (908) 687-4338

Comic Relief at Berkeley
2138 University Avenue
Berkeley, CA 94704
ph: (510) 843-5002

Comics and Da-Kind
1653 Noriega Street
San Francisco, CA 94122
ph: (415) 753-3037
Clearance Outlet Center
same address/ph: (415) 753-9678

Comics for Sale
166 West 75th Street
New York, NY 10023
ph: (212) 787-7943

The Comic Shop
502 Andrew Jackson Way
Huntsville, AL 35801
ph: (205) 536-5186

Comic Source, Inc.
73 South Federal Highway
Boca Raton, FL 33432
ph: (407) 395-7134

The Comic Store
28 McGovern Avenue
Lancaster, PA 17602
ph: (717) 397-8737

Comic Swap
110 South Frasier Street
State College, PA 16801
ph: (814) 234-6005

Comix Connection
Camp Hill Shopping Mall
Camp Hill, PA 17011
ph: (800) 730-0994

Count Dracula's Comic Crypt
226 Merrick Road
Lynbrook, NY 11563
ph: (516) 887-2599

Cyborg 1 Comics and Collectibles
5 South Main Street
Doylestown, PA 18901
ph: (215) 348-1451

Dark Star Books and Comics
237 Xenia Avenue
Yellow Springs, OH 45387
ph: (513) 767-9400

Dark Star II Books and Comics
1410 West Dorothy Lane
Kettering, OH 45409
ph: (513) 293-7307

Dark Star III Books and Comics
1273 North Fairfield Plaza
Beavercreek, OH 45432
ph: (513) 427-3213

Dr. Comics & Mr. Games
4014 Piedmont Avenue
Oakland, CA 94611
ph: (510) 601-7800

Dover Cards & Comics
11 Main Street
Dover, NH 03820
ph: (603) 749-6862

Dreamhaven Books & Comics
1309 4th Street SE
Minneapolis, MN 55414
ph: (612) 379-8924

Dreamscape Comics
310 West Broad Street
Bethlehem, PA 18018
ph: (610) 867-1178

Dreamscape Comics
25th Street Shopping Center
Easton, PA 18045
ph: (610) 250-9818

8 Ball Comics & Collectibles
206 Scotch Road
Ewing, NJ 08628
ph: (609) 883-8899

Fantastic Planet
24 Oak Street
Plattsburgh, NY 12901
ph: (518) 563-2946

Fantasy Books & Games
2247 First Street
Livermore, CA 94550
ph: (510) 449-5233

Fantasy Books & Games
404 Mendocino Avenue
Santa Rosa, CA 95401
ph: (707) 578-7754

Fat Jack's Comicrypt
2006 Sansom Street
Philadelphia, PA 19103
ph: (215) 963-0788

50% AND MORE OFF GUIDE!
31 Nutmeg Drive
Manchester, CT 06040
ph: (203) 643-0453

Flying Colors
2980 Treat Boulevard
Concord, CA 94518
ph: (510) 825-5410

Fourth World Comics
35 Route 111
Smithtown, NY 11787
ph: (516) 366-4440

Funny Pages
739 Route 18 South
East Brunswick, NJ 08816
ph: (908) 257-0863

Galaxy Hobby
2337 Main Street/P.O. Box 414
Stevens Point, WI 54481
ph: (715) 341-4077

Gecko Books & Comics
3613 Waialae Avenue
Honolulu, HI 96816
ph: (808) 732-1292

Golden Memories
250 Broadway
Hicksville, NY 11801
ph: (516) 932-8581

Graham Cracker Comics
369 West Army Trail Road
Bloomingdale, IL 60108
ph: (708) 894-8810

Graham Cracker Comics
120 North Bolingbrook Drive
Bolingbrook, IL 60440
ph: (708) 739-6810

Graham Cracker Comics
5232 South Main Street
Downers Grove, IL 60515
ph: (708) 852-1810

Graham Cracker Comics
5 East Chicago Avenue
Naperville, IL 60540
ph: (708) 355-4310

Graham Cracker Comics
108 East Main Street
St. Charles, IL 60174
ph: (708) 584-0610

The Great Eastern Conventions/NY
  & Philly Shows
225 Everitts Road
Ringoes, NJ 08551
ph: (908) 788-6845

The Great Escape
2433 Bardstown Road
Louisville, KY 60181
ph: (502) 456-2216

The Great Escape
Gallatin Road at Old Hickory Blvd.
Madison, TN 37115
ph: (615) 865-8052

The Great Escape
1925 Broadway
Nashville, TN 37203
ph: (615) 327-0646

Grey Region
226 Queen Street
West Toronto M5V 1Z6, Ontario
Canada
ph: (416) 974-9211

Heroes Aren't Hard to Find
1670 Highway 171
Charleston, SC 29407
ph: (803) 766-6611

Heroes on the Half Shell
93 West Main Street
East Islip, NY 11730
ph: (516) 224-7360

Hot Comics & Collectibles St. Paul
1534 White Bear Avenue
St. Paul, MN 55106
ph: (612) 776-7024

Incredible Pulp
2140 Grand Avenue
Baldwin, NY 11510
ph: (516) 223-0856

Jeff's Comics & Cards, Inc.
227 Sullivan Street
New York, NY 10012
ph: (212) 533-6350

Jim Hanley's Universe
A & P Shopping Center
Fords, NJ 08863
ph: (908) 417-5744

Jim Hanley's Universe
166 Chambers Street
New York, NY 10007
ph: (212) 649-2930

Jim's Hanley's Universe
126 West 32nd Street
New York, NY 10001
ph: (212) 268-7088

Jim Hanley's Universe
350 New Dorp Lane
Staten Island, NY 10306
ph: (718) 351-6299

Joe Sarno's Comic Kingdom
5941 West Irving Park Road
Chicago, IL 60634
ph: (312) 545-2231

L. King Collectibles
3001 Fondren
Houston, TX 77063
ph: (713) 782-2273

Mark's Comics & Collectibles
109 North Central Avenue
Valley Stream, NY 11580
ph: (516) 872-5919

Midway Book & Comic
1579 University Avenue
St. Paul, MN 55104
ph: (612) 644-7605

Mint Condidtion Comic Books &
  Baseball Cards, Inc.
664 Port Washington Boulevard
Port Washington, NY 11050
ph: (516) 883-0631

Montclair Book Center
219-221 Glenridge Avenue
Montclair, NJ 07042
ph: (201) 783-3630

Nan's Games and Comics, Too!
2011 Southwest Freeway
Houston, TX 77098
ph: (713) 520-8700

Not Only Baseball Cards
547 South Broadway
Hicksville, NY 11801
ph: (516) 937-1168

One If by Cards, Two If by Comics,
  Inc.
1107 Central Park Avenue
Scarsdale, NY 10583
ph: (914) 725-2225

Ontario Street Comic Shop
2235 East Ontario Street
Philadelphia, PA 19134
ph: (215) 288-7338

Pac-Rat's, Inc.
1051 Bryant Way
Bowling Green, KY 42103
ph: (502) 782-8092

Paper Escape
205 West First
Dixon, IL 61021
ph: (815) 284-7567

Pastimes
3223 Lake Avenue
Wilmette, IL 60091

Pegasus Enterprises
607 Main Street
Boonton, NJ 07005
ph: (201) 335-3428

Power House Comics and Games
340 North Military Avenue
Green Bay, WI 54303
ph: (414) 496-0191

Queen City Collectibles
1400 South Limit
Sedalia, MO 65301
ph: (816) 826-0166

Showcase Comics
874 West Lancaster Avenue
Bryn Mawr, PA 19010
ph: (610) 527-6236

Showcase Comics
Granite Run Mall
Media, PA 19063
ph: (610) 891-9229

Showcase Comics
3/424 South Street
Philadelphia, PA 19147
ph: (215) 625-9613

Silver Cactus Comics
729 North Neillis Boulevard
Las Vegas, NV 89110
ph: (702) 438-4408

South Miami Comics
5745 Sunset Drive
South Miami, FL 33143
ph: (305) 665-4020

Stand-Up Comics
10020 San Pablo Avenue
El Cerrito, CA 94530
ph: (510) 525-3223

Star Spangled
Route 22 & Green Brook Road
Green Brook, NJ 08812
ph: (908) 356-8338

Time Capsule Comics
2737 Post Road
Warwick, RI 02886
ph: (401) 732-8007

Time Warp Comics and Games
584 Pompton Avenue
Cedar Grove, NJ 07009
ph: (201) 857-9788

Tomorrow Is Yesterday
5600 North Second Street
Rockford, IL 61111
ph: (815) 633-0330

Unicorn Comics & Cards
216 S. Villa Avenue
Villa Park, IL 60181
ph: (708) 279-5777

Village Comics Shop
163 Bleeker Street
New York, NY 10012
ph: (212) 777-2770

The World of Stuff
425 East Main Street
Bound Brook, NJ 08805
ph: (908) 627-9202

Zenith Comics & Collectibles
18200-P Georgia Avenue
Olney, MD 20832
ph: (301) 774-1345

Foreign Shops
As with the domestic shop listing, I include these international comic shops here because I've found them to be "self-publisher friendly." As with the previous foreign listings, I've included the country and city telephone codes, so the phone numbers, where included, are complete.

Ace Comics
1 Headgate Buildings
St. John's Street
Colchester, Essex
UK
ph: 44-12-065-61912

Al Fumetto
Via G. da Montorsoli 55
50142 Florence
Italy
ph: 39-55-717049

Album - Dante
6-8 rue Dante
75005 Paris
France
ph: 33-14-3546709

Album - rue Mr. le Prince
60 rue Mr. le Prince
75005 Paris
France
ph: 33-14-3261932

Alessandro Distribuzioni
Via del Borgo San Pietro 140
40126 Bologna
Italy
ph: 39-51-240168

Alessandro Distribuzioni
Via dell'Archiginnasio 4/g
40124 Bologna
Italy
ph: 39-51-225367

Alfa Antikva
Yliopistonkatu 38
20100 Turku
Finland
ph: 358-21-325989

Alfa Strip
Nieuwstraat 12
2440 Geel
Belgium
ph: 32-14-584380

All American Comics
Via Tarquinio Prisco 89
00181 Rome
Italy
ph: 39-6-7848292

Altra Libreria (L')
Via U. Rocchi 3
06100 Perugia
Italy
ph: 39-75-5736104

Altroquando
C. so Vittorio Emanuele
174 Palermo
Italy
ph: 39-91-6114732

Angolo del Collezionista di Pileri (L')
Via Giordano Bruno 51-53
00195 Rome
Italy
ph: 39-6-39737432

Arkham
Via Tirburtina 52/54
03100 Frosinone
Italy
ph: 39-77-5270612

Armando alla Stazione
Piazza Ededra
00185 Rome
Italy
ph: 39-6-485591

AS Comic Shop
Birkenstrasse 22a
10559 Berlin
Germany
ph: 49-30-3964929

Asterisco
Via Verdi 34/36
40137 Mirandola (MO)
Italy
ph: 39-53-524145

Au Paradoxe Perdu
3, place Grenus
1201 Geneva
Switzerland
ph: 41-22-7325961

(De) Balloon Express
Klein Schavernek 4
BV Leeuwarden 8911
The Netherlands
ph: 31-58-127997

Bancarella de Libro
Via XX Settembre 60
14100 Asti
Italy

BDMania
Rua Gomes Freire 9, 3o dto
1150 Lisbon
Portugal
ph: 351-1-3539994

Beo
Hopland 15
2000 Antwerp
Belgium
ph: 32-3-2332536

Blitz CV
Stormestraat 147
8790 Waregem
Belgium
ph: 32-56-610158

Boekelier Verkerk
Rivierdreef 42
AH Haarlem 2037
The Netherlands

De Boekenhalte
Assendorperstraat 103
DH Zwolle 8012
The Netherlands
ph: 31-38-221077

Boekhandel Brouwer
Noorderbuurt 29
AL Drachten 9203
The Netherlands
ph: 31-51-2012191

Boekie
Reigerstraat 24
VH Van Helder 1781
The Netherlands
ph: 31-22-3012377

Bolster
Koninginnesingel 43
KD Venlo 5911
The Netherlands
ph: 31-77-3544069

Bonnefooi
Westerstraat 154-156
AN Enkhuizen 1601
The Netherlands
ph: 31-22-8019597

Bonte
Heidelbergstraat 5
8200 Bruges
Belgium
ph: 32-50-383578

Book Seller
Via di Serraglio 112
50047 Prato
Italy
ph: 39-574-37102

Borsa de Fumetto (LA)
Via Lecco 16
20124 Milan
Italy
ph: 39-2-29513883

Carapaces
Parijsstratt 16
3000 Leuven
Belgium
ph: 32-16-225840

Carpi Comics
Via Nova 45
41012 Carpi (MO)
Italy
ph: 39-59-640611

Carta Viva
Via Macel Gettesco 48
01100 Viterbo
Italy
ph: 39-761-346925

Casa del Fumetto
Via di Poggio 46
55100 Lucca
Italy
ph: 39-583-557798

Casa del Fumetto
Via Nais 19-21-23-25-27-29
00136 Rome
Italy
ph: 39-6-63723455

Casaforte del Vecchio Papero (LA)
Via Centozone 147-149
98100 Messina
Italy
ph: 39-90-710939

CIA Comics
Zeedijk 31a
AP Amsterdam 1012
The Netherlands
ph: 31-20-620-5078

Collector
Marktstraat 20
LH Apeldoorn 7311
The Netherlands
ph: 31-55-214796

Collezionista (IL)
Via M. Rosi 52
55100 Lucca
Italy
ph: 39-583-491212

Comic Kingdom
148 Church Street
Parramatta 2150, New South Wales
Australia
ph: 61-2-891-6248

Comicland
Via Vescovado 85
35100 Padua
Italy
ph: 39-49-650755

Comics & Games
Via Giambellino 12
20100 Milan
Italy

Comics e Dintorni
Via Bocci 99/101
50127 Florence
Italy
ph: 39-55-415614

Comics Etc.
181 Edward Street
Brisbane 4000, Queensland
Australia
ph: 61-7-229-4446

Comic Showcase
76 Neal Street
London WC2
UK
ph: 44-171-240-3664

Comic Showcase
19/20 Saint Clements Street
Oxford
UK
ph: 44-1865-723680

Comic Strips
Adegemstraat 85
2800 Mechelen
Belgium
ph: 32-15-206970

Comic Treff
Operngasse 14
1010 Vienna
Austria

Comicville - Halifax
54 Piecehall
Halifax HX1 1RE, West Yorkshire
UK
ph: 44-14-223-51119

Comicville - Huddersfield
10 Byram Arcade
Huddersfield, West Yorkshire
UK
ph: 44-14-844-55044

Cosmic Comics
Via Trieste 20
43039 Salsomaggiore (PR)
Italy
ph: 39-524-571920

Cosmic Shop
Via Mezzaterra 18
32100 Bellundo
Italy
ph: 39-43-7942985

Crazy All Comics
Moneda 772
Santiago 402 B
Chile

Destarte
Rua Sto Antonio da Gloria 90
1200 Lisbon
Portugal
ph: 35-13-465155

Dick Bos (Stripspeciaalzaak)
Junolaan 2
PW Rotterdam-Hillegersberg 3054
The Netherlands
ph: 31-10-4613147

Didagiò
Via Cagliari 40
09170 Oristano
Italy

Dolores Records & Comics
Drottningegatan 52
Göteborg
Sweden
ph: 46-31-150818

Donner Boeken
Lijnbaan 150
ER Rotterdam 3012
The Netherlands
ph: 31-10-4132070

Empire
Richard-Wagner Strasse 28
50674 Cologne
Germany
ph: 49-221-251603

Espace BD
Place Fernand Cocq 2
1050 Brussels
Belgium

Fantasia
Gelderlandplein 203
LW Amsterdam 1062
The Netherlands
ph: 31-20-6443261

Figuriamoci
Via S. Massimo 2
10124 Turin
Italy
ph: 39-11-8172662

Flater
Van Woustraat 82
LP Amsterdam 1073
The Netherlands
ph: 31-20-6714903

Forbidden Zone
20 Chaussee d'Alsemberg
1060 Brussels
Belgium
ph: 32-2-5346367

Franka
Torenstraat 9 (Torenpassage)
XV Breda 4811
The Netherlands
ph: 31-76-214153

Fumettaro (IL)
Via Musumeci 99c-d
95129 Catania
Italy
ph: 39-95-312705

Fumetteria
Via Vignola 153
41053 Pozza di Maranello (MO)
Italy
ph: 39-53-6946626

Fumetteria eta Beta
Via F. Orsini 3
47100 Forli
Italy
ph: 39-54-329682

Fumetto Chi Cerchi di
    Saverio e Gianluca
Piazza Bonola
20151 Milan
Italy
ph: 39-2-3087942

Fumetto Club
Via Saluzzo 19/D
10125 Turin
Italy

Fumettomania
C. so Torino 17
28100 Novara
Italy

Fumettomania
Via delle Absidi 12
28100 San Nicolo (Treviso)
Italy
ph: 39-422-56402

Fumettopoli
Via Trasimeno 31-a
52100 Arezzo
Italy
ph: 39-575-907255

Galerie Animation Art
Berenstraat 39
GG Amsterdam 1016
The Netherlands
ph: 31-20-6277600

De Gallier
Beekstraat 46
3800 Truiden
Belgium
ph: 32-11-671739

Gobelijn
Mechelsestraat 35
3000 Leuven
Belgium
ph: 32-16-235586

Gojoker's Strips
Haarlemmerdijk 126
JJ Amsterdam 1013
The Netherlands
ph: 31-20-6237905

The Good Fellows ky
Fredrikinkatu 40
Helsinki
Finland
ph: 358-0-6949864

GOSH Comics
39 Great Russell Street
London WC1B 3PH
UK
ph: 44-171-163-61011

Graffiti
Via Vittani 19
22100 Como
Italy

Haagse Stripshop
Wagenstraat 104-c
AZ The Hague 2512
The Netherlands
ph: 31-70-3634115

The Haunted Store
Nieuwe Binninweg 391b
EL Rotterdam 3023
The Netherlands
ph: 31-10-4768078

Het "B"-gevaar
Greepstraat 15
1000 Brussels
Belgium
ph: 32-2-5131486

Het Eiland Amoras
Lombaardstraat 13-3
3500 Hasselt
Belgium
ph: 32-11-235895

Het Gele Teken
Grote Oost 37
BR Hoorn 1621
The Netherlands
ph: 31-35-233646

Het Paard van Troje
Langevorststraat 2
JP Goes 4461
The Netherlands
ph: 31-11-0014691

Het Perron
St. Janstraat 13
KA Middelburg 4331
The Netherlands
ph: 31-1180-34747

Houtekiet Strips
Dietsestraat 146
3000 Leuven
Belgium
ph: 32-16-238012

Hutterer
Landstrasser Hauptstrasse 126
1030 Vienna
Austria
ph: 43-1-7147706

Imago
Via delle Battaglie 14/b
25122 Brescia
Italy
ph: 39-30-46177

Incontri
Via Cavour 40
75024 Montescaglioso
Italy

Infinity Shop
Via Suor Maria Mazzarello 30
00175 Rome
Italy
ph: 39-6-786010

International Comics Club
Via Odessa 20
16129 Genoa
Italy

Isalber N. e C.
Via R. Marzan 1
37010 Cisano di Bardolino (Verona)
Italy
ph: 39-45-6210458

De Jacobijn
Jacobijnestraat 8-10
TH Haarlem 2011
The Netherlands
ph: 31-23-5320782

J. Ketteler
Javalaan 59
VA Heemstede 2103
The Netherlands
ph: 31-23-5294506

Jowan
Izegemsestraat 8
8500 Kortrijk
Belgium
ph: 32-56-356342

Kapitein Rob
2e Egelantiersdwarsstraat 7
SB Amsterdam 1015
The Netherlands
ph: 31-20-6223869

Kings Comics
Shop 14, Below
Sydney 2000, New South Wales
Australia
ph: 61-2-2675615

De Klare Lijn
Gijsbrecht van Amstelstraat 132A
BC Hilversum 1214
The Netherlands
ph: 31-35-6241190

Kukunor
Rautatienkatu 18
33101 Tampere
Finland
ph: 358-931-131-287

La Bande des Six Nez
179 Chausee de Wavre
1050 Brussels
Belgium
ph: 32-2-5-137258

Lambiek
Kerkstraat 78
GN Amsterdam 1071
The Netherlands
ph: 31-20-6267543

The Land Beyond Beyond
583 George Street
Sydney 2000, New South Wales
Australia
ph: 61-2-2676279

Land van Langvergeten
Nieuwe Ebbingstraat 199
NC Groningen 9712
The Netherlands
ph: 31-50-148540

Leidse Stripshop
Aalmarkt 4
JC Leiden 2311
The Netherlands
ph: 31-71-121802

De Lektuurhal
Nauwe Burgstraat 3
CD Sneek 8601
The Netherlands
ph: 31-51-5015510

Letto Riletto
Via Borgofelino 54A
43100 Parma
Italy
ph: 39-521-202028

Libreria Alzar
Viale del Fante 56
90146 Palermo
Italy
ph: 39-91-6700500

Libreria AR
Via F. la Francesca 26
84100 Salerno
Italy
ph: 39-89-221226

Libreria del Fumetto Usato
Via B. Gigli 5
40137 Bologna
Italy

Libreria Fumettistica
Via N. Sauro 8
46100 Mantua
Italy
ph: 39-376-222535

Libreria Gandalf
Via Ceccarini 58
Riccione
Italy
ph: 39-54-143054

Libreria Giolitti
Via Giolitti 319/321/323
Rome
Italy
ph: 39-6-4464916

Libreria Il Trovalibri
Via A. Cotta 8
00175 Rome
Italy
ph: 39-6-76964332

Libreria Internazionale Rinascita
Via dei Priori 55/57
06100 Perugia
Italy
ph: 39-75-32569

Libreria Iori Daniele
C. so Adriano 40
Modena
Italy
ph: 39-59-0226406

Libreria Millepagine
Via Baldissera 9
20129 Milan
Italy
ph: 39-2-29512974

Libreria Pieroni
Via M. Rossi 52
55100 Lucca
Italy

Libreria Quintliano
Via Arcidiacono Giovanni 9
70124 Bari
Italy
ph: 39-80-5042665

Libreria Rondinella
C. so Umberto I 253
84013 Cava dei Tirroni
Italy
ph: 39-89-341590

Libreria Solaris
Via Cannaregio 2332
30121 Venice
Italy
ph: 39-41-5241098

Libreria Stelle e Strisce
Via Roma 178
48100 Ravenna
Italy

Libro Club
Via F. Cane 21
15033 Casale Monferrato
Italy

Libroteka
Via Mazzini 14
38100 Trento
Italy
ph: 39-461-238530

Little Nemo
Via Montebello 2/0
10100 Turin
Italy
ph: 39-11-8127089

Lungaretta (LA)
Via della Lungaretta 90/E
00153 Rome
Italy
ph: 39-6-5894710

Max
Heembeeksestraat 288
1120 Brussels
Belgium
ph: 32-2-2684192

Max Studio's Amsterdam bv
P.O. Box 15629
NC Amsterdam 1001
The Netherlands
ph: 31-20-6254852

Mekanik Strip
St. Jacobsmarkt 73
2000 Antwerp
Belgium
ph: 32-3-2342347

Michel Strips
Zwarte Markt (Hal-5)
AE Beverwijk 1940
The Netherlands
ph: 31-79-310128

Mieke's Striptiek
Chassestraat 71
RW The Hague 2518
The Netherlands
ph: 31-70-3650738

Milano Fumetto - Kali Comics
Via Volta 20
Milan
Italy
ph: 39-2-6555141

Minotaur
Bourke Street
Melbourne 3000, Victoria
Australia

Modena Fumetto
Viale Monte Kosika 202
41100 Modena
Italy
ph: 39-59-230783

Modern Papier
Pelsterstraat 20
KL Groningen 9711
The Netherlands
ph: 31-50-132521

Mondo del Fumetto (IL)
Via Montevideo 2
16129 Genoa
Italy
ph: 39-10-3629187

Mondo Fantastico
Via Osoppo 13
20149 Milan
Italy
ph: 39-2-4078172

Mondoperaio
Via Tomecelli 141
00186 Rome
Italy
ph: 39-6-6878920

9aArte
Travessa do Charariz de El-Rei
1100 Lisbon
Portugal
ph: 351-1-8882964

Nipponya
Via Muzio 1, ang. M. Gioia 77
20124 Milan
Italy
ph: 39-2-6899359

De Noorman
Koningstraat 43
DH Arnhem 6811
The Netherlands
ph: 31-085-420909

De Noorman
Koningstraat 9
LA Nijmegen 6511
The Netherlands
ph: 31-80-226146

NN Komics
Providencia 2198
Santiago 63
Chile

Non Solo Libri
Piazza Barbacan 1/a-b
34121 Trieste
Italy
ph: 39-40-631562

Noord
Zaagmolendrift 33-41
JX Rotterdam 3036
The Netherlands
ph: 31-10-4664368

Nou En!
Schoterweg 42 zwart
HN Haarlem 2021
The Netherlands
ph: 31-23-5259938

Nuvole Parlanti (LE)
Viale Ippocrate 13
Rome
Italy
ph: 39-6-4402688

Nuvoloso Club
Piazza L. Sabatini 12
00041 Albano Laziale (RO)
Italy
ph: 39-6-9322693

Obelix
Ten Katestraat 26-a
NC Amsterdam 1053
The Netherlands
ph: 31-20-6855100

Olimpo de Fumetto
Via Flavio Stilicone 52
00175 Rome
Italy
ph: 39-6-76965861

Oom Wim
Reestraat 24
DN Amsterdam 1016
The Netherlands
ph: 31-20-6220402

Oud & Nieuw
Wilhelminastraat 52
XK Gouda 2801
The Netherlands
ph: 31-18-2026967

Pa Pinkelman
Oude Kijk in't Jatstraat 62
EL Groningen 9712
The Netherlands
ph: 31-50-133455

Paesi Nuovi
Piazza Montecitorio 59
00186 Rome
Italy
ph: 39-6-6781103

Page 45
9 Market Street
Nottingham NG1 6HY
UK

Paper Mill
Piet Heinstraat 85
CD The Hague 2518
The Netherlands
ph: 31-70-3455889

The Phantom Zone
101 A Argyle Street
Parramatta 2150, New South Wales
Australia
ph: 61-2-8911848

Pierke
Frans van Rijhoverlaan 312
9000 Ghent
Belgium
ph: 32-9-1277086

Piet Snot
Vismarkt 3
KR Utrecht 3511
The Netherlands
ph: 31-30-318472

Plaatjes-Boekjes
Herenstraat 77
CA Hilversum 1211
The Netherlands
ph: 31-35-233646

Plok. Strips en eh…dinges!
Zaagmolen 31
BR Assen 9401
The Netherlands
ph: 31-59-2313292

Pocket 2000
Via Famagosta 39-41
00192 Rome
Italy

Polyester Books
330 Brunswick Street
Fitzroy, Melbourne 3065, Victoria
Australia
ph: 61-3-4195137

De Poort
Nederkouter 137
9000 Ghent
Belgium
ph: 32-9-1253128

Professor Ich
Koninginnewig 218
EL Amsterdam 1075
The Netherlands
ph: 31-20-6755653

Professor Ich
Reestraat 144
EM Beverwijk 1941
The Netherlands
ph: 31-25-1017319

Professor Ich
Anegang 42
SH Haarlem 2011
The Netherlands
ph: 31-23-310168

Rataplan
Grote Markt 195
JE Almere 1315
The Netherlands
ph: 31-36-5343995

Rattekopje
Onderwijsstraat 1
8430 Middelkerke
Belgium
ph: 32-59-305266

Reggio Comics
Via Emilia San Pietro 65
42100 Milan
Italy
ph: 39-2-2430535

Richard
Rombout Hogerbeetsstraat 78
HX Amsterdam 1052
The Netherlands
ph: 31-20-6842923

Rifugio del Fumetto
Via Santo Stefano 3
50013 Campi Bisenzio (FI)
Italy
ph: 39-55-890664

De Robijn
Rommelhaven 26
AS Harlingen 8861
The Netherlands
ph: 31-5178-14357

Rob's Striphoek
Wilgstraat 52
MC The Hague 2565
The Netherlands
ph: 31-70-3605773

Roccaforte (LA)
Via Val Tellina 117
Monteverde (Rome)
Italy
ph: 39-6-58200383

Rotterdam (Noord)
1e Middellandstraat 110-c
BH Rotterdam 3021
The Netherlands
ph: 31-10-4258756

Runch
Esterhazygasse 20
1060 Vienna
Austria
ph: 43-1-5870216

De Schaar
Serpentstraat 26-28
9000 Ghent
Belgium
ph: 32-9-2255091

Seria Paolo
Via Musumeci 99/c-d
95129 Catania
Italy
ph: 39-95-312705

Silvester Strips en Presents
Snellestraat 8
EN Bosch 5211
The Netherlands
ph: 31-73-123529

Sjors +
Voorstraat 313
EP Dordrecht 3311
The Netherlands
ph: 31-78-6310800

Snoek Strips
Eerste van Swindenstraat 545
LC Amsterdam 1093
The Netherlands
ph: 31-20-6684764

Soffitta (LA)
Viale Dante 35b
29100 Piacenza
Italy
ph: 39-52-3457485

Solaris 2
Via Dorsoduro 2920
30123 Venice
Italy
ph: 39-41-5121571

Speciaalzaak Eppo
Kleine Berg 33
JS Eindhoven 5611
The Netherlands
ph: 31-40-441882

Spirit
Hinthamerstraat 90
MS Den Bosch 5211
The Netherlands
ph: 31-73-145530

Stagni Andrea
Via Nomentana 60
00013 Mentana (RM)
Italy
ph: 39-6-9091284

Star Shop
Via Campo di Marte 150
06124 Perugia
Italy
ph: 39-75-32730

De Striep
Katelijnstraat 42
8000 Bruges
Belgium
ph: 32-50-337112

De Strip-Aap
Kuipersdijk 66
CJ Enschede 7512
The Netherlands
ph: 31-53-305261

Stripantiquariaat Panda
Frederikstraat 955-959
LJ The Hague 2514
The Netherlands
ph: 31-70-3635950

Stripboekhandel Bul Super
Breestraat 18-22
RG Delft 2611
The Netherlands
ph: 31-15-126097

Strip en Lektuurshop
Oude Gracht 194
NR Utrecht 3511
The Netherlands
ph: 31-30-334357

De Stripkever
Bruulcenter, Bruul 79
2800 Mechelen
Belgium
ph: 32-15-217605

De Stripomaan
Kardinal Cardijnstraat 3
1500 Halle
Belgium
ph: 32-23-561589

Stripwinkel Blunder
Oude Gracht 203
NH Utrecht 3511
The Netherlands
ph: 31-30-311461

Stripwinkel Blunder
Zadelstraat 14
LT Utrecht 3511
The Netherlands
ph: 31- 30-2311831

Stripwinkel De Lektuurhal
Over de Kelders 10
JE Leeuwarden 8911
The Netherlands

Stripwinkel De Rat
Korfmakersstraat 3
LA Leeuwarden 8911
The Netherlands
ph: 31-58-151600

Stripwinkel Dumpie
Nieuwe Rijn 18
JC Leiden 2312
The Netherlands
ph: 31-71-126404

Stripwinkel Paulus
Verdronkenoord 62
BG Alkmaar 1811
The Netherlands
ph: 31-72-126041

Stripwinkel Sjors
Scheffersplein 1
EJ Dordrecht 3311
The Netherlands
ph: 31-78-142012

Stripzaak DoZo
Hoogstraat 105
BM Vlaardingen 3131
The Netherlands
ph: 31-10-4356293

Supermarket del Fumetto
Via Montesanto 14
80135 Naples
Italy
ph: 39-81-5519738

't Centrum
Korte Singelstraat 20a
GB Schiedam 3122
The Netherlands
ph: 31-10-4262584

Tempi Duri
Via de' Pilastri 20/22R
50121 Florence
Italy
ph: 39-55-242946

't Ezelsoortje
Hemonystraat 48
Amsterdam 10
The Netherlands
ph: 31-20-6767610

't Ezelsoortje
Bakkerstraat 30
JR Roermond 6041
The Netherlands
ph: 31-47-5033782

Tistjen Dop
Paterstraat 120
2300 Turnhout
Belgium
ph: 32-14-428829

Tommy
Nieuwlandstraat 14
SN Tilburg 5038
The Netherlands
ph: 31-13-358319

De Tweede Lezer
Eerste Wormenseweg 102
DK Apeldoorn 7331
The Netherlands
ph: 31-55-427202

Walk In
Fluwelen Burgwal 8a
CJ The Hague 2511
The Netherlands
ph: 31-70-3646336

Wonderland
Paardsdemerstraat 17
3500 Hasselt
Belgium

Wonderland Strips & SF
Soembawastraat 54-a
XC Amsterdam 1095
The Netherlands
ph: 31-20-6943562

Xenia Libri
Via Boccacanale di S. Stefano
44100 Ferrara
Italy
ph: 39-53-2210566

Yendor
Korte Hoogstraat 16
GL Rotterdam 3011
The Netherlands
ph: 31-10-4331710

Zinnebeeld
Pelsterstraat 14
KL Groningen 9711
The Netherlands
ph: 31-50-128472

NATIONAL AND MIDWEST NEWS WIRES

These news wires are all located at the same address, so I've only included the complete address in the first listing; all subsequent listings just have the agency name and contact.

Associated Press
State Capitol Building, Press Room
Springfield, IL 62706
attn: Dennis Conrad, Tom Strong,
 or Seth Perlman

Copley News Service
attn: Matt Krasnowski

Lee Enterprises
attn: Kathy Johnston

WGN/TV
attn: Molly Hall

WLS/TV
attn: Hugh Hill

WMAQ/TV
attn: Dick Kay

INTERNET SERVICE PROVIDERS AND BROWSERS

These are a few of the more popular ISPs, plus the most widely used browser. I list only this one browser because it's the best, and it's free.

Internet Service Providers

American Online
8619 Westwood Center Drive
Vienna, VA 22182-2285

Earthlink Network, Inc.
3100 New York Drive
Pasadena, CA 91117
ph: (800) 395-8425
fax: (818) 296-2470
http://www.earthlink.net

The Microsoft Network (MSN)
One Microsoft Way
Redmond, WA 98052-6399
ph: (800) 386-5550

Netcom
3031 Tisch Way
San Jose, CA 95128
ph: (415) 556-3211
http:/www.netcom.com

Prodigy
445 Hamilton Avenue
White Plains, NY 10601
ph: (800) PRODIGY

Browser

Netscape Communications Corporation
501 East Middlefield Road
Mountain View, CA 94043
phs: (415) 937-2555 for corporate product and sales information (7:00 a.m. to 5:00 p.m. PST)
(415) 937-3777 for individual consumer product and sales information (7:00 a.m. to 5:00 p.m. PST)
(415) 254-1900 for executive offices
fax: (415) 528-4124
http://home.netscape.com

INVESTOR SERVICES

The following lists of investor mailing lists, trade shows, grants, and venture capitalists may help you when trying to build capital to start your business.

Investor Mailing Lists

Quality Lists
Dept. En-157, Wholesale List Section
P.O. Box 6060
Miller Place, NY 11764
ph: (516) 744-7289

Seed Capital Network, Inc.
Operations Center
8905 Kingston Pike, Suite 12
Knoxville, TN 37923-9925
ph: (615) 573-4655

Investor Trade Shows

These trade shows travel the United States with a variety of investment options, information, and potential contacts. Check your local small-business publications for a list of upcoming events.

Q. M. Marketing, Inc.
Franchise & Business Investment Shows
1515 West Chester Pike, Suite B-2
West Chester, PA 19382
ph: (215) 431-2402

Grants

You can obtain a publishing grant in much the same way that academics apply for research grants. However, in this case, it's for the betterment of the arts. It's *free* money from the government—certainly worth a try, right? The National Endowment for the Arts application deadline is in May of every year.

National Endowment for the Arts
Literature Program, Room 722
Nancy Hanks Center
1100 Pennsylvania Avenue, NW
Washington, DC 20506-0001
ph: (202) 682-5451

Venture Capitalists

The following capital firms are interested in newborn businesses, acquisitions, and expanding companies in the comic book industry. You can find a list of local venture capital firms at your local library or through word-of-mouth references from lawyers as I did.

Capital Strategy Management
P.O. Box 06334
232 South Wacker
Chicago, IL 60606
ph: (312) 444-1170
attn: Eric Von Bauer

Dresner Capital Resources, Inc.
29 South LaSalle Street, Suite 1040
Chicago, IL 60603
ph: (312) 726-3600
attn: Alan Bernstein

Edwards, Liss & Murray
43 East Ohio Street, Suite 1030
Chicago, IL 60611
ph: (312) 755-0239
fax: (312) 321-9420

Frontenac, Co.
208 South LaSalle Street, Suite 1900
Chicago, IL 60604
ph: (312) 368-0044
attn: Tom Salentine

Inroads Capital Partners
525 West Monroe, 21st floor
Chicago, IL 60661
ph: (312) 902-5347
attn: Jerry Carrington

Marquette Venture Partners
520 Lake Cook Road, Suite 450
Deerfield, IL 60015
ph: (708) 940-1700
attn: Jim Simmons

McFarland/Dewey
230 Park Avenue, Suite 1450
New York, NY 10169
ph: (212) 867-4949
attn: Jack Hyland

National Venture Capital Association
1655 North Fort Myer Drive, Suite 700
Arlington, VA 22209
ph: (703) 528-4370

Nebraska Business Development Center
1313 Farnam Street, Suite 132
Omaha, NE 68182
ph: (402) 595-2381

LAWYERS

Mitch Berger, Esq.
68 Surrey Commons, P.O. Box 150
Lynbrook, NY 11563
ph: (516) 593-1061

Cesario & Walker
211 West Chicago Avenue, Suite 118
Hinsdale, IL 60521
ph: (708) 920-8800
attn: Dan Walker, Jr.

Vedder, Price, Kaufman & Kammholz
222 North La Salle Street
Chicago, IL 60610
ph: (312) 609-7500
fax:(312) 609-5005
attn: Robert Brown

Winston & Strawn
175 Water Street
New York, NY 10038
ph:(212) 858-6741
fax:(212) 952-1474
attn: Robert W. Ericson

INDEX